Africa & Madagascar

Total Eclipse 2001 & 2002

contributing editor
Aisling Irwin

additional authors
Matthew Bokach
Hilary Bradt
Philip Briggs
Chris McIntyre
Mike Slater

eclipse consultant
Sheridan Williams

Bradt Publications, UK
The Globe Pequot Press Inc, USA

First published in 2000 by Bradt Publications,
19 High Street, Chalfont St Peter, Bucks SL9 9QE, England
web: www.bradt-travelguides.com
Published in the USA by The Globe Pequot Press Inc, 246 Goose Lane,
PO Box 480, Guilford, Connecticut 06475-0480

The authors and publishers have made every effort to ensure the accuracy of the
information in this book at the time of going to press. However, they cannot accept any
responsibility for any loss, injury or inconvenience resulting from the use of information
contained in this guide.

British Library Cataloguing in Publication Data
A catalogue record for this book is available from the British Library
ISBN 1 84162 015 7

Library of Congress Cataloging-in-Publication Data
Africa & Madagascar : total eelipse 2001 & 2002 / contributing editor,
Aisling Irwin ; contributors, Matthew Bokach ... [et al.] ; eclipse adviser,
Sheridan Williams.
        p.cm.
Includes bibliographical references and index.
ISBN 1-84162-015-7
1. Solar eclipses—2001—Observers' manuals. 2. Solar eclipses—2002—
Observers' manuals. 3. Africa. Southern—Guidebooks. 4. Madagascar—
Guidebooks. I. Title: Africa and Madagascar. II. Title: Total eclipse 2001
& 2002. III. Irwin, Aisling. IV. Bokach, Matthew. V. Williams, Sheridan.
QB545.01.A4 2000
523.7'8—dc21
                                                                00-041107

Cover Concise Artisans
Back cover *left* 30 minutes before totality (Mike Foulkes)
centre left A few seconds before totality (Mike Foulkes)
centre right An enlarged diamond ring (Paul Coleman; tel: 020 8946 8830)
right A solar maximum corona (Paul Coleman)
Illustrations Susan Bethune
Maps and diagrams Steve Munns, based on sources supplied by the authors

Typeset from the author's disc by Wakewing
Printed and bound in Spain by Grafo SA, Bilbao

Authors/Acknowledgements

AUTHORS

Matthew Bokach has lived and worked in Zimbabwe for over three years and is originally from Michigan in the United States. He began work in Zimbabwe as a secondary school science teacher, and is currently a full-time volunteer in the office of the government ornithologist. He will be returning to the States later this year to pursue his graduate education, with the intention of making a career in ornithological research in the southern African region.

Hilary Bradt is the proprietor of Bradt Travel Guides which she has run since 1974. She is author of *Madagascar: The Bradt Travel Guide* and co-author of Bradt's *Madagascar Wildlife*. Her idea for this guide followed the exhilarating viewing of the 1999 total eclipse in the Isles of Scilly.

Philip Briggs (philari@hixnet.co.za) is a travel writer specialising in sub-Saharan Africa. He is the author of eight highly successful Bradt travel guides covering South Africa, Tanzania, Uganda, Ethiopia, Malawi, Mozambique, Ghana and East & Southern Africa. Based in Johannesburg, Philip is married to the photographer Ariadne Van Zandbergen, in collaboration with whom he has contributed more than 50 features to the British and South African travel press. He spends up to seven months of the year travelling around Africa.

Aisling Irwin is an award-winning journalist specialising in science and travel. She has been science correspondent on *The Daily Telegraph* and the *Times Higher Education Supplement*. She has published two travel books based in Africa - *In Quest of Livingstone: a Journey to the Four Fountains*, and *Cape Verde Islands: The Bradt Travel Guide*. She is now freelance, based in Indonesia.

Chris McIntyre (africa@sunvil.co.uk) went to Africa in 1987 after reading physics at Queen's College, Oxford. He taught with Voluntary Service Overseas in Zimbabwe for three years and travelled extensively. In 1990 he co-authored the UK's first guide to Namibia and Botswana, before spending three years as a business analyst in London. He is now managing director of specialist African tour operator Sunvil Discovery. He has written acclaimed guides for Bradt on Zambia and Namibia and is now researching and writing the new Bradt guide to Botswana.

Mike Slater (slaterm@iafrica.com) was born in Johannesburg where he still lives. He first went to Mozambique (by bicycle) in 1992 during the civil war, and he stayed for six months. Since then he has spent an accumulated period of around two years there, diving its reefs, climbing its mountains, rafting its rivers and learning Portuguese. Although he has travelled extensively in a dozen other African countries, Mozambique remains his favourite. He also runs a consultancy advising investors, prospectors, tourists, movie-makers, engineers and researchers about the country.

Sheridan Williams (sheridan@clock-tower.com) is a member of the British Astronomical Association. He worked for seven years as a rocket scientist with the Ministry of Defence, then for ten years as a lecturer in mathematics/computing. He now runs computer and publishing companies. His hobby of travel has taken him to see the total eclipses of 1988 (Sumatra), 1990 (Finland), 1991 (Mexico) 1994 (Peru), 1997 (Siberia), 1998 (Antigua) and 1999 (England). Sheridan has written and broadcast about eclipses and is author of *UK Solar Eclipses from Year 1 to 3000*.

ACKNOWLEDGEMENTS

Matthew Bokach thanks Eric, Sally and Dr P Mundy for giving him the time to work on this project; Val at the Bulawayo Publicity Association, Anthony at River Horse Safaris, and especially Gillian at UTc for all their helpful information; Fatima and Mercy for help with the Shona translations; and finally, his family for all their support.

Hilary Bradt would like to thank Claude Rambelson of Madamonde and Nivo Ravelojaona of Za Tours for local information, Frankie Kerridge for inside information on the east coast sites, and Scott Grenfell for details on the newly opened Andringitra National Park. As always, Derek Schuurman provided a stream of invaluable emails.

Aisling Irwin would like to thank Gert Esselink for invaluable help with Angola, Francis Podmore of the University of Zimbabwe for his help with eye safety concerns, Victoria Beatty for her information on African Sun and Moon lore; and Jay Anderson, Francisco Diego and Paul Maley, all eclipse specialists, for their scientific input.

Chris McIntyre owes special thanks to Ilse Mwanza, of Lusaka, who is always terrifically helpful with information on Zambia and helped considerably with the language sections and with stories.

Mike Slater is indebted to Petra Bester for such comprehensive updates about Quelimane.

Contents

Introduction

Aisling Irwin

'There is nothing in Nature to rival the glory of a total eclipse of the Sun.
No written description, no photograph, can do it justice.'

Patrick Moore, veteran British astronomer, 1999

For many of those who witness one, a total solar eclipse is the most moving
experience on Earth. While some feel unrestrained joy at the sight of totality,
others feel an equally powerful sense of desolation, such as an observer in England
in 1927:

'It was as if the whole Earth were smitten with a moral sickness ... It was
all inexpressibly sad and utterly desolate, and when the small golden
crescent appeared again behind the Moon, I involuntarily uttered the
words "Thank God for the Sun".'

No-one can really explain why a total eclipse of the Sun has the power to unleash
such varied emotions, leaving us so momentously disorientated. After all, the
movements of the Earth, Moon and Sun have been predictable for thousands of
years – and explicable for hundreds. They are hardly a surprise any more.

Yet they still overwhelm us. I believe it is because of the instinctive realisation,
as the eclipse unfolds, that nothing whatever can prevent it. We already know this
in a rational way, of course, but the eclipse drives it into our understanding with
unequalled drama. Another observer wrote in 1927:

'It is well that we should now and then be made to realise the might and
majesty of the universe in which we are the greatest and the least.'

I thought I was well briefed when I travelled to Alderney in the English Channel
to view the total solar eclipse of August 1999. As *The Daily Telegraph*'s science
correspondent I had written thousands of words about eclipses in the preceding
weeks, although I had never actually seen one.

But I discovered that I was not prepared at all. My response to the Moon gliding
in front of the Sun, as I watched with jubilant crowds from atop the island's
crumbling fort, was totally unexpected: it was fear. Suddenly, I did not want the
eclipse to happen.

But it did, and gradually my fear disappeared, to be replaced by exhilaration,
echoed and intensified by the screams and cries of my fellow viewers.

These emotions will be magnified during the southern African eclipses as you
watch them from some of the most beautiful landscapes on Earth. You may gaze
in delicious loneliness from some unknown crag on the Zambezi escarpment; or
join the crowds and the animals in a magnificent Zambian game park; or watch
morning fade from the stunning Xai-Xai beach in Mozambique. Perhaps you will
gaze from the western shores of Madagascar as the eclipsed Sun begins to set in the

Mozambique Channel. Wherever you go, you will be joining a distinguished club of 'eclipse-chasers' whose history is at least 200 years old and arguably dates back as far as Captain Cook. Their numbers are exploding as word spreads about this natural wonder.

Before you go, however, read this book. Then take it with you. It will guide you around the pitfalls of eclipse-chasing – choosing a country and viewing site, and taking calculated risks with the weather. This book will help you select your setting, record memorable images and protect your eyes.

We – the authors and editors – have done everything we can to make your eclipse a splendid one. But there is one thing we cannot do – as I know too well – and that is to prepare you for your own reactions.

Prologue

COWRIES OF THE ECLIPSE
David Njoku

The story I am about to tell you happened not too long ago – before most of you were born, I admit, but not too long ago – and happened at not too tiring a distance from here. You can investigate the place yourselves in the morning when the Sun returns sight to your eyes: go beyond the chief's millet farm, and along the dense, verdant strip that guides the stream, and you'll be there before your water-kegs are empty. But on second thoughts, perhaps it would be wiser to give that place the wide berth of a cemetery; strange dramas have been known to take place there, in the eye of the floodlight of the Moon.

The tribe this tale is about, the Mako tribe, was not, strictly speaking, a tribe distinct from ours; after all, they spoke a dialect of our language. Any differences, I suppose, were due mainly to their religion. You see, the Makos worshipped the Sun, and this even affected the way they acted. I remember, in our village then, you wouldn't say someone was behaving like a Mako unless you wanted knives to shed their sheaves and dance naked. They were that strange.

As I said, they worshipped the Sun, believed that all energy came from it – without it plants wouldn't grow, and people wouldn't talk, walk or farm. Consequently, as soon as the Sun dipped behind the hills at night to unplug itself, they stumbled to bed, silently as ghosts, only to arise, well into the morning, to stagger about like befuddled drunks until their god could warm a fresh dose of energy in them. And on rainy days when the face of the Sun was hidden by a curtain of dark cumulus, the Makos would lie out in the weather, comatose for want of energy, until their god was resurrected from his watery grave. We used to watch them as children; believe me it was eerie.

And because the Sun shone on one and all without discrimination, their religion preached a sort of communalism, and robbed them of the concept of self. That was partly why they mutilated our language so: they had three words for 'we', but not one for 'I'. They were a strange lot, were the Makos.

How strange? I'll tell you. Their women were tall, they often grew into the thinning air while the men were broad, and frequently short enough to look up their womenfolk's skirts without squatting too much. Their children played curious games – they either spent countless hours hunting snakes, or rolled in the dust pretending to be reptiles themselves.

And the tribe had a pair of twins, Mara and Rama, who, growing in the same swaddle, had somehow developed a peculiar language of their own – distinct from the Mako dialect, and distinct from our language. I don't know how they did it, but that was the kind of thing one saw in Mako town. They were a strange lot, I tell you.

It was in 1956, during the census, that Mako town was first 'discovered' by the rest of the country, and loud cries went up in newspaper editorials calling on the

Government to civilise immediately these barbarians – whatever that meant. Within weeks European missionaries had swooped down on the town, to do battle with their heathen religion; and linguists came in droves too to study their strange dialect. Both groups met stony-faced uncooperation, and the missionaries left empty-handed, while the linguists left with the twins I just told you about.

'*Evak aka kuara!*' called Rama in their private language; and as no one had yet deciphered it, no one could say if this was a cry of farewell, or a cry for help.

'*Evak aka kuara!*' called Mara too, but no one could understand him any better.

Civilisation's next onslaught came in the form of a jeepful of health officials, spurred on by a United Nations grant to hunt down yellow fever to the remotest cranny and to gun it down with vaccines and stuff like that. They also met a refrigerated reception, flavoured, this time, with a pinch of curiosity.

'What do you want with us?' Mako's chief asked of the team's leader.

'There is a sickness called yellow fever, and it kills,' began the health official, talking slowly, allowing his interpreter time to garnish his words with figures of speech and the spidery gesticulations the Makos were much given to. 'However there is an injection which we can give your people that would protect you all from this disease.'

As he spoke, a cloud yawned the Sun in for a moment, and, as if assaulted, the Mako people collapsed as shadows spilled on to the grass about them for the span of that second. Then their God showed his face again, and they regained their feet, unsteadily.

'God,' roared the old chief, raising his hands to the god he meant, 'has answered you! We do not need your kind of protection.'

'The Sun is your god?' the doctor asked incredulously.

'The Sun is the source of all life, of all energy,' the chief said simply.

'Can't argue with that,' the doctor said, 'but why did you all fall down just now?'

'You have no right to ask such a question,' the chief said. 'You aren't young enough to be stupid, nor old enough to be senile; you have no right to ask unintelligent questions.'

The health official flushed on the translation of this.

'Oh, you mean that because the Sun is the source of energy, you are weakened when it blinks out even for a moment. Why didn't I fall too, or my men?'

'You are pagans,' the chief said simply.

'OK, what about night-time – what do you do then?'

'We sleep,' the Mako chief replied, and favoured the doctor with a pitying look.

'OK, imagine this. What if sometimes during the day the Sun were to go out like a candle for a few minutes – what would happen to your tribe then?' the doctor asked sharply, his eyes gleaming.

'That situation is called an eclipse,' the chief said, startling the other man with his knowledge and enjoying it. 'We have an eclipse in our history, and our religion teaches that, at the time of the second coming of the eclipse, God shall call his children to his ever-lit bosom. There shall be those minutes of darkness, but when the world is lit again, all true children of the Sun will have disappeared. But that day shall come like a thief in the night; why talk of it?'

The doctor beckoned one of his aides, and they conferred excitedly behind the screen of an open newspaper. Finally the aide withdrew, with the paper folded under his arm, and the doctor addressed the Mako, smiling.

'This is a remarkable coincidence, remarkable! We have ways – and we know as a fact that an eclipse shall be sighted in this part of the world at noon on the day after tomorrow. What do you have to say to that?'

'Then the day after tomorrow, the Makos will be no more,' the old chief replied with simple logic.

'But if you don't ascend into heaven or whatever,' the doctor insisted, 'then would you allow us to inoculate your people?'

'You have no right to ask unintelligent questions. Of course we will disappear into the Sun's bosom.'

'But what if...?'

'But if we don't, you may do whatever you want with us, for our lives would have ceased to have a meaning. How would you feel if you found out that your god was no more than a dry twig that chanced upon a flame? Now excuse me, I have to go and prepare my people.'

As the Mako chief turned his back and began to shuffle away from the health officials, they slapped their hands excitedly, celebrating perhaps the imminent triumph of science over superstition – or maybe the possibility of further UN grants – but probably just the taming of an annoyingly simple village chief. In two days, they were sure, they would immunise the Mako people and make the first inroad for civilisation. There could be no doubting that, could there?

Time passed on a snail-drawn chariot; it seemed like an eternity had shouldered its way in and separated every tick of the clock from its tock: an eclipse was always a memorable event, but this time it would represent the death of a world, or the hacking-down of a way of life. We couldn't wait. The day before the eclipse, the people of my village queued up and went 'Ouch!' in turn, as the health officials occupied themselves by shooting us full of antibodies.

But finally the day was upon us, the hour was upon us, and the minute was just around the corner. We were all tense – the health official began talking too much, explaining eclipses, while the Mako chief swallowed mouthfuls of nothing, feeding it to his faltering nerve. The Mako people stood around, the really tall women, the really short men, quiet in their faith in their god. Eyes darted anxiously from sky to wrist-watches, and back upwards.

Suddenly, a dimness crept on to an edge of the Sun and began to spread across its face, like an eager rash. Mothers from my village rushed their kids into their arms, screaming. And then the Sun was no more. Screaming, the Makos dropped to the grass, lifeless. Darkness. Would they disappear? Wouldn't they disappear? Would they disappear? I could feel everyone's thoughts buffeting me in that midday dusk.

Then just as suddenly it was over and, like a bad penny, the Sun was back. And there, lying at our feet, were the Makos, as invisible as the mountains, as our noses, as the health department jeep, as invisible as anything that was not invisible.

'We told you! We told you!' jubilated one of the health team, but our looks silenced him.

Before us, we saw the ruins of a religion, lying in the dust like a cripple who had lost control of his crutches; we saw the desolation of a hope discovered to be false, the bewilderment of a trust betrayed; we saw lives just proven to be wasted. Lying in the dust before us, we saw the disciples of a Christ who had failed to resurrect. How could we laugh at that?

The Mako chief finally climbed to his feet wearily; defeat and disillusionment had aged him horribly. Slowly, he pulled himself over to the health official and, silently, he proffered his shoulder for his jab. The doctor gave him his yellow fever vaccine silently, too; victory was not sweet.

The Makos crawled past the health team, one by one, in a straggly queue, but by sunset only half of their population had been inoculated. Fearing they might pass out on him for want of sunlight as their disgraced god dimmed from orange to cola-red and slunk off behind the hills, the health official ordered the Makos to bed for the day. And that was the last ever seen of them.

That's right, not one Mako has ever been seen to this day since that night, not even the twins, Mara and Rama. Did they run away? Did they disappear? I don't know; I am now old and wise but I still don't know that. What I do know is that a cowrie was found in the bed of each Mako, two in the beds of couples. If this is a clue, I don't...

'What's a cowrie?' one of the listeners asks the storyteller.

'It's a kind of sea-shell,' he answers.

'Why a cowrie?' the listener insists. 'Why not something else?'

'That I don't know.'

'Is this the end of the story?' another asks.

'No, that was merely the ... what's-it-called, prologue. Strange things began to ...'

But a voice calls from inside the hut: 'Husband, come and eat. Supper is ready.' The storyteller shrugs, rises and enters the hut. There is always tomorrow.

Winner of BBC Worldwide Magazine short story competition, December 1995

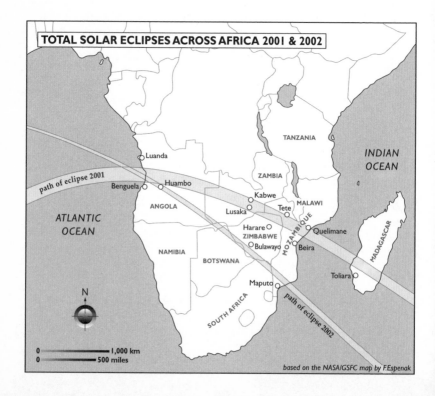

TOTAL SOLAR ECLIPSES ACROSS AFRICA 2001 & 2002

TANZANIA

INDIAN OCEAN

Luanda

path of eclipse 2001

ZAMBIA

Benguela   Huambo

Kabwe

ATLANTIC OCEAN

ANGOLA   Lusaka   Tete   MALAWI

Harare   Quelimane

ZIMBABWE

Bulawayo   Beira

NAMIBIA

BOTSWANA

MOZAMBIQUE

MADAGASCAR

N

Maputo   Toliara

SOUTH AFRICA   path of eclipse 2002

0 ———— 1,000 km
0 ———— 500 miles

based on the NASA/GSFC map by F.Espenak

Total Solar Eclipse

Aisling Irwin

INTRODUCTION

Every time the Moon passes between the Earth and the Sun, casting its shadow on our planet, the experience for the humans who watch it is different from the last. Every solar eclipse is governed by a multitude of rhythms and subtleties that guarantee its individuality. The Sun's activity, its flares and prominences, the exact positions of the Moon and the Earth – all these factors conspire with numerous others to ensure that each eclipse is unique. Similarly, the aesthetics of an eclipse are influenced by the time of day, the region of the world, the weather and, to a surprising extent, the surrounding crowds or emptiness.

Yet, despite this capacity for infinite variation, eclipses are governed by the enduring laws of celestial mechanics that guarantee us totalities for hundreds of millions of years to come.

EXPLANATIONS
Why eclipses happen

A total solar eclipse occurs when the Moon moves between the Sun and the Earth, fully blocking our view of the Sun.

This happens because of a heavenly coincidence: the Sun and the Moon, when viewed from the Earth, appear to be the same size. The Sun may seem at first to be the larger but this is because it is so bright. If you stick your thumb and forefinger out to gauge their apparent (or angular) sizes you will find they are the same.

In reality the Sun's diameter is 400 times that of the Moon. But, with perfect compensation, it sits 400 times further away. This symmetry has not always existed but scientists have calculated that things will remain this way for another 650 million years, after which the Moon will drift too far from the Earth for it ever again to be able to cover the Sun completely.

During the year the Earth takes to complete its journey around the Sun, the Moon speeds around the Earth about 12 times. Once in each of these cycles (known as synodic months) the Moon passes between the Sun and us and we see a new Moon. We do not see a monthly solar eclipse, though, because the Moon's orbit is at a slight angle to that of the Earth – so the Sun and Moon 'miss' each other as they pass across our skies.

To understand the orbits relevant to an eclipse it is easier to consider a model in which the solar system is inverted, with the Earth at its centre. This model, still in use for some purposes today, represents not the reality of planetary orbits but what we actually see when we look at the skies. In this model, the Sun's apparent path across the sky is known as the ecliptic.

What we see from Earth is the the Moon circling us every 27.5 days, and the Sun circling every 346.62 days – a period known as an eclipse year. The Moon catches up with the Sun every 29.5 days and would pass between it and Earth, causing a solar eclipse, if it weren't for those inclined orbits (see diagram). But the two orbital paths do, of course, intersect at two points. These points – or nodes – represent two periods each year during which the Moon can indeed pass in front of the Sun.

If the Sun, creeping along its yearly path, happens to be exactly at one of the two intersections when the Moon is racing round on its monthly cycle, there will be a total solar eclipse. If the Sun is just approaching or leaving the intersection there may yet be a total solar eclipse because the Moon is often large enough to cover it anyway. If the Sun is a little further from the intersection there is still the chance that the Moon will at least overlap with it, creating a partial solar eclipse.

In fact, the Sun moves so slowly that it is impossible for it to get past either intersection without the Moon catching up with it at least once, and therefore guaranteeing a solar eclipse of some sort. Sometimes the Moon manages to travel all the way round and catch up with the Sun before it has fully left the intersection – causing two partial eclipses a month apart. Whatever happens during these eclipse 'seasons', there will always be at least two solar eclipses of some sort each year.

Those are the basics behind a solar eclipse. In practice, however, there are various distortions and complexities that give each eclipse its signature. For example, both the Sun and the Moon follow elliptical paths around the Earth rather than circular ones, with the result that their distances from our planet vary. If a solar eclipse occurs when the Moon is at its furthest from the Earth and the Sun at its closest, a rim of Sun remains around the black disc of the eclipse – and we see an annular eclipse.

Eclipses pursue other, more long-term rhythms, the most distinctive of which is the Saros cycle, discovered by the Chaldeans possibly as early as 400BC and used over subsequent millennia to predict eclipses. The Chaldeans found that eclipses follow 18-year cycles, with each new solar eclipse bearing similarities to the one that occurred 18 years previously.

An eclipse casts a shadow in an arc across the Earth. For that shadow to be identical to the shadow cast by another eclipse, the relative orientations of the Earth, Moon and Sun would have to be exactly the same. This can occur only on the rare occasions when the Moon's position in its orbit around the Earth, and the Earth's position in its orbit around the Sun, are repeated. This does not happen every time. For example, when one eclipse year has passed and the Earth begins its orbit around the Sun again, the Moon is three-quarters of the way through a cycle round Earth; so it is not back in the same position as it was when the Earth last began an eclipse year. But after the passage of 18 years the Moon is just coming to the end of its monthly

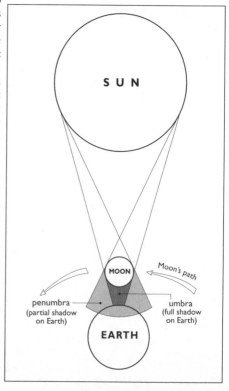

SUN

Moon's path

MOON

penumbra
(partial shadow
on Earth)

umbra
(full shadow
on Earth)

EARTH

cycle when the Earth is coming to the end of its yearly cycle – and they pass through positions very similar to those of 18 years previously. Thus, when an eclipse occurs over a certain region of the Earth, we can predict that, 18 years later, an eclipse will occur at a similar latitude. Because this synchronisation is not perfect the eclipse will be displaced from its 18-year-old sister by about one third of the world to the west. The eclipses in a Saros series also gradually shift northward or southward – about 1,000km every three cycles or so.

The 2001 total solar eclipse is a member of Saros cycle 127 and the 2002 eclipse belongs to Saros cycle 142.

Anatomy of the Sun

Our knowledge of the Sun has grown magnificently in recent years, partly because of the spacecraft *Soho* which creates a permanent eclipse between itself and the Sun, allowing constant monitoring of its outer layers.

The core of the Sun is a furnace of burning hydrogen of 15 million °C, hidden from view by a shell of opaque gases 696,000km thick. Working outwards, through layers of radiation and convection, we reach the **photosphere**. This is the Sun's visible surface – a boiling sea of rising and sinking gases of 5,500°C. It is the layer where sunspots emerge and vanish. The photosphere is only about 300km deep.

Above this layer is the **chromosphere**, a vivid orange colour, just 2,500km thick. Its temperature varies strangely, the lower levels being about 4,000°C and the upper layers hotter, at about 10,000°C. The chromosphere is not smooth but covered with sporadic projections of gas which can reach 700km high, as far as the next layer – the **corona**.

The corona is a haze stretching far from the Sun, growing ever thinner and still detectable as a tenuous haze beyond Earth.

Those parts of the chromosphere which stretch into the corona soar in temperature to 1 million°C. This heat accelerates charged particles outwards, imbuing them with enough speed to escape the Sun's gravitational field. The gases rising from the surface of the Sun expand as they go and so their density decreases and they are more easily warped by the Sun's magnetic fields. This twists them into loops and arches known as **prominences**. Sometimes a magnetic loop breaks and billions of tons of gas shoot into space, creating a coronal mass ejection.

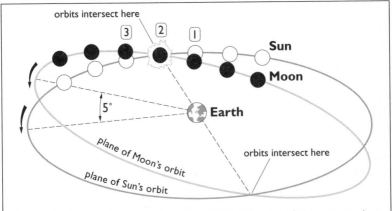

The moon's orbit is at a 5° angle to the Sun's orbit. At positions 1 and 3 there is a partial solar eclipse. At position 2 there is a total solar eclipse.

X-ray pictures reveal the Sun's outer layer to be full of roller-coaster loops and exploding gases interspersed with darker, quieter regions known as **coronal holes**. The beauty of a total solar eclipse is that, with the glare of the photosphere obscured, you can for once witness the chromosphere and corona.

What to watch for as the eclipse unfolds

'...An unearthly gloom enveloped us, and the atmosphere grew chill, so that we shivered perhaps as much with awe as with the cold...'

Quoted in *1927: a British Eclipse* by R A Marriott

Once you are well inside the path of totality (which you can work out using the maps and tables in this book) you can settle down to watch the spectacle unfold. Do not worry too much about memorising the precise timings of the stages of the eclipse – so long as you know roughly (to the nearest 15 minutes) when to look, nature will guide you through the experience.

When the Moon first encroaches on the Sun, the moment known as **first contact** has arrived. It is followed some time later by **second contact** – the moment when the Moon drifts fully in front of the Sun and totality begins. **Third contact** heralds the end of totality because the Moon starts to shift away from the Sun. **Fourth contact** is when the two discs finally part.

At first an eclipse is almost unnoticeable, just a shallow scoop from one edge of the Sun which hardly diminishes the daylight. The fading of the day happens very slowly and, until the Sun is more than half covered, there is little more than a faint dullness. Even when the Sun is 80% covered most of us will notice little change in the light because our brains are so used to compensating for the effects of heavy cloud. But the Moon crawls relentlessly onwards and, when it has covered 90% of the Sun, the light will fail noticeably and the land will turn a bluish grey. With about ten minutes to go, some people will shield one eye to accustom it to darkness, so they will be better able to appreciate the wisps and auras that characterise totality.

From about five minutes before totality you should start watching for brighter planets such as Venus, near the Sun.

The shadow cast by the Moon in 2001 and 2002 will appear on the western horizon like the approach of a giant, silent thunderstorm. You may spot it racing towards you when there are about three minutes to go before totality, when it is roughly 120km away.

During the last few minutes before second contact, daylight will disappear fast. Now is the moment to watch the ground for **shadow bands** rippling across lightly coloured surfaces, as if on a lake. The ripples appear because of a lensing effect caused by the Earth's upper atmosphere which bends and focuses the light streaming towards Earth from the Sun's thin remaining crescent. You can see them more easily if you lay a white sheet on the ground. Note also tiny crescent shapes projected on to the ground through gaps between the leaves of trees and bushes.

About 15 seconds before the Sun is completely eclipsed, you will see specks of light appear around the dark disc of the Moon, just like a string of pearls. These are **Baily's Beads**, the last few rays of sunlight shining through valleys on the edge of the Moon. They will swiftly die away until just one remains – a dazzling jewel known as the **diamond ring** which glints for just three or four seconds and then vanishes.

From the moment of the diamond ring's appearance it is safe to view with the naked eye, though you may pay a penalty for viewing the diamond by being unable at first to distinguish the features of the ensuing **totality**.

You will know when totality has arrived. Suddenly the Moon's shadow rushes across the land towards you and your world is plunged into twilight.

Now the secrets of the Sun's outer layers, usually hidden by the glare of its fiery centre, are briefly revealed. For the first few seconds of totality you may see a vibrant, pinkish-red rim at the edge of the Sun. This is the light from the Sun's lower atmosphere, the chromosphere. As the Moon moves onwards it will swiftly cover this too (during very short eclipses the chromosphere never really disappears because the Moon is only minutely larger than the Sun).

An effect that should last a little longer will be the appearance of several deep red clouds, like smoke drifting from the surface of the Sun. These are the **solar prominences**, stretching to a distance of up to one-twentieth of the Sun's diameter.

At full totality you will see the black disc of the Moon perfectly surrounded by the pearly light of the Sun's corona. Wispy plumes and streams of coronal light will dance outwards. In 2001, it will be only 18 months after the maximum of the Sun's 11-year cycle, so you may instead see a vast and complete aureole, like a cushion behind the Moon. It may be hard to see streamers because of the Sun's high level of activity so near the solar maximum. Streamers may be easier to distinguish 18

THE STAGES OF A TOTAL SOLAR ECLIPSE

First contact: The moment when the edge of the Moon first encroaches on the Sun.

The moon approaches 50% coverage of the Sun but the ambient light has changed little.

Second contact: Just before second contact the Sun's rays still leak through the valleys of the Moon creating Baily's Beads.

Diamond ring: A gleam from the Sun lingers until the Moon fully covers the Sun.

Totality: The eclipse is total. When it ends we have third contact. The diamond ring will appear on the other side.

Fourth contact: The Moon takes its leave of the Sun. The eclipse is over.

NB: The Sun's orientation to the Moon is as it will be for Plumtree, Zimbabwe, in 2002

months later, during the 2002 eclipse. However, these rules do not always apply and large streamers have been witnessed during total solar eclipses that occur around the solar maximum.

If you can drag your eyes away from the eclipse itself, you will have an unprecedented opportunity to view the daytime positions of planets and stars (see diagrams) which began to emerge just before totality.

Don't forget to check the **landscape**, where nature will respond as if night has fallen. Flowers will close their petals and disorientated bees will cease their flight. Insects, maintaining their

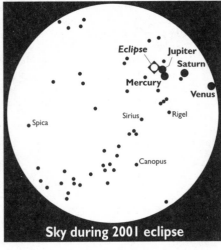

Sky during 2001 eclipse

daytime silence until the moment of totality, will suddenly sing as if it were night, and mosquitoes will start biting. Elephants which were grazing peacefully may become nervous and confused, while the birds above them will flock into the trees with great fuss. In general, animals go to waterholes or begin their nightly foraging. Cows have been known to line up and walk home.

In the distance, where the eclipse is only partial, the horizon will be an evening pink. The temperature plunge will be noticeable.

When the diamond ring emerges again at the opposite edge of the Sun from before, totality has finished and the sequence will begin again in reverse. At its appearance look away or use your eclipse viewer.

At fourth contact, the eclipse is over.

If the day is thick with cloud then most of these sights will be hidden, but partial cloud and thin cloud will not necessarily spoil the experience. The eclipse carries

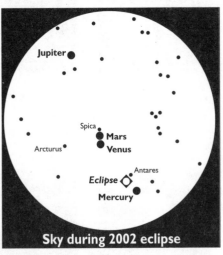

Sky during 2002 eclipse

with it its own weather patterns, caused by the wild temperature variations that the moving shadow creates on Earth. This can cause clouds miraculously to disperse during the seconds leading up to totality – but more often it can cause them swiftly to materialise out of a previously clear sky (rapid cooling of the air can have either effect, depending on the humidity and pressure). Trying to catch a glimpse of totality through the spaces between thick clouds has its own thrills – even one fleeting view seems a tremendous achievement and is deeply exciting. If there is broken cloud you may see patterning and colours in the sky. If there is thin cloud, the corona may still be visible. Finally, for those besieged by the weather, watch out for a shadow that the Moon may cast on to the cloud above you.

ECLIPSES IN HISTORY
Humans and eclipses

'The Sun...
In dim eclipse disastrous twilight sheds
On half the nations, and with fear of change
Perplexes monarchs.'

John Milton, *Paradise Lost*, Book I, lines 587–600 (1667)

Milton's sentiment remains true today. A total solar eclipse bypasses the brain, with its scientific understanding, and speaks primitively to the heart. It reminds us of our cosmic insignificance.

Eclipses caused far more perturbation when they were unpredictable – and historians have studied ancient responses to them.

The oldest known eclipse tale comes from China and relates to two astronomers, Hsi and Hoe, who became drunk and failed to respond adequately to a total solar eclipse, a crime which was punished by death. If this were true it would mean that the first recorded eclipse occurred between 2159 and 1948BC. But it is almost certainly a myth, perhaps a morality tale aimed at civil servants of the time.

The first person to predict totality with success was thought for a long time to have been Thales of Miletus. He is said to have foretold the year and position of an influential eclipse that plunged a battlefield into darkness during an encounter between the Lydians and the Medes. Chastened by the experience, the two sides laid down their arms and agreed a peace deal. Today astronomers cannot see how Thales could have predicted an eclipse given the limited knowledge at the time. It is generally agreed that, while the solar drama may well have ended a war, probably on May 28 585BC, it was not actually predicted.

Ancient civilisations such as the Egyptians, the Chinese and the Babylonians all developed methods for tracking the motions of the Sun and Moon, and had thorough constellation maps. The best-known eclipse archive was developed by the Chaldeans who began to keep precise historical records from 750BC to AD75. They developed mathematical theories from these records and, in the 4th century BC (the Hellenistic period), they made the breakthrough of examining past records to look for repeating cycles: eclipse prediction had begun.

Even today those Babylonian records, stored on thousands of clay tablets, are useful. In 1997 F Richard Stephenson, an astronomer from Durham University in Britain, used a discrepancy between the records of 136BC and today's calculations to show that the Earth's rotation is slowing by 2.3 milliseconds per century. His work was published in *Historical Eclipses and the Earth's Rotation* (see *Further Reading*).

Scientific study of the Sun during eclipses began in the early 19th century with Francis Baily, who gave his name to the 'string of bright beads' that fringes the Moon just before totality. After his successful public relations activities for total solar eclipses scientists began their modern pursuit of eclipse-chasing, pointing all manner of instruments at the Sun to exploit the rare moment when its faint corona could be viewed unimpeded.

Eclipses in Africa

Since a region may go for hundreds of years between solar eclipses, the people's knowledge of previous eclipses will be scant if they have not passed down written records or travelled extensively.

One solar eclipse in Africa is well remembered because it presided over an important moment in the history of a powerful tribe. The Ngoni are Bantu-speaking people who are today scattered throughout eastern Africa. In the early 19th century they lived further south but were forced to flee into what is today east Zambia to escape Shaka Zulu, the warrior behind the Zulu empire. On the day the Ngoni crossed the Zambezi during this epic migration the Moon passed in front of the Sun.

Eclipse fanatics from other continents have periodically assailed Africa, bent on solving the burning scientific riddle of the day by means of balloon, boat and even Concorde.

Jules Janssen was a physicist who became the first to point a spectroscope at an eclipse, in 1868. He was desperate to continue his studies two years later, below an eclipse that was due to pass over Algeria. When it came to the moment for departure, however, the Franco-Prussian war was in progress and Paris was under siege. So Janssen took to a balloon, piloting it by himself and surviving powerful winds. He landed safely in Algeria but failed to see the eclipse because of cloud.

Perhaps the most famous African eclipse in scientific history was that of 1919, three years after Albert Einstein published his complete theory of general relativity. Scientists knew there was an observation they could make during an eclipse which could test one of the predictions of relativity theory – that the Sun bends the light coming from any nearby star. To detect such weak starlight coming from close to the Sun it was necessary to wait for the Moon to blot it out. The 1919 eclipse crossed the island of Principe and the tip of West Africa, afterwards passing along a path a little north of the June 2001 eclipse, taking in Gabon, Congo, Zambia and Tanzania on the way. Arthur Eddington, the British physicist, elected to study it from Principe and despite relentless cloud obtained the first measurements of starlight deflection, supporting Einstein's theory.

Khartoum was the next African venue, in 1952, where scientists wanted to study the emissions of the solar corona. A team led by Professor Madwar, of the Egyptian Royal Institute, and Bernard Lyot, battled its way to Anglo-Egyptian territory, unperturbed by the riots, martial law and strikes that marked Egyptian resistance to British troops. Working with scientists from the Helwan Observatory in Egypt they set up their equipment to the west of Khartoum and at the Fort Stanley site east of the town. Three days before the eclipse was due, a desert sandstorm blew up and blotted out the sky for a day. But they saw a magnificent eclipse on February 25.

On June 30 1973 it was the turn of the Sahara desert to host a team of scientists with burning questions to answer. Since 1916, when the warping of starlight was first measured, there had been numerous attempts to repeat the observations and produce definitive evidence that it did happen. The Saharan eclipse promised to be an ideal setting. It was to have the second longest totality of the 20th century – 7 minutes 3 seconds at its maximum. A team of Americans made elaborate preparations and turned up there – only for a dust storm to begin just before the eclipse, choking the atmosphere and blocking over 80% of the light. Another team had better luck overhead. Scientists commandeered Concorde 001 to travel with the eclipse across Africa at supersonic speeds and thus witness totality for 74 minutes. They set off from Las Palmas in the Canaries and flew across Africa as the eclipse passed over ten African countries, from Mauritania via Niger and Sudan, leaving the continent at Somalia.

African Sun and Moon myths

The Sun and Moon are key figures in creation myths across much of the world including Africa. Many myths and folktales from the 46 or so African tribes have themes in common and refer to a Golden Age in which the earth needed no cultivation, there was no war, and humans lived without sorrow. As with other cultures, explanations of the creation of the world assume that the Earth is at the centre of the story. The Sun and Moon generally began their existence on Earth and the myths explain how they ended up in the sky.

One Nigerian myth describes the Sun living with his wife, the Moon, on Earth. The Sun was good friends with the ocean and would often visit, but the ocean would never return the compliment on the grounds that the Sun's house was too small. Eventually the Sun built a huge yard and persuaded the ocean to visit. The water, fish and all, filled the yard and the house, driving the Sun and Moon on to their roof. Eventually they were forced to retreat to a refuge in the sky, and have remained there ever since, taking it in turns to gaze down on their old house back on Earth.

In similar vein, the Bushmen have a myth entitled 'The Sun and the Children' which depicts the Sun living on the Earth. This time a group of children wait until he is asleep and then throw him into the sky where he can do useful work warming them.

The Boshongo, a Bantu tribe of central Africa, ascribe even less dignified beginnings to the Sun and Moon. Their story describes how the great god Bumba vomited up the Sun and then the Moon, followed by assorted animals and then humans.

For the Dogon, the Sun and Moon were fashioned by the supreme God Amma, using two white earthenware bowls, one encircled with red copper, the other with white copper. Black people were born under the Sun and white people under the Moon.

Mythology specific to eclipses is less common. In Zimbabwe several tribes, including some in Matabeleland and the Sotho people in Gwanda district, believe that an eclipse of the Moon occurs because the Moon is decaying away, only to be immediately replaced by a brand new Moon. In Nambya (a tiny tribe concentrated in Hwange district) they call it *kubola mweji* - the rotting of the Moon.

The Fon people of West Africa have a myth about Liza, associated with the fierce and harsh Sun, who is inseparable from his partner, Mawu, associated with the Moon. Liza was also the god of day, heat, work and strength. Mawu was the goddess of night, fertility, rest and motherhood. When there is an eclipse, it is said that Mawu and Liza are making love.

Planning and Preparation

Aisling Irwin

WHERE TO GO
The eclipse paths

The June 21 2001 eclipse appears at sunrise over the Atlantic Ocean near the South American coast. It travels for 37 minutes across these waters, starting at a speed of 3km/sec, and reducing to 0.5km/sec, passing its maximum (with 4 minutes 57 seconds of totality) before it reaches the west coast of Africa.

Its shadow will fall on the African landmass at 13.39 local time, and will leave Madagascar just over 2 hours 11 minutes later. During that time it will follow a shallow, southeasterly curve across Angola and on into remote western Zambia after which it will reach the only capital city on its path: Lusaka. At early afternoon it will cross the Zambezi and move into some of the most beautiful parts of northern Zimbabwe, straddling the border between that country and Mozambique. Racing now towards the coast at 0.8km/sec, it will clip the most southern tip of Malawi and reach the Mozambique Channel at Quelimane. After presenting Madagascar's west coast with a spectacular sunset, the eclipse will depart from the island's east coast and the Moon's shadow will depart from the Earth's surface at the Indian Ocean.

The December 4 2002 eclipse follows a remarkably similar path, shifted to the east and tilted to the south. It, too, starts in the Atlantic Ocean but this time much nearer the African coast, with first contact reaching land just before 06.00 local time. Taking a steeper, more southeasterly course through Angola it flirts with southwest Zambia and nips across Namibia's Caprivi Strip. Narrowly missing the Victoria Falls it slips down the border between Botswana and Zimbabwe, darkens the northern part of Kruger National Park in South Africa and passes over southern Mozambique. Fourth contact leaves Africa just after 09.45 and heads towards its maximum, 2 minutes 4 seconds, on the Indian Ocean. From there it journeys towards a sunset in Australia.

Choosing your eclipse

The 2001 eclipse has a number of advantages. It occurs during the dry season, so there is an excellent chance of clear skies. Its path is broad – a corridor 200km wide

THE BRADT WEBSITE

Inevitably, travel information about the eclipses will alter as new viewing sites open, others become fully booked, and the security situation changes. To help our readers plan good trips, Bradt has set up an eclipse page on its website (www.bradt-travelguides.com/eclipse) which our specialist authors will keep up to date. If you come across new information yourself, please help us to make it one of the most useful 2001 and 2002 sites by sending brief details to info@bradt-travelguides.com

ECLIPSE-CHASERS
Sheridan Williams

You've heard of trainspotters – well, there are people whose sole aim in life is to go to the ends of the Earth (literally) to see a total solar eclipse. These people have names such as eclipse-chasers, ecliptomaniacs, eclipsoholics and umbraphiles. We (I admit that I class myself as one) take total solar eclipses very seriously. For example I use total solar eclipses to plan my holidays, so in 1988 I went to Sumatra, 1990 to Finland, 1991 to the Baja Peninsula in Mexico, 1994 to Peru, 1997 to Siberia, 1998 to Antigua and 1999 to Cornwall in England. Future holidays will be Madagascar in 2001, South Australia in 2002, Antarctica in 2003, on a boat in the Pacific off the coast of central America in 2005, either Libya or Turkey in 2006, Mongolia or west China in 2008, east China in 2009, and Easter Island in the Pacific in 2010. If I should live for another 20 years I will be able to see the next total eclipse to traverse British waters in 2015 – this eclipse passes right next to the tiny island of Rockall on March 20.

Umbraphiles will go to any lengths to find the best location to maximise the chance of seeing totality, and for the March 1997 eclipse most tours went to Mongolia. I decided that the eclipse would be too short and low on the horizon when seen from Mongolia, but the problem was that maximum duration and altitude was at latitude 60°N in northern Russia – inaccessible in March and unbelievably cold. I chose Chita in Siberia near Lake Baikal as the best bet. To cut a long story short, when I arrived in Chita I was walking past the station and who should get off the Trans Siberian Express but Glenn Schneider, adding to other unplanned encounters with him in 1988 and 1991. According to my survey, Glenn currently leads the world's umbraphiles, having seen 21 total solar eclipses, and has been in the Moon's umbral shadow for 63 minutes. I rate a mere 12th tied in this table (see my website: www.clock-tower.com).

Glenn is renowned for his exploits, which include a hike up a mountain on Atka island in the Aleutians to see the 1990 eclipse. However, his most extraordinary endeavour was on October 3 1986. A solar eclipse was due to happen but unfortunately it was only to be annular from the surface of the Earth – and an annular eclipse is no good for an umbraphile as the Moon is not big enough to cover the Sun completely. It just so happened that the Moon's umbral shadow (the only place in which a total solar eclipse can be seen)

at its maximum compared with 87km for 2002. And totality will last for longer – the maximum totality over Africa is 4 minutes 34 seconds (Angolan coast) compared with 1 minute 31 seconds for 2002 (Mozambique coast). In each country the eclipse occurs in the afternoon, allowing plenty of time for viewers to set up beforehand.

The 2002 eclipse occurs during the wet season so the chance of clear skies is less. But it has other advantages. It appears over some choice venues, including Kruger National Park in South Africa, the Matobo Hills of Zimbabwe and Xai-Xai beach in Mozambique. The best positions from which to watch happen to be accessible – unlike in 2001 where Angola is unlikely to attract more than a handful of people. In South Africa, Mozambique and Zimbabwe the eclipse falls during high season for local holiday-makers so the atmosphere in places like Xai-Xai beach is bound to be exuberant.

stopped 12km above the Earth's surface. A group of nine umbraphiles led by Glenn arranged to charter a Cessna Citation aircraft to fly up into the arctic air near Greenland and rendezvous with the Moon's tiny shadow, which was probably only a few hundred metres across. If their calculations were correct, and the pilot could fly accurately, they would witness a fleeting glimpse of totality, maybe only one or two seconds, but long enough to notch up another total eclipse.

This feat was successful and, as soon as totality ended, Glenn and his team looked down at the cloud tops and saw a cigar-shaped shadow of the Moon racing off into the distance, secure in the knowledge that they were the only living creatures to see this totality. To read more about this amazing feat look at the website: http://nicmosis.as.arizona.edu:8000/ECLIPSE_WEB/ECLIPSE_86/ECLIPSE_86.html.

There can be problems if you are a fanatical umbraphile. I recall that in July 1991 we were relaxing in luxury at a beach hotel in San Cabo at the southern tip of the Mexican Baja Peninsula, waiting for an eclipse that was to last 6 minutes 43 seconds. It was to be the longest remaining eclipse in the lifetime of everyone on this planet. A group of umbraphiles amongst us had previously calculated that a 50km trip into the desert would yield an extra 11 seconds of totality, so off they set at dawn armed with kit to allow them to survive many hours with no shelter, with the midday Sun directly overhead.

Meanwhile we sat on the beach, occasionally taking half a dozen steps into our hotel rooms to collect another beer from the fridge. We saw a magnificent, full-duration eclipse in total luxury – unaware that the group that had set out earlier had a cloud drift in front of the Sun for over a minute. For all their extra (life-threatening) efforts they saw less totality than we did.

The fanatical umbraphile will be armed with a laptop computer and global positioning system as well as a detailed chart of the Moon's valleys and mountains. Using these, it is often found that maximum totality can be some way away from the centre-line, allowing a valuable second or two to be added to the viewing log. The best locations are frequented by hundreds of umbraphiles, which itself attracts the media, local dignitaries and others. This prevents umbraphiles from making exaggerated claims about their times under totality.

If you succeed in seeing totality in 2001 or 2002, I assure you that you will want to see another. And then you will have become an umbraphile.

Choosing your country

You should select your viewing point from a compromise between length of totality, weather, ambience, safety, practicality and budget.

Most importantly, you must be within the path of totality – that is, within the corridor from which you can see the Moon covering the Sun 100%. The Sun is so bright that if even 0.1% remains exposed its light will submerge such glories as the diamond ring and the wonders of the corona. So do not be tempted by the promise of a 98% eclipse over the Victoria Falls – that is like going to the opera but remaining in the foyer, according to Jay Pasachoff, an eclipse specialist in the United States. Get well into the path of totality. As the Moon's surface has mountains and valleys, it is not possible to define the exact edge of its shadow on the Earth. It is therefore safer to avoid those places that appear to be just on the edge of totality.

ESSENTIAL FACTS

Date	June 21 2001	December 4 2002
Passes over	Angola, Zambia, Zimbabwe, Mozambique, Madagascar	Angola, Zambia, Namibia, Botswana, Zimbabwe, South Africa, Mozambique, southern Australia
Eclipse begins	Atlantic Ocean, 400km east of Uruguay, South America	Atlantic Ocean, 1,800km west of Luanda, Angola
Eclipse ends	Indian Ocean, 850km east of Madagascar	Australia, southwest tip of Queensland
Maximum totality	Atlantic Ocean, 1,100km west of Lobito, lasting 4min 56sec	Indian Ocean, 3,000km southeast of Mozambique, lasting 2min 3sec
Maximum width of path of totality	201km	87km
Altitude of Sun at greatest eclipse	55°	72°
Time at greatest eclipse (GMT)	12.04	07.31
Saros cycle number	127	142

Perfectionists will want to consider how to maximise their experience of totality. There are two ways of doing this. The first is to choose a position as near to the point of maximum eclipse as possible. In 2001 the maximum eclipse occurs before the Moon's shadow reaches Africa – so the further west you are, the better. In 2002 the eclipse reaches its maximum after it has departed from Africa – so the further east you are, the better. The other trick is to be as close to the centre-line as possible. However, the duration of totality does not taper away significantly until you are quite near the borders of the path of the total eclipse.

In the case of the 2001 eclipse, people may want to sacrifice length of time spent in totality for the intriguing spectacle of an eclipse that finishes exactly at sunset, which can be witnessed from the west coast of Madagascar, where fourth contact and sunset are at precisely the same time. You can use the table (page 16) to help guide your choice.

Ensuring a high chance of clear skies is the next most important consideration. The 2001 eclipse occurs while southern Africa is in the midst of its winter with plenty of fine, mid-June weather. Meteorologists predict that the chance of cloud gradually increases the further east you go from about 5% in Angola to 20% in west Zambia, to 40% in Mozambique. Southwest Madagascar is the exception with only a 20% chance of cloud. One of the reasons for this gradation is that as you get closer to the Mozambique channel, trade winds blow in, bringing clouds on to the land; and cloud bubbles up over the Zambezi. The 2002 eclipse occurs during the wet season in most of its countries and so cloud is more likely. However, in several countries the typical pattern is cloud build-up during the day with rain in the afternoon, so the early eclipse may avoid this.

Skies can also become obscured by dust storms and smoke. Seasonal forest fires, which add a haziness to the sky, may detract from the view of the 2001 eclipse, particularly in central Angola and central Zambia.

The third consideration is maximising your panorama. A panorama to the west is best, as watching the Moon's shadow approach is invariably more exciting than seeing it depart. So head for hills, preferably adjacent to an expanse of flat land or ocean. Avoid valleys and spots with vegetation that might get in the way. This is particularly important if the Sun is low in the sky as it will be in Madagascar in 2001 and in Angola in 2002.

Then there are personal factors. You may want to be somewhere you know to be beautiful – such as the Zambezi escarpment or Kruger National Park. You may want to witness the eclipse with crowds – collective emotion is an essential part of the experience for many people – who could head for Mana Pools in Zimbabwe or Xai-Xai beach in Mozambique. If you prefer to be alone or only with local people you might try some of the village visiting schemes in Zimbabwe or head to remoter parts of Zambia. Jay Anderson, a Canadian eclipse veteran, says: 'Get out of the big cities, get into the small towns, hold hands with the local people and enjoy it with them and you will have friends for life.'

There are also practical considerations. A country with a good tourist infrastructure will be less likely to let you down at the last minute with a bus breakdown. Security issues as this book goes to press rule out much of Angola, whose conflict also leaks over the border with Zambia and Namibia. Some people prefer not to visit Johannesburg because of its high crime levels. Recent unrest in Zimbabwe means that you should check the security situation before deciding to go there.

Finally: plan a holiday that will be a success even if you have an eclipse disaster. A rogue cloud is bound to obscure the eclipse for some, and transport problems will prevent others reaching totality on time. Make sure your holiday has another highlight as well.

Cruises are an option for some. In June 2001, the region of the Atlantic which is near the eclipse maximum is very cloudy and even a ship may not be able to escape large amounts of cloud cover. The situation in 2002 will be better. The advantage of a cruise is that, should cloud appear, the ship can belt off unimpeded towards clear skies. Some people will enjoy the freedom from the hassles of being on land in a strange country. But those on cruises will not see the response of nature or of local people to the eclipse, and photography will be limited by the undulations of the boat.

The idea of chartering a light aircraft may tempt others. It seems an exotic way of viewing an eclipse but from the air you will miss a lot of the atmosphere, so consider it only in cloudy conditions. Even then, light planes cannot always get above the clouds.

GETTING THERE AND AROUND
Planning your own trip

This guide is designed to be used in conjunction with a country guide, for it would be impossible to talk you through the arrangement of an entire holiday in each country without producing a book of encyclopaedic size. This book tells you how to see the eclipses, which often entails visiting places not usually covered in guidebooks. You will also find plenty of pointers to general holiday information sources and suggestions for sightseeing in the regions of the eclipses.

Do plan your trip as soon as possible. The June 2001 eclipse has attracted a wealth of interest in Zambia and Zimbabwe, with many popular sites already fully booked. However, in many cases, it is tour operators rather than real visitors who have booked the places – so in reality they may still be available. Do not be put off

ECLIPSE TIMINGS: WEST TO EAST (all times are local)
June 21 2001

Country	Location	GMT+	Lat (S)	Long (E)
St Helena	*Island*	0	*15° 55'*	5° 44'W
240km N of St Helena		0	13° 18'	4° 50'W
Angola	Egito	1	11° 57'	13° 46'
Angola	Santa Filomena	1	11° 38'	13° 46'
Angola	Sumbe	1	11° 12'	13° 50'
Angola	Tete	1	10° 55'	14° 09'
Angola	Waku-Kungo	1	11° 25'	15° 07'
Angola	Gungo	1	10° 49'	15° 33'
Angola	Silva Porto	1	12° 22'	16° 55'
Angola	Kuito	1	12° 22'	16° 56'
Angola	Luena	1	11° 47'	19° 54'
Angola	Lumbala	1	12° 39'	22° 35'
Angola	Chinde	1	12° 42'	22° 51'
Zambia	Zambezi	1	13° 32'	23° 06'
Zambia	Kabompo	1	13° 36'	24° 12'
Zambia	Lusaka	2	15° 24'	28° 16'
Zimbabwe	*Kariba*	2	*16° 31'*	28° 47'
Zimbabwe	Chirundu	2	16° 05'	28° 55'
Zimbabwe	*Makuti*	2	*16° 18'*	29° 14'
Zimbabwe	Mana Pools	2	15° 42'	29° 20'
Zambia	Mana Pools	2	15° 53'	29° 25'
Zimbabwe	*Karoi*	2	*16° 48'*	*29° 41'*
Mozambique	Zumbo	2	15° 36'	30° 26'
Zimbabwe	Mushumbi Pools	2	16° 08'	30° 33'
Zimbabwe	Guruve	2	16° 39'	30° 41'
Zimbabwe	Muzeza	2	16° 05'	30° 50'
Zimbabwe	Siyalima Farm	2	16° 39'	30° 50'
Zimbabwe	*Mvurwi*	2	*17° 02'*	*30° 55'*
Zimbabwe	*Harare*	2	*17° 49'*	*31° 03'*
Zimbabwe	Musengedzi	2	16° 05'	31° 05'
Mozambique	Hoya River (Zim'we border)	2	15° 58'	31° 08'
Zimbabwe	Bindura	2	17° 18'	31° 19'
Zimbabwe	Mount Darwin	2	16° 49'	31° 34'
Zimbabwe	*Murewa*	2	*17° 38'*	*31° 46'*
Zimbabwe	Bullnoze	2	16° 26'	31° 51'
Zimbabwe	Mutoko (Mtoko)	2	17° 24'	32° 13'
Zimbabwe	Ruangwe	2	16° 37'	32° 50'
Zimbabwe	Nyamapanda	2	16° 59'	32° 55'
Mozambique	Centre-line on route 103	2	16° 53'	33° 05'
Mozambique	Changara	2	16° 50'	33° 16'
Mozambique	Centre-line on route 102	2	17° 05'	33° 22'
Mozambique	Guro	2	17° 25'	33° 30'
Mozambique	*Tete*	2	*16° 09'*	*33° 35'*
Mozambique	Sena Bridge	2	17° 26'	35° 03'
Mozambique	Caia	2	17° 48'	35° 20'
Mozambique	Mopeia	2	17° 58'	35° 42'
Mozambique	Marromeu	2	18° 16'	35° 55'
Mozambique	Chinde	2	18° 34'	36° 28'
Mozambique	Quelimane	2	17° 52'	36° 52'
Madagascar	Morombe	3	21° 44'	43° 21'
Madagascar	Ihosy	3	22° 23'	46° 07'
Madagascar	Vangaindrano	3	23° 21'	47° 36'

• Locations in *italics* will not witness totality, so there will be no second and third contacts. For these place
** Altitude of the Sun at mid eclipse

1st contact	2nd contact	Mid	3rd contact	4th contact	Duration* (min:sec)	Alt**
10:03:30	N/A	11:35:11	N/A	13:15:12	96.5%	49°
10:05:47	11:36:32	11:38:54	11:41:15	13:19:48	00:04:43	52°
11:57:11	13:37:07	13:38:05	13:39:04	15:08:30	00:01:57	48°
11:57:18	13:36:16	13:38:12	13:40:07	15:08:35	00:03:50	48°
11:57:41	13:36:12	13:38:30	13:40:48	15:08:54	00:04:35	49°
11:58:42	13:37:25	13:39:36	13:41:46	15:09:36	00:04:20	49°
12:01:47	13:39:56	13:42:11	13:44:27	15:11:12	00:04:30	47°
12:03:17	13:41:52	13:43:30	13:45:07	15:12:05	00:03:14	47°
12:07:24	13:45:20	13:46:42	13:48:04	15:13:54	00:02:44	45°
12:07:30	13:45:24	13:46:47	13:48:10	15:13:54	00:02:46	45°
12:17:18	13:53:05	13:54:36	13:56:06	15:18:42	00:03:00	42°
12:25:30	13:58:52	14:00:29	14:02:07	15:21:54	00:03:15	39°
12:26:17	13:59:31	14:01:05	14:02:40	15:22:11	00:03:09	38°
12:26:54	13:59:30	14:01:24	14:03:17	15:22:17	00:03:47	38°
12:30:18	14:01:52	14:03:48	14:05:44	15:23:36	00:03:52	47°
13:41:36	15:09:15	15:10:53	15:12:32	16:26:59	00:03:17	31°
13:42:36	N/A	15:11:17	N/A	16:26:54	98.8%	30°
13:43:06	15:11:07	15:11:42	15:12:16	16:27:11	00:01:08	30°
13:43:54	N/A	15:12:11	N/A	16:27:24	99.9%	29°
13:44:24	15:10:55	15:12:36	15:14:17	16:27:41	00:03:22	30°
13:44:36	15:11:08	15:12:41	15:14:14	16:27:48	00:03:06	29°
13:45:00	N/A	15:12:41	N/A	16:27:29	99%	29°
13:47:18	15:12:54	15:14:30	15:16:05	16:28:41	00:03:11	28°
13:47:23	15:12:49	15:14:30	15:16:10	16:28:35	00:03:20	28°
13:47:42	15:13:30	15:14:30	15:15:29	16:28:30	00:02:00	28°
13:48:11	15:13:11	15:14:53	15:16:35	16:28:48	00:03:24	28°
13:48:05	15:13:32	15:14:41	15:15:50	16:28:35	00:02:17	27°
13:48:05	N/A	15:14:41	N/A	16:28:23	99.6%	27°
13:48:11	N/A	15:14:30	N/A	16:28:06	97.7%	27°
13:48:47	15:13:36	15:15:17	15:16:59	16:29:00	00:03:23	28°
13:48:59	15:13:51	15:15:29	15:17:08	16:29:05	00:03:17	28°
13:48:59	N/A	15:15:12	N/A	16:28:35	99.3%	27°
13:49:54	15:14:22	15:15:48	15:17:14	16:29:05	00:02:52	27°
13:50:00	N/A	15:15:42	N/A	16:28:41	98.9%	26°
13:50:42	15:14:43	15:16:24	15:18:04	16:29:23	00:03:20	27°
13:51:11	15:16:19	15:16:30	15:16:40	16:29:12	00:00:20	26°
13:52:59	15:16:14	15:17:48	15:19:21	16:30:00	00:03:07	25°
13:53:05	15:16:04	15:17:42	15:19:19	16:29:54	00:03:15	25°
13:53:29	15:16:22	15:17:59	15:19:37	16:30:00	00:03:15	25°
13:54:00	15:16:43	15:18:17	15:19:52	16:30:12	00:03:07	25°
13:54:12	15:16:40	15:18:17	15:19:55	16:30:05	00:03:15	25°
13:54:17	15:16:53	15:18:23	15:19:54	16:30:05	00:03:00	24°
13:55:05	N/A	15:19:05	N/A	16:39:41	99.4%	25°
13:58:00	15:19:05	15:20:30	15:21:54	16:30:59	00:02:48	23°
13:58:23	15:19:09	15:20:42	15:22:15	16:30:59	00:03:06	22°
13:59:11	15:19:33	15:21:05	15:22:38	16:31:06	00:03:04	22°
13:59:30	15:19:40	15:21:11	15:22:43	16:31:06	00:03:02	21°
14:00:35	15:20:13	15:21:42	15:23:10	16:31:11	00:02:58	21°
14:01:48	15:21:57	15:22:36	15:23:14	16:31:48	00:01:18	21°
15:12:06	16:25:47	16:26:59	16:28:11	17:52:00	00:02:23	13°
15:16:00	16:27:31	16:28:41	16:29:52	17:32:11	00:02:21	10°
15:17:30	16:27:52	16:29:05	16:30:19	17:31:48	00:02:28	8°

shows the percentage of the Sun that is covered rather than the duration of totality.

ECLIPSE TIMINGS: WEST TO EAST (all times are local)
December 4 2002

Country	Location	GMT+	Lat (S)	Long (E)
Angola	Santa Filomena	1	11° 38'	13° 46'
Angola	*Sumbe*	*1*	*11° 12'*	*13° 50'*
Angola	Huambo	1	12° 45'	15° 43'
Angola	Nova Lisboa	1	12° 42'	15° 54'
Angola	*Serpa Pinto*	*1*	*14° 48'*	*17° 52'*
Angola	Mavinga	1	15° 50'	20° 10'
Angola	Nriquinha	1	16° 00'	21° 25'
Angola	Rivungo	1	16° 19'	22° 01'
Angola	Luiana	1	17° 25'	22° 30'
Angola	Kongola	1	17° 46'	23° 22'
Angola	Ngwezumba	1	18° 26'	24° 51'
Botswana	Sebe	2	18° 47'	25° 31'
Botswana	*Sebutu*	*2*	*18° 42'*	*25° 41'*
Zimbabwe	*Victoria Falls*	*2*	*17° 55'*	*25° 50'*
Zimbabwe	*Hwange*	*2*	*18° 21'*	*26° 29'*
Botswana	Tsuli	2	19° 52'	26° 30'
Botswana	*Francistown*	*2*	*21° 09'*	*27° 29'*
Botswana	Habangan	2	20° 33'	27° 32'
Zimbabwe	Plumtree	2	20° 29'	27° 48'
Zimbabwe	*Matobo (Matopos)*	*2*	*20° 25'*	*28° 28'*
Zimbabwe	*Bulawayo*	*2*	*20° 10'*	*28° 34'*
Zimbabwe	*Gwanda*	*2*	*20° 56'*	*29° 00'*
Zimbabwe	Tuli	2	21° 58'	29° 13'
South Africa	*Louis Trichardt*	*2*	*23° 03'*	*29° 26'*
South Africa	*Pietersburg*	*2*	*23° 54'*	*29° 28'*
Zimbabwe	Beitbridge	2	22° 12'	29° 59'
South Africa	Messina	2	22° 20'	30° 02'
South Africa	*Thohoyandou*	*2*	*22° 57'*	*30° 04'*
South Africa	Nwanedi Reserve	2	22° 39'	30° 24'
South Africa	Punda Maria	2	22° 43'	31° 02'
South Africa	Pafuri Picnic Site	2	22° 34'	31° 04'
South Africa	Pafuri Gate	2	22° 36'	31° 04'
South Africa	Punda Maria	2	22° 45'	31° 05'
South Africa	*Phalaborwa*	*2*	*23° 57'*	*31° 09'*
South Africa	Bataleur	2	23° 14'	31° 12'
South Africa	Babalala Picnic Site	2	23° 05'	31° 15'
Mozambique	*Pafuri*	*2*	*22° 27'*	*31° 19'*
South Africa	Shingwedzi	2	23° 06'	31° 25'
South Africa	Mopane Camp	2	23° 31'	31° 25'
South Africa	Mooiplas Picnic Site	2	23° 34'	31° 26'
South Africa	Mopani	2	23° 02'	31° 26'
South Africa	Shingwedzi	2	23° 07'	31° 27'
Mozambique	Babalala	2	22° 55'	31° 30'
South Africa	*Letaba*	*2*	*23° 51'*	*31° 34'*
South Africa	*Satara*	*2*	*24° 24'*	*31° 45'*
South Africa	*Olifants Camp*	*2*	*24° 00'*	*31° 45'*
Mozambique	Massingir	2	23° 50'	32° 04'
Mozambique	Chibuto	2	24° 40'	33° 31'
Mozambique	Xai-Xai	2	25° 02'	33° 38'
Mozambique	Chonguene	2	24° 59'	33° 47'
Mozambique	Manjacaze	2	24° 42'	33° 52'
Mozambique	Chongoene-Chidengiele	2	24° 58'	33° 58'
Mozambique	Max on coast	2	24° 55'	34° 02'
Mozambique	*Maalamba*	*2*	*24° 25'*	*34° 48'*

* Locations in *italics* will not witness totality, so there will be no second and third contacts. For these places
** Altitude of the Sun at mid eclipse

1st contact	2nd contact	Mid	3rd contact	4th contact	Duration (min:sec)	Alt
05:58:29	06:55:48	06:56:11	06:56:35	08:00:48	00:00:46	18°
05:58:06	N/A	06:55:47	N/A	08:00:18	99.8%	18°
05:59:11	06:57:28	06:57:53	06:58:19	08:03:47	00:00:51	21°
05:59:06	06:57:28	06:57:53	06:58:19	08:03:47	00:00:51	21°
06:01:06	N/A	07:00:54	N/A	08:08:24	98.8%	24°
06:01:59	07:02:44	07:03:06	07:03:28	08:12:11	00:00:44	27°
06:02:17	07:03:30	07:03:53	07:04:17	08:13:42	00:00:47	29°
06:02:35	07:04:19	07:04:35	07:04:51	08:14:47	00:00:32	29°
06:03:54	07:05:57	07:06:30	07:07:02	08:17:29	00:01:06	31°
06:04:29	07:06:52	07:07:18	07:07:44	08:18:47	00:00:52	32°
06:05:23	07:08:06	07:09:06	07:10:05	08:21:24	00:01:58	34°
07:05:58	08:09:28	08:09:59	08:10:30	09:22:48	00:01:02	34°
07:05:53	N/A	08:09:59	N/A	09:22:53	99.99%	35°
07:04:54	N/A	08:09:00	N/A	09:21:54	97.8%	34°
07:05:36	N/A	08:09:59	N/A	09:23:24	97.8%	35°
07:07:30	08:11:45	08:12:18	08:12:50	09:25:53	00:01:04	36°
07:09:29	N/A	08:14:53	N/A	09:29:24	99.1%	38°
07:08:41	08:13:24	08:13:59	08:14:35	09:28:29	00:01:11	38°
07:08:36	08:13:27	08:14:05	08:14:43	09:28:42	00:01:15	38°
07:08:41	N/A	08:14:30	N/A	09:29:36	99.5%	39°
07:08:23	N/A	08:14:11	N/A	09:29:17	98.8%	39°
07:09:36	N/A	08:15:48	N/A	09:31:11	99.8%	39°
07:11:06	08:17:14	08:17:29	08:17:46	09:33:17	00:00:32	40°
07:12:42	N/A	08:19:24	N/A	09:35:23	97.9%	41°
07:13:59	N/A	08:20:48	N/A	09:36:47	95.6%	42°
07:11:36	08:17:54	08:18:36	08:19:16	09:34:48	00:01:22	41°
07:11:47	08:18:09	08:18:47	08:19:25	09:35:05	00:01:15	41°
07:12:47	N/A	08:19:48	N/A	09:36:12	99.2%	42°
07:12:24	08:19:00	08:19:35	08:20:11	09:36:18	00:01:11	42°
07:12:42	08:19:37	08:20:17	08:20:57	09:37:23	00:01:19	43°
07:12:35	08:20:17	08:20:17	08:20:17	09:37:30	00:00:00	43°
07:12:35	08:19:41	08:20:11	08:20:41	09:37:17	00:01:00	43°
07:12:47	08:19:43	08:20:23	08:21:03	09:37:30	00:01:19	43°
07:14:35	N/A	08:22:23	N/A	09:39:36	98.7%	43°
07:13:29	08:20:42	08:21:18	08:21:53	09:38:30	00:01:11	43°
07:13:18	08:20:23	08:21:05	08:21:48	09:38:18	00:01:25	43°
07:12:24	N/A	08:20:06	N/A	09:37:23	99.6%	43°
07:13:24	08:20:35	08:21:18	08:22:00	09:38:35	00:01:26	43°
07:14:05	08:21:57	08:22:00	08:22:03	09:39:17	00:00:05	44°
07:14:05	08:21:50	08:22:06	08:22:21	09:39:29	00:00:31	44°
07:13:18	08:20:30	08:21:12	08:21:53	09:38:35	00:01:23	43°
07:13:29	08:20:35	08:21:18	08:22:00	09:38:41	00:01:26	43°
07:13:12	08:20:33	08:21:05	08:21:38	09:38:30	00:01:04	43°
07:14:35	N/A	08:22:36	N/A	09:40:05	99.6%	44°
07:15:30	N/A	08:23:41	N/A	09:41:23	98.7%	44°
07:14:53	N/A	08:23:05	N/A	09:40:41	99.6%	44°
07:14:48	08:22:27	08:23:05	08:23:43	09:41:00	00:01:15	44°
07:16:41	08:25:08	08:25:53	08:26:39	09:44:47	00:01:30	46°
07:17:18	08:26:01	08:26:36	08:27:09	09:45:42	00:01:07	47°
07:17:18	08:25:58	08:26:42	08:27:25	09:45:48	00:01:26	47°
07:16:53	08:25:36	08:26:17	08:26:58	09:45:29	00:01:22	47°
07:17:18	08:26:08	08:26:54	08:27:40	09:46:05	00:01:31	47°
07:17:18	08:26:08	08:26:54	08:27:39	09:46:11	00:01:30	47°
07:16:53	N/A	08:26:54	N/A	09:46:42	98.4%	48°

shows the percentage of the Sun that is covered rather than the duration of totality."

by rumours of rampant eclipse fever – they often fail to fulfil their promise. For December 2002, flights and hotels will be booked up quickly in South Africa and Mozambique because it is high season.

If you are planning a day-trip to the eclipse it is important to organise reliable transport because the Moon will wait for no-one. Put some thought into this, allow plenty of time for delays and devise an alternative plan. It would be better to be in place the night before. An added luxury would be to have transport on hand during the eclipse, and a driver or guide who is knowledgeable about local roads. Then you can make for clear patches of sky if it becomes cloudy overhead. Some eclipse-chasers who have had bad experiences careering around at the last minute advise the opposite: stay in one place, because by the time you have moved, the cloud may have drifted over your new location leaving the previous one cloud-free.

Use the tables (pages 16–19) to help select your site. You should aim to arrive well before first contact so you can choose a position, and set up equipment if necessary. But do not get too concerned about precise timings in the position you choose – it is enough to know to within about 15 minutes when your eclipse will start.

Organised tours

There are several tour operators that specialise in eclipse-chasing, some with the patronage of leading eclipse experts. You have a choice between travelling with one of these or with one that specialises in the country you want to visit. Eclipse specialists are mostly American companies that offer larger group trips. These are often led by an astronomer, and will also include a few days sightseeing, perhaps a trip to Victoria Falls and some time spent in a national park. Astronomy lectures and talks are usually included, and participants will often be keen astronomers or veteran eclipse-chasers. The safari arrangements on these trips tend to be subordinate to the prime task of seeing and photographing the eclipse, and hence some of the companies may not be able to differentiate between the better and the poorer safari camps.

Country specialists are generally organising smaller groups, emphasising the natural environment, and spending more of their time visiting small, dedicated safari camps. However, they will be less skilled in the essentials of a good eclipse, such as being within totality and paying close attention to continental and local weather patterns. And few will have astronomers accompanying the trip, so you will not have detailed explanations of the celestial events.

The eclipse specialists are listed below and the Africa specialists are listed chapter by chapter. Most of those listed below will cater for tourists from outside their country of operation.

Explorers Tours Tel: (44) 01753 681999; email: feedback@explorers.co.uk; web: www.explorers.co.uk/astro/astro_tours_1999.htm. Using its 22 years of experience with eclipse trips, the company plans to take 600 people to Harare in 2001 and transport them in a fleet of buses to a site on the Ruya River, close to the border with Mozambique, as well as to various camps along the Zambezi valley. All trips include a visit to the Victoria Falls and optional extensions to Botswana, Cape Town, Tanzania and Namibia. Price: from £1,095. 2002 trip planned

Hole in the Sky Tours Tel: (1) 562 594 6067 or through Giselle's Travel, (1) 916 922 5500; email: eclipse98@earthlink.net; web: www.holeinthesky.com/esafari.htm. Ten-day trip to South Africa and Victoria Falls in 2001 culminating in eclipse-viewing near Lusaka in Zambia, and possibly at other venues. May organise a cruise off the west coast of Africa, so that viewers can experience nearly 5 minutes of totality. For 2002 a trip to the Victoria

Falls and Okavango Delta region is planned, which may also include Cape Town, Port Elizabeth and Durban in South Africa.

Ring of Fire Expeditions Future Travel Inc, 1085 Hercules Av, Houston, Texas 77058; tel: (1) 281 480 1988; fax: (1) 281 480-2587; email: paul.d.maley1@jsc.nasa.gov; web: www.eclipsetours.com. This firm is affiliated to the NASA Johnson Space Centre Astronomical Society, which has logged 23 expeditions so far, organised by eclipse veteran Paul Maley. It will use Lusaka as its base for the 2001 eclipse with buses ferrying its 30 guests, on the day, to a site 40km to the north. It will also run a 2002 expedition and hopes to offer cruises for both eclipses. Cost from around £3,400/US$5,500 per person sharing.

Sandveld Sebastian Silio, Mathystr 21, D-76133, Karlsruhe, Germany; tel (49) 721 9822083; fax: (49) 721 9822084; email: service@sandveld.de; web: www.sandveld.de. Offering a 24-day tour through many destinations including Namibia and Botswana, with eclipse-viewing north of Lusaka in Zambia, for 2001. 2002 plans are in the pipeline.

Sita Tours 16250 Ventura Boulevard, Suite 300, Encino, CA 91436; tel (1) 818 990 9530; fax: (1) 818 990 9762; email: sitatours@sitatours.com; web: www.sitatours.com. Offering 3 nights in Lusaka with eclipse-viewing outside the city with 11 different bolt-on tours to various southern African countries.

Sky and Telescope Scientific Expeditions 227 West Miami Avenue, Suite #3, Venice, FL 34285; fax: (1) 941 485 0647; email: scienex@aol.com; web: www.skypub.com/store/scienx/africa2001.html. Will view the 2001 eclipse in Zambia on an 11-day trip that includes trips to game reserves and the Victoria Falls. Sample cost: US$5,200 per person.

Spears Travel PO Box 1256, 500 S. Keeler, Bartlesville, OK, 74005; tel: (1) 918 336 2360; fax: (1) 918 337 3630; email: cralph@spearstravel.com; web: www.spearstravel.com. An 8-night trip with eclipse veteran Fred Espenak, taking in Hwange National Park in Zimbabwe and the Victoria Falls before viewing the eclipse from Lilayi Lodge, 30 minutes from Lusaka in Zambia. Sample cost: US$4,500–5,000 per person.

Total Solar Eclipse email: 2001@totalsolareclipse.com; web: www.totalsolareclipse.com. A 12-night trip which will take viewers to a spot on the Zimbabwe-Mozambique border to view the 2001 eclipse, with other possible Zimbabwe viewing sites at Mount Darwin and near the Zambian border.

TravelQuest International 570 Skyview Drive, Prescott, Arizona; tel: (1) 520 445 7754; fax: (1) 520 445 8771; email: tours@tq-international.com; web: www.tq-international.com. Working with eclipse meteorologist Jay Anderson, TravelQuest is organising an 11-night trip to Zambia and will view the eclipse at Chisamba Safari Lodge north of Lusaka. There is the option of staying there (48 places) or staying in Lusaka with a transfer on the day (100 places). There will be buses available for an escape to the west if it is cloudy. There are also 48 places on an 11-night trip to Morombe in Madagascar. They plan to be in Australia rather than Africa for 2002. Sample cost: Madagascar US$5,295 per person; Zambia US$4,850 per person.

WHAT TO TAKE

Eclipse viewers are vital (see *Viewing eclipses safely*, below). If you plan to take photographs you need to give some time and thought to equipment (see *Photography*, below). You may also want to take binoculars with the appropriate solar filter. You could also consider taking 12in x 12in sheets of mylar which can be cut into viewing strips and handed around, or to fit binoculars, cameras and telescopes. They are available from Beacon Hill Telescopes, 112 Mill Road, Cleethorpes DN35 8JD, UK; tel: 01472 692959, or from many astronomical suppliers in the USA. A tape recorder might seem like a strange thing to bring to a visual spectacle but the responses from the people around you will be tremendously vocal, and you can add your own adjectives and descriptions as you watch. (Alternatively, some people prerecord minute-by-minute instructions about what they should look for and when, and then play the tape recorder when the eclipse starts.)

Thin sheets of cardboard from which to make a pinhole camera (see *Safety*, below) may be useful. In addition, a seat or rug, a torch, protection from the Sun, mosquito repellent (for when the insects emerge in the twilight) and a water bottle may be useful.

Finally, particularly for rural areas, consider bringing some photocopies of the eclipse warnings in local languages (*Appendix 1*) and the cartoons below and on page 24.

HEALTH AND SAFETY
General health

You must take precautions against malaria and check you are up to date with the relevant immunisations. For more information consult country guides and specialist health guides (see country chapters and *Further Reading*).

THE RISK-FREE WAY TO VIEW THE ECLIPSE

1   Stand with your back to the Sun.

2   Hold a card, with a pin hole in the middle, up and to the side so that the Sun's rays pass through the hole in the card.

3   Do not look through the hole at the Sun.

4   Adjust the card so that the image is projected on to another piece of white card, or a pale wall.

LOCAL EYE SAFETY

For the locals, solar eclipses have great potential for edification but also for eye damage. For once, a majestic work of physics conducted in the biggest laboratory of all will happen right in front of the most isolated of African schoolchildren. The problem is that if these children watch the celestial drama unprotected they could damage their eyesight for life.

Several groups are working to help local people make the most of the eclipses while safeguarding their sight.

One person who has done a formidable job of collecting viewers used during previous eclipses is Dr Francis Podmore, a member of the Astronomical Society of Southern Africa. After the total solar eclipse of August 1999, which passed over much of Europe, Dr Podmore appealed for people's eclipse viewers. They arrived by the mailbag and he believes he has collected well over 100,000. The ASSA plans to produce educational packs for schools, each of which will include viewers, for distribution around Zimbabwe. Meanwhile Oxfam Solidarity in Belgium has collected around 200,000 viewers for distribution in Mozambique.

There are several ways in which you can help get viewers and information to local people.

- Take several viewers with you.
- Even if you have only one viewer with you, lend it to those without them. You will find you want to look at the partial eclipse only briefly, once every ten minutes or so. One viewer can therefore serve several people.
- Find out the official eye safety advice in the country you are visiting (if any) and try to work with this rather than confusing people by contradicting it.
- Use the language appendix and viewing cartoons in this book to help get your message across.
- Remember the golden rule: do not look at any stage of the partial eclipse except through specially made viewers.
- The primary method of viewing the eclipse in Africa is likely to be smoked glass. This is very dangerous (though better than watching with the naked eye). Offer the use of your viewers instead.
- Consult the Bradt and 'zimastro' websites (see *Further Reading*) in case there are new ways in which you can help.

Most first-time visitors to Africa experience a degree of culture shock for the first few weeks, unless they are cocooned inside first-class hotels and whisked through the countryside in luxury coaches. You might find it hard to cope with the noise, dirt and poverty of the cities, and with the simple standards of living in rural areas. More importantly, think twice before the eclipses lure you off the beaten track unless you know from experience how to prepare for such ventures. In every one of the eclipse countries there are regions where simple mistakes, like forgetting the drinking water or getting stuck in sand, can turn into disasters. The usual means of recovery – shops, telephones, medical facilities, other vehicles – may simply not be there.

Travel clinics
UK/South Africa
British Airways Travel Clinic and Immunisation Service Tel: 01276 685040
BA clinics all around Britain and three in South Africa. To find your nearest one, phone 01276 685040.

Nomad Travel Pharmacy and Vaccination Centre Tel: 020 8889 7014.
Trailfinders Immunisation Centre Tel: 020 7938 3999 (London); 0141 353 0066 (Glasgow).
MASTA (Medical Advisory Service for Travellers Abroad) Tel: 09068 224100.

USA
Centers for Disease Control Tel: 877 FYI TRIP; 800 311 3435; web: www.cdc.gov/travel.

Australia/New Zealand/Thailand
TMVC Tel: 1300 65 88 44; web: www.tmvc.com.au. 20 clinics in Australia, New Zealand and Thailand.

Security
It is increasingly difficult to obtain balanced advice about a country's safety as official recommendations from the UK and US governments become more conservative. It is worth asking tour operators for their opinions as well, to obtain a middle line between the two.

In the **UK**, try Foreign Office Travel Advice; tel: 020 7238 4503 or 4504; web: www.fco.gov.uk. In the **US** try www.travel.state.gov/travel_warnings.html.

Viewing eclipses safely
It is dangerous to look at the Sun **at any time** except for the brief period of totality, when it is fully covered by the Moon. Some eye experts argue that you should never look at an eclipse, even during totality, because it is all too easy to make a mistake, such as looking too soon, and cause permanent damage to your eyes. Most astronomers say sensible adults should easily be able to follow the basic viewing rules to witness one of the great sights of nature.

If you stare at the Sun you are looking directly at a huge, thermonuclear explosion spewing out ultraviolet and infrared rays. Evolution has honed us to find it painful to look at the Sun – if your gaze accidentally settles on it, discomfort quickly forces you to look away. During a partial eclipse, illumination is low and it is easier and more tempting to stare at the Sun, but it is just as dangerous because its rays are still sufficiently powerful to cause damage. Infrared is heat, and heat cooks the delicate tracery of blood vessels at the back of the eye. Ultraviolet and blue rays can activate chemicals in the retina which then cause damage. If your retina is damaged you will feel nothing at first, but could become blind at the spot where images are focused, making it hard to read or recognise people's faces. Nothing in medical science can reverse this. Even at 99% eclipse the Sun is 4,000 times stronger than the Moon. That is why watching eclipses can be dangerous.

The one time when it is safe to watch the eclipse is during totality – the few minutes when the Sun is totally covered by the Moon. The Sun is then only as bright as the full Moon and cannot cause damage. For the rest of the eclipse you must not look with the naked eye. Watching the *screen* of a video camera is safe as you are seeing an electronic image and not the real thing. It takes mighty screening power to block the Sun's rays and the only suitable materials are specially made, generally coated with a thin layer of metal such as silver or aluminium. Often the material is aluminised mylar. Welders' goggles with a rating of 14 or higher are also suitable. Nothing else is safe, and that includes sunglasses, smoked glass, compact discs, exposed black and white film and the Sun caps, or solar eyepieces, provided with binoculars and amateur telescopes (you need special metal-coated solar filters for these).

You can order eclipse viewers from many companies. Three well-known ones are ECLIPSE99 Ltd, Belle Etoile, Rue du Hamel, Cantel, Guernsey GY5 7QJ; tel: (44) 01481 264 847; fax: 01481 264 871; email: eclipse99ltd@dial.pipex.com; American Paper Optics, email: optics3d@lunaweb.net; and Rainbow Symphony,

6860 Canby Av, #120, Reseda, CA 91335; tel: (1) 818 708 8400; fax: (1) 818 708 8470; web: www.rainbowsymphony.com.

Test your viewer beforehand against a bright light source such as a reading lamp. If there are any pinhole pricks throw the viewer away. It would be good to take several in case one becomes damaged – keep them where they cannot get scratched.

Watch the stages of the partial eclipse through the approved viewer but, even with this protection, do not stare for longer than half a minute. This is the braces and belt approach – a tiny hole you have missed might otherwise cause harm (damage from gazing directly at the Sun has been reported with less than a minute's viewing). When the diamond ring appears you can remove the viewer, replacing it when the ring returns at the end of totality.

Eye experts worry that the slightest accident when following the above protocol could lead to permanent damage. They fear, in particular, that a viewer could slip from a child's face or an adult could forget the rules amidst the tremendous excitement of the eclipse. They point out that the only totally safe way to view an eclipse is using a pinhole projector. This can be made by piercing a hole in a piece of card and viewing, on another piece of white card, the light that shines through it (see diagram page 22).

For more on safety see *Further Reading*.

Safety for local people

Ophthalmologists say there is bound to be an epidemic of eye damage among people who are not aware of the dangers of viewing the eclipse. Tourists can act for good or evil here. Your presence may encourage people to stay outside and watch the eclipse instead of running indoors which is the instinctive response. Alternatively, you can be a source of information (and viewers) so that those who would otherwise have stared long and hard at the eclipse learn how to view it safely. For ideas on how to be a help rather than a hindrance, see the box on page 23.

PHOTOGRAPHY

> 'I well remember that I wished I had not encumbered myself with apparatus, and I mentally registered a vow, that, if a future opportunity ever presented itself for my observing a total eclipse, I would … devote myself to that full enjoyment of the spectacle which can only be obtained by a mere gazer.'
>
> Warren De La Rue, on the total solar eclipse in Spain of July 18 1860, quoted on the website www.MrEclipse.com.

If this is your first total solar eclipse, consider first whether you want to be distracted during the precious few minutes of totality by the need to focus cameras and adjust settings. You may absorb the moment better if you forget about photography and buy professional photographs later – there will be many of them and they will be superb.

If you decide to go ahead, do not use a compact camera for anything other than general panoramic shots taken a minute before totality, at totality and just after totality. Even then, the Sun will appear no more than a tiny dot in your snapshot; you may damage your eyes looking through the viewfinder and the flash may irritate others who are trying to accustom their eyes to the darkness.

You must use either a single lens reflex (SLR) camera or a camcorder.

Don't forget that gazing through your camera viewfinder at the Sun is dangerous – the rays will fry your retina as well as the electronics inside your camera. You must have a neutral density filter that cuts out light and heat by a factor of 100,000. This translates to an ND5.0 filter. You must use it even when the Sun is 99% covered, removing it only when the eclipse is 100%. Aluminised mylar filters show a blue-grey Sun while the more expensive metal-coated glass filters give a more realistic orange. Large filters for camera and telescopic work can be ordered from Beacon Hill (see above) or, in the USA, from Thousand Oaks Optical (www.thousandoaksoptical.com). Be sure to place your order in good time.

The simplest pictures for the novice to take are of the diamond ring and totality. Set the SLR camera on to automatic exposure and load it with an ordinary ISO 400 colour negative film. You will probably over-expose the inner corona and prominences but you will produce reasonable pictures. This approach has the great advantage of being simple and leaving you time to watch the eclipse properly.

For eclipse close-ups you will need a telephoto lens or telescope with a focal length of 500mm or more. (A 500mm lens will yield a 4.5mm diameter image on an ordinary print.) Experts recommend 1,000mm to produce the largest image possible while leaving space to accommodate the corona, prominences and wisps around the Sun. To work out the size of the image on the resulting photograph, divide the focal length of the lens (in mm) by 110.

The final essential piece of equipment is a tripod. Lightweight tripods frequently cause blurred eclipse photographs. The tripod's legs should be extended not more than half way. Try adjusting the height so that you can easily reach the camera controls while sitting on a chair, to minimise the vibrations you transmit. You can further decrease vibrations by suspending a weight under the tripod – rocks or sand in a sack. Use a cable release and bring a spare.

Specialist camera shops will sell adaptors for connecting cameras to telescopes. Do not use the eyepiece filter provided with some small telescopes. It is not safe.

Once you are equipped, the golden rule is preparation. First, decide what kind of picture you want – evocative scenes of the Sun fringed by trees and people or a close-up of the flaring prominences? Try out all new equipment beforehand and rehearse the procedure so it will work perfectly at the crucial (and dark) moment.

If you are photographing the partial eclipse you should calculate the shutter speed and f-ratio appropriate to your solar filter and telephoto lens by setting up the apparatus on a sunny day beforehand. Point the camera to the Sun (using your solar filter) and set the aperture to its widest. Take a reel of film – a frame for every shutter speed you have – record the settings and develop the film to see which worked best.

Before the eclipse begins, fit the filter, set the focus to infinity, set the lens to the widest aperture and switch off the automatic exposure and flash. Do not hunt through the sky for the Sun without the filter fitted. Some 30 seconds before Baily's Beads you can remove the filter. This will give the camera time to settle before taking shots. You will need to increase the exposure from 1/500 second to 1 second, 2 seconds or even 4 full seconds to get all the corona. Each eclipse phenomenon has a different brightness value so exposures will vary according to what you want to photograph. For example, to capture the solar prominences during the total eclipse with an ISO 400 film and an f-stop of 8 you need an exposure time of at least 1/1000. The solution is to bracket your exposures.

Once totality is finished, do not forget to replace the filter.

If you are using a camcorder, put it on a tripod with the zoom at its widest setting to record the observing site and people around.

At sea, eclipse photography is constrained by the movement of the ship. You cannot use a focal length of more than 1,000mm because of this. You must also contend with vibration from the ship's engines, wind across the deck and other passengers' footsteps. It is safest to use a fast film such as ISO 400. Notice the range of motion of the ship and attempt to snap the picture when it reaches one extreme.

For more specialist information see *Further Reading*.

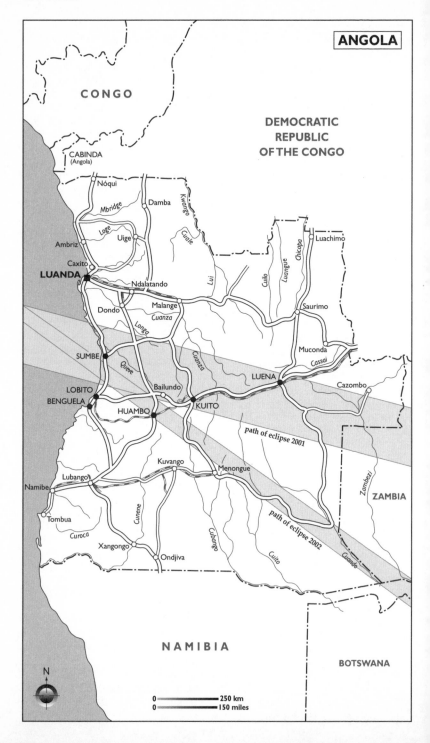

Angola

Aisling Irwin

Visiting the eclipse areas
OVERVIEW
Last total solar eclipse: February 1980
Next total solar eclipse after 2002: August 2046

Angola hosts over a third of the 2001 mainland Africa eclipse and nearly half of the continent's 2002 eclipse. By unusual coincidence, a small region – near Santa Filomena on the west coast – will experience both eclipses. This duplication is entirely the product of chance, although it may seem as if more than mere chance is at work to the people who witness both. A total solar eclipse passes, on average, over the same patch of land every 375 years. But this figure is the mean – Jerusalem once went for 1,109 years without one while the Outer Hebrides will experience a total eclipse in 2289 and again in 2290. Jean Meeus, the world's leading eclipse mathematician, calculates that a small region in the desert of southern Egypt will experience five total solar eclipses in 32 years from 2325 to 2356.

Geographically, Angola is the best place from which to watch the 2001 eclipse. From a narrow coastal plain mountains rise impressively to the broad Bié plateau over 1,000m above. Both low and high regions experience clear skies in the winter month of June. The chance of cloud is as little as 5% on much of the plateau area over which the eclipse passes. Elsewhere in the path it does not exceed 10%. Angola's flat interior records a huge amount of daily sunshine in June; the only cloud on the horizon is the prospect of a smoky haze from fires.

In addition, Angola will experience the longest stretch of totality in 2001 – 4 minutes 34 seconds on the west coast, and 4 minutes 19 seconds at its eastern border. The sun will be above 45° in the sky – higher than over the countries further east. Watching the Moon's shadow approach over the Atlantic Ocean promises to be an aesthetic treat.

The 2001 eclipse will first strike the African landmass at Santa Filomena, at 11.57 local time. Sumbe will be almost directly in the centre-line. The Moon's shadow will swiftly fall over the plateau, passing over the town of Kuito at the mountains' eastern edge, where first contact will arrive at 12.07. From there it will pass in a very shallow southeasterly curve, taking in Luena to the north (first contact at 12.17), before disappearing over the Zambian border.

The 2002 eclipse does not have such good prospects. Totality will be shorter and it will be the middle of the wet season. In addition, the eclipse has still a long way to go before it reaches its maximum far away in the Indian Ocean.

The 2002 eclipse appears over Santa Filomena in the early morning, with first contact arriving by 05.58. It moves southeast to the town of Huambo on the plateau, and races over the lowlands until it reaches the most southern part of the border with Zambia, which it will straddle until it reaches the Caprivi Strip.

SECURITY

Sadly, the geographical pluses and minuses are likely to be irrelevant. Angola's civil war, which has raged on and off since it gained independence in 1974, has made it one of the most dangerous countries on the planet, scattered with up to 15 million landmines which will leave it highly unsafe for many years.

Angola's civil war has shattered its infrastructure and its social fabric. The longest period of relative peace since 1974 was the period between 1994 and 1998. More than 100,000 Angolans have been killed since the fighting began. The war has affected much of the country, with flashpoints emerging unpredictably. The landmine problem is nationwide. Virtually everything written below, therefore, could change, especially in areas thought to be reasonably safe at present. For updated information try your country's travel advisory service or consult the Bradt website, www.bradt-travelguides.com. Angola's international telephone code is 244.

GATEWAY TOWNS
Luanda

The capital city of Luanda swarms with people displaced from elsewhere in the country and parts of it are no-go areas. But it has attractions related to its rich colonial history, with a pleasant boulevard and other sights, and it feels reasonably safe to walk about. Sights include the Cidade Alta, the old Portuguese part of the city, which includes the beautiful church Igreja da Nossa Senhora da Nazzare. The fortress contains the Museum of the Armed Forces. There is also the National Museum of Anthropology (Rua Frederico Engels 59) and the Museum of Slavery, 25km along the coast at Luanda Sul.

Danger areas include the Roque Santeiro market and the shanty towns housing thousands of displaced people. Do not loiter at the castle or in the military zone on the Ilha de Luanda. The beaches at Ilha de Luanda are unsafe because of pollution and currents. Those at Ilha do Mussolo are beautiful if somewhat unclean, and there are bars and cafés as well as Vietnamese, Chinese and French restaurants. Get there by taking a ferry from the marina at the end of Estrada da Samba.

Where to stay

Forte Hotels' **Le Presidente Meridien** (Largo 4 De Fevereiro) is in the centre of town with views over the beach. It and the **Intercontinental** (both US$150–200) are the two top hotels in town. **Avenida** has good reports (US$90) and there are some good bed and breakfasts (about US$50–60). On the Ilha do Mussolo there is **Hotel Panorama**. A popular restaurant is **Rialto**, an Italian venue, famous for its ice-cream.

For further information try the **Empresa Angolana de Turismo** (ANGOTUR), Al Manuel Van Dunen 109, Hotel Alameda, CP 5531, Luanda; tel: 2 343614/343616/346034/394735; fax: 2 343616. It can supply you with a tourist map of the town.

GETTING THERE

International flights go to the capital, Luanda. TAAG Angola Airlines departs from Lisbon and Rome in Europe, and Windhoek (Namibia), Harare (Zimbabwe), Johannesburg (South Africa) and Lusaka (Zambia) in Africa.

To enter you need a visa, which is hard to obtain. At times it has only been possible to obtain five-day visas – and these only in Johannesburg and Harare by residents of those countries. At other times the short visa option has been open to other nationals. However, you must get your sponsor in Angola (organisation or company) to send an invitation letter to the Angolan embassy where you are trying to obtain a visa. If done by fax this could take as little as a week, but allow more time. Sometimes, people have obtained visas simply by presenting a return ticket and a confirmed hotel reservation at their local embassy.

There are embassies in neighbouring Namibia, Botswana, Zimbabwe, Zambia and Congo as well as South Africa. The airport, 4km out of town, is intimidating, with officials ready to charge a fine for the slightest irregularity in your documentation. There are few taxis around so you must be met by your sponsor.

Nipping into the country overland is out of the question at the time of going to press because the war – or its armed effluvia – periodically spills over the Namibian border (2002 eclipse) and the Zambian border (2001 eclipse).

GETTING AROUND
By air
The safest way of travelling in Angola is by plane and there is a network of airports worked by TAAG (5th Floor, Rua da Missão 123, Luanda).

Flights go to many towns, including Benguela, Sumbe, WakuKungo, Kuito, Huambo and Luena. Flights are regularly overbooked so turn up at the airport several hours in advance. Many flights are in aircraft chartered by the United Nations and other such bodies: you might find a spare seat if you chat them up.

By train
The railway network is at a virtual standstill and none of the stretches which function will take you to the eclipse path.

By road
Angolan roads can be both dismal and terrifying. Road travel outside Luanda is dangerous because of the landmines. Check before you travel what the latest news is about the roads you want to take.

Means of travel is also a problem. Although it is possible to hitch a lift on the occasional truck, there is a fair chance, say people who have tried it recently, that you will be arrested by soldiers or paramilitaries as a spy.

ECLIPSE CENTRES
The 2001 eclipse
The best option, from the points of view of both viewing and safety, is to stick to the coast. The coast road south from Luanda is safe at the time of writing as far as Sumbe, and local expatriates often venture down it to the beaches. Beyond Sumbe, on the way to Benguela, it is not safe. You could also fly to Sumbe or you could enquire about taking a boat down the coast from Luanda.

The other town you could try is Kuito. It is safe enough to stay in but there is little accommodation. Various aid agencies have permanent bases there and may be able to advise you where to stay.

Other possible venues are WakuKungo and Luena. Check in Luanda whether it is safe to go to these places. At the time of writing the outskirts of both Luena and Kuito are filled with the camps of thousands of displaced people.

The 2002 eclipse
For 2002 the only obvious airport is Huambo, another town whose fringes are packed with displaced people. It is secure enough as a place to stay – if you can find accommodation. You could also try flying to Benguela and travelling on towards the eclipse path, though the coast road just north of the town is not safe at the time of writing.

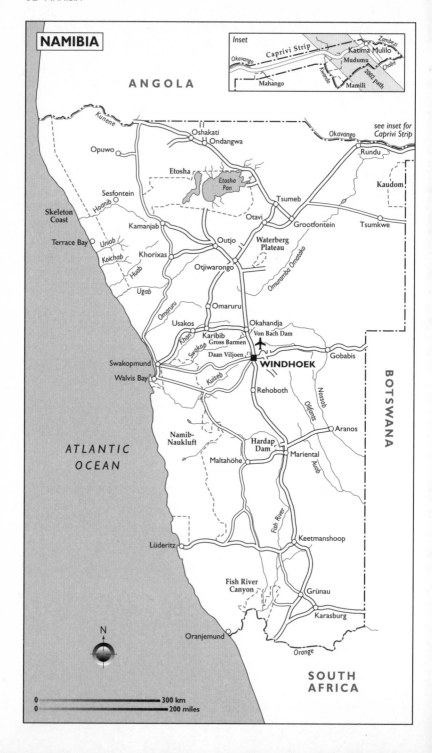

Namibia

Chris McIntyre

4

Visiting the 2002 eclipse areas

OVERVIEW

Last total solar eclipse: August 1886
Next total solar eclipse after 2002: November 2030

Namibia's Caprivi Strip is probably the first landfall site of the 2002 eclipse which it is practical to visit. Totality should cross the corridor at 07:07 local time on December 4.

However, before making further plans, the first thing that any potential eclipse-watcher ought to do is take safety advice. Although the greater part of Namibia is one of the safest areas for travel on the continent there are localised problems in a narrow belt along the Angolan border. Currently the UK foreign office, among others, advises 'against travel to border areas from Ruacana (in the Kunene Region) eastwards, and the Caprivi and Kavango Regions'. These are fundamental problems resulting from the long-running instability in Angola, and are unlikely to be resolved quickly. For the latest information try the Bradt eclipse website: www.bradt-travelguides.com.

Assuming that it's once again safe to go, then there are really only three roads running through the area of the eclipse. The main B8, known as the 'golden highway', cuts the centre line about 60km west of Katima Mulilo, near to where the D3501 turns off south. Alternatively the very rural D3511 cuts the centre line just east of the small village of Linyanti. You could stop and watch on any of these roads – the important thing would be to find a rise or a small hillock that rises above the bush.

If you're on holiday in the Victoria Falls area then a few days exploring here could be fun. The lodges along the Kwando River are excellent and cost a fraction of those over the border in Botswana. You're very unlikely to hit any tourists on 'eclipse supplements', or indeed many other visitors at all.

At the beginning of December the weather is a bit of a lottery. With luck, it'll be a lovely morning that's largely clear and cloudless – as is often the case. However, December is the start of the rainy season so some rain is likely. The normal pattern is a gradual build up of clouds during the day, before a short deluge in the late afternoon. Hence there's a fair chance that cloud cover in the morning will be sparse.

The country telephone code is 264.

ORGANISED ECLIPSE TRIPS

The usual eclipse operators may well have small trips running – see *Planning and Preparation*, page 20. The safari specialists, below, haven't organised many group trips, thus leaving open a perfect opportunity for you to organise your own trip with a good chance of finding accommodation – or to have a tailor-made trip organised for you (see *Namibia specialists*, below) to include a few days in the Caprivi.

The ideal might be a fly-drive trip starting in mid-November in Windhoek, heading across the Namib to Swakopmund, and then up to Damaraland. After that, spend time in Etosha, before driving northeast and into the Caprivi, stopping at one of the Kwando Lodges around the time of the eclipse. Then you could continue driving to Victoria Falls, drop the car and depart from there.

Namibia specialists

The Caprivi is quite an offbeat destination by Namibian standards, so if you're not organising your own trip then find a company that knows the country well. Specialists recommended by the author include:

UK

Art of Travel 21 The Bakehouse, 119 Altenberg Gardens, London, SW11 1JQ; tel: 020 7738 2038; fax: 020 7738 1893; email: safari@artoftravel.co.uk

Okavango Tours and Safaris Marlborough House, 298 Regents Park Rd, London N3 2TJ; tel: 020 8343 3283; fax: 020 8343 3287; email: info@okavango.com

Sunvil Discovery Upper Square, Old Isleworth, Middlesex TW7 7BJ; tel: 020 8232 9777; fax: 020 8568 8330; email: africa@sunvil.co.uk; web: www.sunvil.co.uk/africa. I run this specialist African operator, which has the UK's widest range of options in Namibia, including fly-drive trips and fly-in safaris.

The overland truck operator **Bukima Expeditions** (15 Bedford Rd, Great Barford MK44 3JD; tel: 01234 871329; fax: 01234 871886; email: bukima@compuserve.com; web: www.bukima.com) will pause on its 3-week Victoria Falls to Cape Town trip, to view the partial eclipse from the Skeleton Coast in Namibia. Cost excluding flights: £360 + US$200 local payment.

USA

Adventure Center 1311 63rd St, Suite 200, Emeryville, California 94608; tel: 510 654 1879; fax: 510 654 4200; email: sandy@adventure-center.com

David Anderson Safaris 4635 Via Vistosa, Santa Barbara, CA 93110; tel: 800 733 1789 or 805 967 1712; fax: 805 964 8285

Australia

African Wildlife Safaris 1st Floor, 259 Coventry St, South Melbourne, Victoria 3205; tel: 3 9696 2899; fax: 3 9696 4937; email: office@africasafaris.com.au

GETTING AROUND

Internal air links are good and reasonably priced, and long-distance coach services are excellent. However, the Caprivi is often less well served than the rest of the country, and there are no trains there. Local buses are limited in their scope. Getting away from the main roads can be difficult without your own transport.

By air

The scheduled internal flights are sufficiently infrequent that you need to plan your trip around them and do so far in advance to be sure of getting seats. But this approach runs the risk of your trip being thrown into disarray if the airline's schedule changes.

Namibia has a good network of scheduled internal flights, run by Air Namibia (tel: 61 298 2552; fax: 61 221382), which link the outlying towns to Windhoek. The main regional airport in the Caprivi Strip is Katima Mulilo's M'pacha airstrip (airline code MPA).

The prices and timetables of the internal flights change regularly; currently there is a flight which links M'Pacha to Victoria Falls, Mokuti (Etosha) and Windhoek.

For chartered internal flights, there are several smaller companies chartering small 4- and 6-seater planes, and many lodges have their own bush airstrips. If you have the budget and want to make the most of a short time in the country, then perhaps a fly-in trip would suit you. Of course, if you've a private pilot's licence and an adventurous streak, then Namibia's skies are marvellously open and free of hassles. Contact one of the larger charter companies, like Namibia Commercial Aviation (tel: 61 223562; fax: 61 234583), or a good tour operator.

By bus
There are not many cheap local buses useful for travellers. Small Volkswagen combis (minibuses) ferry people between towns, providing a good fast service at about N$16 per 100km, but these operate only on the busier routes between centres of population. In more remote areas local people hitch.

Intercape Mainliner operates luxury vehicles on long-distance routes covering most of the main towns. One route is Windhoek–Victoria Falls (US$75) running twice a week, departing Windhoek on Fridays and Mondays, departing Victoria Falls Saturdays and Tuesdays. The coach calls at Rundu and Katima Mulilo, among other places, en route. Book through the reservations office in Windhoek: tel: 61 227847; fax: 61 228285, or through the booking agent in Rundu: the Tourism Centre, tel: 67 255911.

There is also the NamVic shuttle, aimed at tourists, departing Windhoek on Thursdays and Victoria Falls on Sundays. To check if it is running, phone 61 248185.

Driving
Namibia suits self-drive trips. The roads are generally excellent and smooth, the signposting is clear and there's very little traffic. Almost all of Namibia's major highways are tarred and the small amount of traffic makes journeys easy. Less important roads are often gravel, but even these tend to be easily passable.

Only people going off the beaten track – into Kaudom, Bushmanland or the Kaokoveld – really need to join an organised group. The only safe way to conduct such a trip is to go in a convoy of two 4WDs, each with experienced bush drivers. Without extensive experience of using a 4WD, you may get into dangerous situations.

Technically, an international driving permit is required.

Hitchhiking
Hitchhiking is feasible and can be speedy and cheap. Some of the gravel roads, however, have very little traffic, and you can wait days for even a single car to pass. The important part is to set off with enough food and (especially) water to be able to wait for this long. For the sake of courtesy, and those who come after you, it's important not to abuse people's kindness. Offer to help with the cost of fuel (most people will refuse anyhow) or pay for some cold drinks on the way. Listen patiently to your host's views and, if you choose to differ, do so courteously – after all, you came to Namibia to learn about a different country.

The 2002 eclipse area
OVERVIEW
The zone of totality extends to cover Kongola and a slice of (generally unvisited) eastern Mudumu in its western section, and Lake Liambezi in its eastern section. It misses Katima Mulilo and most of the lodges along the Kwando (Mazambala is an honourable exception to this).

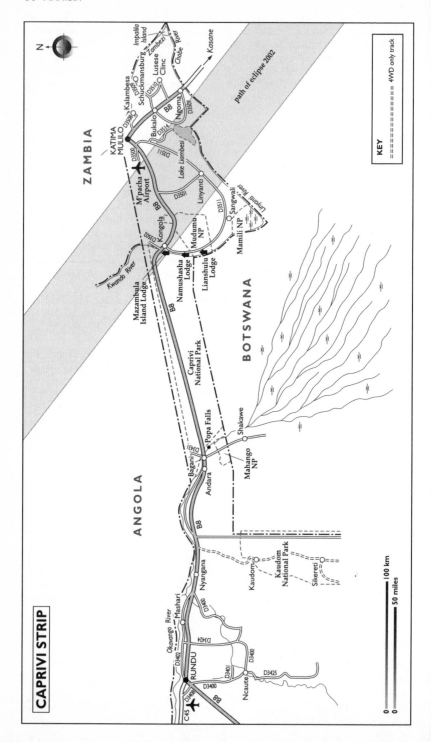

The best plan is probably either to camp in the bush or to get up very early and drive from Katima, or one of the Kwando Lodges, to see the event. Then it will make an excellent side-show to your holiday in Africa.

GATEWAY TOWNS
Katima Mulilo

Established by the British in 1935, Katima is the regional capital of the eastern Caprivi. It is a large town with good facilities, beautifully placed on the banks of the Zambezi. There is an open central square, dotted with trees. As western Zambia has started to open up, Katima has taken on the role of frontier town, with a little of the wild-west air: a base for supplies and communication for the new camps on the Upper Zambezi river in Zambia. It is close enough to the eclipse zone for you to base yourself here and drive out (very carefully, watching for animals on the road) a few hours before dawn for the eclipse.

Getting there

About 18km west of town is the M'Pacha airport. This receives the odd private flight for Lianshulu or Namushasha, and several Air Namibia services a week calling at Windhoek, Mokuti Lodge and Katima Mulilo, before continuing to Victoria Falls.

To reach the Zambian border, continue west past the Zambezi Lodge until the tar road turns left towards Rundu. Continue straight on to a gravel road for about 6km, passing the rubbish dump. The border post here at Wenella opens 06.00–18.00 every day.

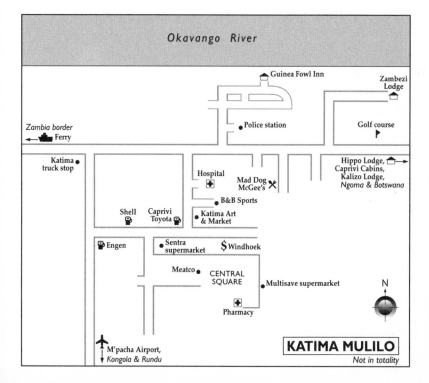

Where to stay

Recommendations include:

Zambezi Lodge PO Box 98; tel: 67 73203 or 73149; fax: 67 73631. A few hundred metres from the main road as it enters Katima from Ngoma, it is the area's best lodge. There's an adjacent camping site. N$260 single, N$160 per person sharing

Hippo Lodge PO Box 1120; tel: 67 352685. East of town (just beyond the turn to Caprivi Cabins), it has some of Namibia's lushest gardens. N$180 single, N$130 per person sharing, N$340 for a family room taking four. Camping N$20 per person

Caprivi Cabins PO Box 2029, Ngwezi-Katima Mulilo; tel: 67 72288 or 3300; fax: 67 73158. About 800m from the main road, east of the Zambezi Lodge, a super place. N$200 single, N$250 double

Kalizo Restcamp PO Box 1854, Ngweze-Katima Mulilo; tel/fax: 61 234342; fax: 67 73453. Beside the Zambezi, about 25km downstream from Katima. A simple camp in a lovely spot – but you may need a 4WD to get there and it is too far from totality to drive there in the early morning. N$220 single, N$200 per person sharing. Camping N$20 per person.

Rundu

This town was expanding, with many new lodges, until hit by the security problems of the Caprivi Strip, which have caused visitor numbers to drop and may lead to the closure of lodges. It has fuel stations and a bank (though Grootfontein is better endowed with these).

Getting there

The main Shell fuel station is located on the corner where you turn off the B8 and into Rundu. This is the best place for lifts if you are hitchhiking, but watch for thieves.

Where to stay

Most lodges are clearly signposted and offer activities like boating on the Okavango. Here is just a selection:

Kavango River Lodge PO Box 634, Rundu; tel: 67 255244; fax: 67 255013. Situated in a superb (and secure) spot on Rundu's western edge. N$210 single, N$290 double.

Omashare River Lodge PO Box 294, Rundu; tel: 67 256101; fax: 67 256111. In the centre of town, its rooms overlook the river. N$250 per room, maximum two people.

Sarasunga River Lodge PO Box 414, Rundu; tel: 67 255161; fax: 67 256238. Beautifully rustic. N$280 single, N$180 per person sharing. Camping N$27.50 per person.

Ngandu Safari Lodge PO 519, Rundu; tel: 67 255911; fax: 67 255910. Off the main road by the river, beside the turn-off to Sarasungu, Ngandu is a large new restcamp. N$70–150 single, N$120–230 per person sharing.

N'Kwazi Lodge PO Box 1623, Rundu; tel/fax: 67 255467; cell: 081 127 4010. 20km east of Rundu, n'Kwazi is an impressive, comfortable lodge. N$285 single, N$230 per person sharing. Camping N$25 per person per night.

Mayana Lodge PO 519, Rundu; tel: 67 255911; fax: 67 255910. Not to be confused with Mayana Happy Lodge, this is 1km further northeast than the turn signposted to n'Kwazi. Small, simple and friendly. N$120 single, N$80 per person sharing, for the en-suite rooms. Camping N$15 per person.

PRE- AND POST-ECLIPSE EXCURSIONS

If the Caprivi is again safe and open to visitors then consider driving yourself here. Simply plot out a two- or three-week itinerary, starting and finishing in Windhoek or Victoria Falls (ie: places that you can leave a hire car). The area is then your oyster – choose your own route, pre-book the lodges (preferably 9–12 months in advance), and drive. The two main places worth seeking out near the eclipse are Mudumu National Park, beside the Kwando, and Popa Falls. Mamili National Park would also be an option, but only for those with several well-equipped 4WDs as it's remote and has no facilities.

Campsites at any of these can be booked through the Ministry of Environment and Tourism (MET) in Windhoek (P Bag 13267, Windhoek; tel: 61 236975–8, 233845, 223903 or 224097; fax: 61 224900). The lodges must be booked individually in advance.

Mudumu National Park

The more northerly of the region's two new reserves, Mudumu, covers 850km² of riverine forest south of Kongola, either side of the D3511. Bordered by the Kwando River on the west, the reserve has good populations of a large variety of animals. Together with Mamili and the Triangle, Mudumu is notable for its buffalo (otherwise uncommon in Namibia), roan and sable antelope (both generally uncommon species), the water-loving lechwe and sitatunga, and often large herds of elephant.

Although the eastern corner of the reserve is in the zone of totality, it's usually the western side, beside the Kwando River, which is visited on safari. The dense, dry bush in the park's interior is generally much less interesting than the lush vegetation beside the river.

Mudumu can be explored on foot or by 4WD, though don't expect much organisation or many clearly marked game drives. To stay here, the choice is either an unfenced campsite with river water and basic sanitation – Nakatwa Nature Conservation Camp – or one of the lodges by the river. If you opt to camp, then follow the signs and note that the reserve, which is not fenced or clearly demarcated, borders with hunting areas. Ask the scouts exactly where the boundaries are.

Mamili Reserve

This unfenced swampland reserve of about 350km² was created shortly before independence and consists largely of marshland, veined by a network of reed-lined channels. It includes two large islands: Nkasa and Lupala. Together with Mudumu National Park, it has most of Namibia's population of sitatunga, red lechwe and puku.

Mamili is located in the southwest corner of the eastern Caprivi Strip, where the Kwando sharply changes direction to become the Linyanti. As yet there are no facilities for visitors and few passable roads, even by 4WD. The MET issues camping permits, so check with them for the latest information and buy a permit before you leave Windhoek or Katima Mulilo.

Approaching along the D3511, the turning to Mamili National Park is at Sangwali village. This community, together with the nearby villages of Samudono and Nongozi, is in the process of setting up a conservancy just outside the park with plans for a simple campsite. There is already a small craft stall, Sheshe Crafts, about 4km from the D3511 as you head into Mamili. This sells locally produced baskets, carvings, reed mats and some authentic fishing traps.

Popa Falls

This is a simple government restcamp next to some lovely rapids in the Okavango River. They mark where the river drops 2.5m over a rocky section, caused by a geological fault. After passing over this, the Okavango begins gradually to spread out across the Kalahari's sands until eventually, in Botswana, it forms its remarkable inland delta.

The camp's area by the riverside is thickly vegetated with tall riverine trees and lush green shrubs, which encourage waterbirds and a variety of small reptiles. Footbridges have been built between some of the islands, and it's worth spending a morning island-hopping among the rushing channels, or walking upstream a little where there's a good view of the river before it plunges over the rapids. In a few hours you can see all of this tiny reserve, and have a good chance of spotting a leguvaan (water monitor), a snake or two, and many different frogs. Note that Popa's gates usually open at sunrise and close at sunset.

Lizauli traditional village
This small village is well signposted on the D3511 just north of Lianshulu. The entrance fee is N$20, for which visitors are guided around the village to see traditional arts and crafts practised. This is just one of several important community projects in this area.

ECLIPSE ZONE
Overview
The eclipse zone itself covers a stretch of the B8 road between Kongola and Katima Mulilo. There is very little in this area apart from some delightfully rural African bush, dotted with occasional small villages and homesteads. Perfect for getting away from it all and watching the spectacle on your own.

Getting there
From Rundu in the west
The main B8 road from Rundu to Katima, known as the Golden Highway, is tar. A word of warning though: distances on the Caprivi are deceptively long. The maximum distance you should attempt in one day is from Victoria Falls or Kasane to Mudumu, or from Katima Mulilo to Popa Falls, or from Mudumu to Rundu.

From Rundu to Divundu (204km) is a pleasant drive, the road often surrounded by green, irrigated fields against the backdrop of the Okavango River. The entry point to the Caprivi Game Park is a bridge over the Okavango. A few hundred metres before the river the road forks. The right fork goes to Botswana, via Popa Falls and Mahango. Just after the fork, on the left of the Popa road, is a service station, the only reliable source of fuel for hundreds of kilometres.

From Divundu to Kongola (191km) you will be bisecting the undeveloped Caprivi Strip Game Reserve. While it is home to much wildlife, it has no facilities and no marked game-viewing side roads, so most visitors just pass through, saving their time for other parks. Drive carefully, though, in case something does appear on the road. There are only two larger settlements within this park: the Omega Shopping Centre, 70km from Bagani; and Babatwa, 23km further on.

You do not need any permits to cross the strip and the people manning the control posts will usually just ask where you are going and wave you on with a smile.

From Kasane in Botswana
Coming from Botswana, you'll leave the new tar road and smart customs and immigration building on the south side of the Chobe River, and cross over the bridge into Namibia. This crossing is fine for 2WD vehicles, and opens 06.00–18.00.

The gravel road from Ngoma to Katima is gradually being tarred.

Where to stay in the eclipse zone

Until the end of 1999, when Caprivi became an inadvisable destination for tourists, there were several camps there, all accessed from the D3511. When the area becomes safe again, these should re-open. They include:

Mazambala Island Lodge PO Box 1935, Ngweze-Katima Mulilo; tel: 61 229075; fax: 61 263224. The turning to Mazambala is a few kilometres east of the Kongola Bridge across the Kwando. This is the most northerly of the Kwando camps, and the only one within the zone of totality. It also has several campsites, spread out near the river. N$180 single, N$150 per person sharing. Camping N$30 per person.

Open Skies Campsite P Bag 1072, Ngweze-Katima Mulilo; tel: 67 72029; fax: 67 72029. Clearly signposted 26km south of the Katima–Kongola road, along the D3511, and then 3km west from that, it has a few simple shelters where you can eat and drink, and helpful caretakers. It's ideal if you have your own food and camping kit but like having toilets and a bar nearby. Camping N$35 per person

Namushasha Lodge PO Box 21182, Windhoek, tel/fax: 61 240375; email: namsha@iwwn.com.na. Standing above the Kwando on a high bank, Namushasha is well signposted 16km off the B8 along the D3511, and then 4km west off that. It's on the edge of the zone of totality, but has fine views north and west. N$580 single, N$550 per person sharing, including activities.

Lianshulu Lodge PO Box 142, Katima Mulilo; fax: 64 207497. Probably the best lodge in the area, and the only one inside Mudumu. It stands beside the Kwando, about 5km down a good bush track off the D3511, 40km from the B8 turn-off. US$221 single, US$135 sharing, including activities.

Where to watch the eclipse

The bridge over the River Kwando ought to be quite a good place to view totality. Although it's not so close to the centre-line, it is elevated above the surrounding area. However, there are always soldiers guarding it, so be careful that you explain exactly what you are doing before you start setting up anything as suspicious as a telescope.

FURTHER READING FROM BRADT

Africa by Road, Charlie Shackell and Illya Bracht
East and Southern Africa: The Backpacker's Manual, Philip Briggs
Namibia: The Bradt Travel Guide, Chris McIntyre
Southern Africa by Rail, Paul Ash

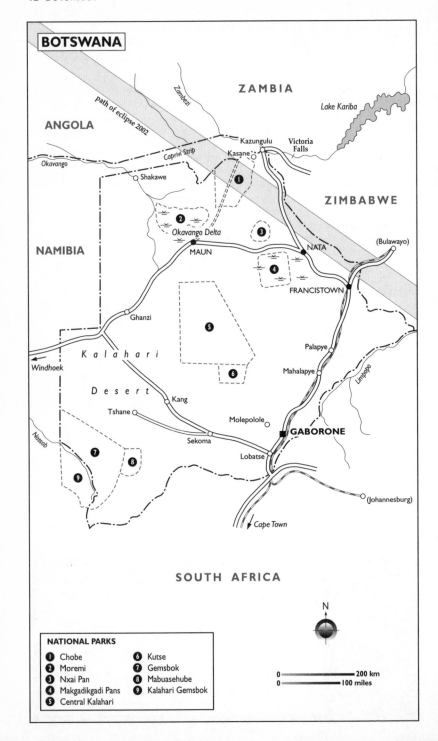

BOTSWANA

ANGOLA

ZAMBIA

Zambezi

Lake Kariba

path of eclipse 2002

Okavango

Caprivi Strip

Kazungulu

Victoria
Falls

Kasane

Shakawe

❶

ZIMBABWE

❷

Okavango Delta

❸

NAMIBIA

MAUN

NATA

(Bulawayo)

❹

FRANCISTOWN

K a l a h a r i

Ghanzi

❺

Windhoek

❻

Palapye

D e s e r t

Mahalapye

Limpopo

Kang

Tshane

Molepolole

GABORONE

Nossob

Sekoma

Lobatse

❼

❽

❾

(Johannesburg)

Cape Town

SOUTH AFRICA

N

NATIONAL PARKS

❶ Chobe
❷ Moremi
❸ Nxai Pan
❹ Makgadikgadi Pans
❺ Central Kalahari

❻ Kutse
❼ Gemsbok
❽ Mabuasehube
❾ Kalahari Gemsbok

0 — 200 km
0 — 100 miles

Bradt Travel Guides

Africa & Madagascar: Total Eclipse 2001 &
2002 Aisling Irwin et al
Africa by Road Charlie Shackell & Illya
Bracht
Albania: Guide and Illustrated Journal
Peter Dawson/Andrea Dawson/
Linda White
Amazon, The Roger Harris/
Peter Hutchison
Antarctica: A Guide to the Wildlife
Tony Soper/Dafila Scott
Australia and New Zealand by Rail
Colin Taylor
Belize Alex Bradbury
Brazil Alex Bradbury
Britain, Eccentric Benedict le Vay
Cambodia Anita Sach
Canada: North – Yukon, Northwest
Territories, Nunavut Geoffrey Roy
Cape Verde Islands Aisling Irwin/
Colum Wilson .
Chile and Argentina: Backpacking and
Hiking Tim Burford
China: Yunnan Province Stephen
Mansfield
Cuba Stephen Fallon
Cyprus see North Cyprus
East and Southern Africa: The Backpacker's
Manual Philip Briggs
Eccentric Britain see Britain, Eccentric
Eclipse see Africa & Madagascar
Ecuador, Climbing and Hiking in
Rob Rachowiecki/Mark Thurber
Ecuador, Peru and Bolivia: The Backpacker's
Manual Kathy Jarvis
Eritrea Edward Paice
Estonia Neil Taylor
Ethiopia Philip Briggs
Galápagos Wildlife David Horwell/
Pete Oxford
Georgia Tim Burford
Ghana Philip Briggs
Greece by Rail Zane Katsikis

Haiti and the Dominican Republic
Ross Velton
India by Rail Royston Ellis
Latvia Stephen Baister/Chris Patrick
Lithuania Gordon McLachlan
Madagascar Hilary Bradt
Madagascar Wildlife Hilary Bradt/
Derek Schuurman/Nick Garbutt
Malawi Philip Briggs
Maldives Royston Ellis
Mali Ross Velton
Mauritius, Rodrigues and Réunion
Royston Ellis/Derek Schuurman
Mozambique Philip Briggs
Namibia Chris McIntyre
North Cyprus Diana Darke
Palestine, with Jerusalem Henry Stedman
Peru and Bolivia: Backpacking and Trekking
Hilary Bradt
Philippines Stephen Mansfield
Poland and Ukraine, Hiking Guide to
Tim Burford
Romania, Hiking Guide to Tim Burford
Russia and Central Asia by Road
Hazel Barker
Russia by Rail, with Belarus and Ukraine
Athol Yates
South Africa Philip Briggs
Southern Africa by Rail Paul Ash
Spitsbergen Andreas Umbreit
Switzerland: Rail, Road, Lake Anthony
Lambert
Tanzania Philip Briggs
Uganda Philip Briggs
USA by Rail John Pitt
Venezuela Hilary Dunsterville Branch
Vietnam John R Jones
Your Child's Health Abroad
· Dr Jane Wilson-Howarth/
Dr Matthew Ellis
Yunnan see China
Zambia Chris McIntyre
Zanzibar David Else

Bradt guides are available from bookshops or by mail order from:
Bradt Travel Guides
19 High Street, Chalfont St Peter, Bucks SL9 9QE, England
Tel: 01753 893444   Fax: 01753 892333
Email: info@bradt-travelguides.com   www.bradt-travelguides.com

Travelling to see the eclipse in 2001 or 2002?
SAVE £2 OFF A BRADT GUIDE!

To order your copy of one or more of the Bradt guides listed in this book, post or fax us your order on the form below, together with the appropriate remittance, and we will despatch the book(s) within two working days.

Please send me a copy of each of the following Bradt guides at £2 off the retail price, post and packing free in the UK and Northern Ireland:

No.	Title	Special price	Total
☐	Africa by Road (December 2000)	£11.95	. . . . .
☐	Botswana: The Bradt Travel Guide (summer 2001)	£11.95	. . . . .
☐	East & Southern Africa: The Backpacker's Manual	£11.95	. . . . .
☐	Madagascar: The Bradt Travel Guide	£11.95	. . . . .
☐	Mozambique, Guide to	£9.95	. . . . .
☐	Namibia: The Bradt Travel Guide	£10.95	. . . . .
☐	South Africa: The Bradt Budget Guide (summer 2001)	£9.95	. . . . .
☐	Southern Africa by Rail	£10.95	. . . . .
☐	Zambia: The Bradt Travel Guide	£10.95	. . . . .

Sub-total . . . . .
Post & packing outside UK
(£2 per book Europe; £3 per book rest of world) . . . . .
TOTAL . . . . .

Name . . . .

Address . . . .

Telephone . . . .   Email address . . . .

☐ I enclose a cheque for £. . . . . . made payable to Bradt Publications

☐ I would like to pay by VISA or Mastercard

   Number. . . . .   Expiry date . . . .

☐ Please add my name to your catalogue mailing list.

Send your order on this form to:
Bradt Travel Guides/ECL
19 High Street, Chalfont St Peter, Bucks SL9 9QE
tel: 01753 893444; fax: 01753 892333
email: info@bradt-travelguides.com
web: www.bradt-travelguides.com

Botswana

Chris McIntyre

Visiting the eclipse areas
OVERVIEW
Last total solar eclipse: March 1820
Next total solar eclipse: November 2030

At 07.07 local time first contact begins to pass over a thin slice of northeastern Botswana. It enters the country in the far north, between the Linyanti campsite and Muchenje, covering virtually all of the Chobe Forest Reserve.

Swiftly, totality moves southeast, passing over most of the Sibuyu Forest Reserve but missing both Nata and Francistown. Then it leaves the country to enter southeastern Zimbabwe.

Within this short time, the zone of totality will pass over a tremendous area of open bush, including a large swathe of Chobe National Park – one of southern Africa's greatest reserves. It's all wild, untamed stuff. At the start of December it is likely to be hot but the green shoots will already have sprouted and if there has been any rain, the air will be clear and the bush alive with promise.

This bush will be difficult to reach, but where the eclipse passes over the main Nata–Kasane road, it'll be easily seen. There you can easily drive yourself in a normal car, or even hitchhike and camp nearby. It's fairly open and even desolate in places.

Maps are useful if you are driving your own 4WD into the parks, and essential if you are planning to explore at all. You can obtain them in Gaborone or in Maun (the Surveyor General's Office is at the back of an apparently unused building to the right of the stylish Air Botswana office near the airport).

The country telephone code is 267.

ORGANISED ECLIPSE TRIPS
See *Planning and Preparation*, page 20, for comments on companies specialising in eclipse trips. Safari companies that specialise in Botswana using small, dedicated safari camps include:

UK
Abercrombie & Kent Sloane Square House, Holbein Place, London SW1W 8NS; tel: 020 7730 9600; fax: 020 7730 9376; email: info@abercrombiekent.co.uk
Africa Travel Centre 21 Leigh St, London WC1H 9QX; tel 020 7387 1211; fax: 020 7383 7512; email: chris@africatravel.co.uk; web: www.africatravel.co.uk. Tailor-makes trips on request for 2002. A suggested 9-night trip includes Zimbabwe and viewing of the eclipse from Muchenje Lodge, near Chobe National Park in Botswana. Cost: £2,695 per person.
Art of Travel 21 The Bakehouse, 119 Altenberg Gardens, London SW11 1JQ; tel: 020 7738 2038; fax: 020 7738 1893; email: safari@artoftravel.co.uk

Cazenove & Lloyd 3 Alice Court, 116 Putney Bridge Rd, London SW15 2NQ; tel: 020 8875 9666; fax: 020 8875 9444; email: enquiries@caz-loyd.com
Grenadier Safaris 11/12 West Stockwell St, Colchester CO1 1HN; tel: 01206 549585; fax: 01206 561337; email: james@grenadir.demon.co.uk
Okavango Tours and Safaris Marlborough House, 298 Regents Park Rd, London N3 2TJ; tel: 020 8343 3283; fax: 020 8343 3287; email: info@okavango.com
Sunvil Discovery Upper Square, Old Isleworth, Middlesex TW7 7BJ; tel: 020 8232 9777; fax: 020 8568 8330; email: africa@sunvil.co.uk; web: www.sunvil.co.uk/africa. Sunvil's African operations are run by the author. They have 2 trips to the 2001 eclipse that incorporate Botswana. Falcon A (max 10 people) features 3 nights in the Linyanti, 3 in Victoria Falls, 4 in Hwange, with a flight into Mana Pools and a riverside picnic for the eclipse. Cost: £3,830 per person sharing.

USA
David Anderson Safaris 4635 Via Vistosa, Santa Barbara, CA 93110; tel: 800 733 1789 or 805 967 1712; fax: 805 964 8285

Australia
African Wildlife Safaris 1st Floor, 259 Coventry St, South Melbourne, Victoria 3205; tel: 03 9696 2899; fax: 03 9696 4937; email: ofice@africasafaris.com.au
The Classic Safari Company Town Hall House, Level 11/456 Kent St, Sydney NSW 2000; tel: 01 800 351 088 or 02 9264 5710; fax 02 9267 3047; email: tracey@africatravel.com.au

National parks accommodation
Campsites are very limited in number and must be reserved and paid for in advance. Reservations for Chobe are through Parks and Reserves Reservations Office, PO Box 20364, Boseja, Maun, Botswana (tel: 661265; fax: 661264). If you don't have a reservation then you won't normally be allowed in.

GETTING AROUND
By air
Air Botswana is a reliable airline on the global flight reservations systems and so it is easy to book internal flights. The airline connects Maun and Kasane with Victoria Falls, Gaborone and Johannesburg.

Botswana also has a plethora of small charter flight companies. These are generally high-quality operations ferrying visitors between small, remote safari camps. They are normally booked through tour operators.

Some useful charters are based around Maun airport: Air Kavango PO Box 169, Maun (tel: 660393; fax: 660623, next to the tourist office); Elgon Air PO Box 448, Maun (tel: 660654; fax: 660037); and Wildlife Helicopters (P Bag 161, Maun; tel/fax: 660664; the ultimate in game-viewing flights – at a cost).

By road
Botswana's local buses are cheap but fairly infrequent. Most major arteries, and roads in the towns, are good tar. However, away from these main arteries, the 'roads' are usually little more than unmarked ruts in the sand which require negotiation by a tough 4WD with high ground clearance. If you're even thinking of driving across Chobe National Park, or the Forest Reserve, then this is the kind of vehicle that you'll require.

Hitchhiking is a practical way to get around the main roads. Waiting times are seldom too long, as there is quite a bit of traffic on the three main roads of interest to visitors: Nata–Maun, Nata–Kasane and Nata–Francistown. Carry a few litres of water and some food with you, both for standing beside the road, and for lifts where you can't stop for food. You usually pay for your trip. Hitchhiking cannot be recommended for single women, or even two women travelling together.

By bicycle and on foot

Distances in Botswana are very large, and there are rarely stops for shade or drinks. So cyclists will find the going tough, and walking isn't practical.

The 2002 eclipse

OVERVIEW

Because the sun will be so low in the sky in the early morning, it's vital that observers find either an elevated position or at least a wide open expanse with a clear view to the east, and also preferably a good view to the west so that you can see the approaching shadow.

GATEWAY CITIES
Gaborone

Gaborone is not a bad city, but it is generally uninteresting. Most visitors are in transit, normally between Maun and Jo'burg – the main flight route into Botswana.

If you do have to overnight here then be prepared for a general lack of cheap accommodation. Campsites are particularly difficult to find.

Francistown

This is Botswana's second largest town, and one of the country's oldest settlements, although there remains little to interest visitors. Francistown is only three hours' drive from Bulawayo, to which it has many close cultural and trading links. Now it functions as a shopping centre, especially for Zimbabweans whose own shops are much more limited. It is an obvious stopover on the tar road north from Gaborone, to Maun and Kasane, but seldom merits more than a night.

Getting there and away
By bus

The main bus station is south of the main city centre, beside the railway line, from where buses leave in the morning for Gaborone, Maun and Kasane. Get there by 09.00.

Hitching

Take a taxi out of town and then hitching is relatively easy along the main tar arteries.

Where to stay

Francistown doesn't have many places to stay, but the usual place has for years been the **Marang Hotel** (PO Box 807, Francistown; tel: 213991; fax: 212130; email: marang@info.bw). This is 5km from the centre on the Old Gaborone Road. It has thatched chalets, rooms and a camping site. It opened in 1981 and is still run by the same family.

Alternatively, and with a little less character, the **Best Western Thapama Hotel & Casino** (Blue Jacket Street, P Bag 31, Francistown; tel: 213872; fax: 213766) is near the centre of town and the bus station. It has over 90 rooms from around US$80 each. To the north of the centre the **Grand Lodge** (PO Box 713, Francistown; tel: 212300; fax: 212309) has just 15 rooms.

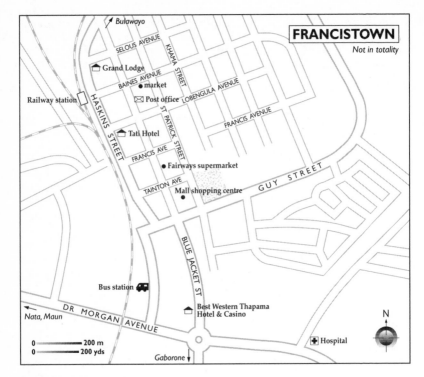

Maun

This dusty, sprawling town has been the start of expeditions into the wilds since the turn of the century, and it is now the safari capital of the country. Maun's elongated centre is dotted with modern shops and offices, while its suburbs are mainly traditional, thatched rondavels. A little of its rough-and-ready frontier feel remains – contemporary cowboys still ride into town for their supplies in battered 4WDs, even if the main roads are now sealed tar rather than dusty gravel.

For the visitor, this is the base for trips into the Okavango Delta, Moremi Reserve and Chobe. There are banks, including a Barclays and Standard Chartered, garages, well-stocked supermarkets and a number of travel agents and operators. Maun is important as a communications centre for all the camps, so it is the best place from which to organise a last-minute trip.

The tourist information office, opposite Riley's Hotel, is small but useful. It opens during the week, 07.30–12.30 and 13.45–16.30. If you arrive with no trip organised, and are travelling on a tight budget, then ask the booking agents in town what is available. Shopping around can be disappointing, however, as some safari operators are not enthusiastic about helping and choices are limited.

Getting there
By air
Air Botswana connects Maun with Gaborone, Victoria Falls and Kasane. Air Namibia occasionally connects with Windhoek. Maun airport buzzes with private flights to remote safari camps throughout northern and central Botswana.

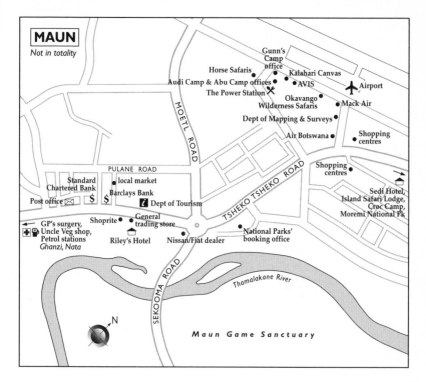

By road

The Nata to Maun road is tarred, as is the road up to Shakawe and the Namibian border, but the road from Ghanzi is not complete yet. The route from Kasane through Chobe National Park is strictly for those with time and 4WDs. Daily buses run from Francistown to Maun via Nata in the mornings. Hitchhiking to Maun via Nata from Kasane or Francistown is not difficult in a day, and is usually faster than the bus. Hitching to or from Ghanzi is rather more tricky, and will require quite a wait. Hitching to or from Kasane through Chobe is not really possible – you need a pre-arranged lift.

Where to stay

Nowadays most visitors to the Delta just pass through Maun's airport, arriving from scheduled air services and connecting to small six-seater planes for a flight to one of the camps. Thus several of the lodges near Maun have been forced to close. Those remaining open include:

Riley's Hotel PO Box 1, Maun; tel: 660204; fax: 660580. Riley's, founded in 1910, has always been more of an institution than a hotel, though now it's a luxury venue owned by Cresta, so has lost a little of its quirkiness.
Sedi Motel PO Box 29, Maun; tel: 660177. About 800m off the main road, on the east side, a few kilometres north of Maun.
Island Safari Lodge PO Box 116, Maun; tel/fax: 660300. On the northern bank of the Thamalakane River. Take the signposted turning about 7km north of Maun and follow the well-used track a further 3km to the camp. Hitching to the beginning of this track is easy. Good value camp and rambling riverside campsite.

Crocodile Camp PO Box 46, Maun; tel/fax: 660265. Small and well organised with a separate camping site. The turn-off to Croc is about 3km further north of that for Island Safari.

Nata

Nata is a tiny settlement, with little more than a large petrol station (a good hitching spot) and a few small houses. Nata Lodge, P Bag 10, Francistown (tel: 611210) is about 10km south of Nata, beside the road.

Kasane

Standing on the Chobe River in the northeast corner of the country, Kasane is a gateway to Namibia's Caprivi Strip, Zimbabwe and Zambia – and a springboard for trips into Chobe National Park. It has several places to stay, garages for vehicle repairs, a few shops for supplies and a very picturesque river front. Kasane is the best place to stay if you are arranging a day-trip into Chobe or a budget mini-safari around the Serondela area.

There's a Barclays bank, a post office and basic grocery shops. The tourist information office is well stocked with brochures and has some ancient maps of Chobe, Nxai and the Okavango. On the west side of the small centre, a new, wide tarred road leads up and away from the river to join the inland road to the Namibian border at Ngoma Bridge. The main road continues to the Kasane filling station and the Chobe Safari Lodge. It no longer continues into the park. .

Getting there and away

From Francistown, Kasane is about 495km of variable tarred road away. Nata, the only fuel stop on the route, is 195km from Francistown. If you are hitching in either direction then this is an easy route with lots of traffic by Botswana's standards – make an early start from Francistown and you can expect to reach Kasane by nightfall. Arriving from the south, the road proceeds northeast to the Zimbabwean border post at Kazungula, while the left turn signals the start of the road to Chobe. Taking this turning, on the right you pass the town's new commercial centre, an embryonic industrial area that lies between Kubu Lodge and the main road. Shortly afterwards, a clearly marked right turn points the way to Kasane, leaving the good tar road to continue to the Namibian border at Ngoma, some 65km away. If you want to speed your way to southern Chobe (avoiding Chobe's riverfront) you could take this road, turning left before the border post at Ngoma.

From Zimbabwe there is an excellent tarred road to Kasane. This brings the Victoria Falls, only 75km away and a major centre for travellers, within a convenient day-trip from Kasane. There is a regular transfer service which shuttles between the two centres every day. It can be booked through any local agent in either town, or by overseas tour operators.

To Zambia there is a ferry over the river at Kazungula – just turn left before the Zimbabwean border post. Most visitors go via Victoria Falls in Zimbabwe, rather than directly across, since getting to Livingstone is much less difficult from there. If you want to hitch across, there are occasional lorries. Try standing where the Zimbabwean and Zambian roads fork, hitching on both of them.

For Namibia there is a good tar road to Ngoma Bridge, 65km away. The road passes the grand new entrance to the main game-viewing area around the riverfront of Chobe National Park before cutting inland through Chobe, and over the Chobe River. Some 2km before you reach the bridge, report to the border post.

Where to stay
Chobe Safari Lodge PO Box 10, Kasane; tel: 250336. Camping on pleasant sites along the river, and a range of accommodation. Daily river cruises (departing 15.00) give excellent game-viewing.
Kubu Lodge PO Box 43, Kasane; tel: 650312; fax: 650412. About 10km east of Kasane, this is a beautiful camp set on lawns that stretch down to the river. Alternatively there is camping on riverside sites. River cruises offered.
Cresta Mowana Lodge PO Box 266, Kasane; tel: 650300; fax: 650301. A typically Botswanan, luxury hotel, conceived on a grand scale and built around a baobab tree. River views.

PRE- AND POST-ECLIPSE EXCURSIONS
Kasane
Most of the lodges run trips along the river. The town's only attraction is probably its Reptile Park. This is near Kubu Lodge, and holds guided tours around its collection of fauna at 09.00, 11.00, 14.00 and 16.00.

Moremi
Gazetted as a game reserve by the Batawana people (a sub-group of the Batswana 'tribe') in 1962 in order to combat the rapid depletion of the area's game, Moremi is certainly one of the most beautiful and interesting reserves in southern Africa. It includes regions of permanent swamp, flood plain, islands and two large areas of dry land: Chief's Island and the Mopane Tongue. Both have excellent populations of big game. Never relax your vigilance for animals when walking or camping here.

Okavango Delta
From its source in the Angolan highlands, the Okavango River flows southwest across Namibia's Caprivi Strip and into the sands of the northern Kalahari. Here it spreads out, forming a unique inland delta – 16,000km² of water wilderness, dotted with islands and laced with a network of channels.

It's an unusual and relaxing environment, where you can glide silently along in a *mokoro* (dugout canoe, made from a single tree trunk) through a maze of reeds, watching the wildlife at eye level and soaking up the sun. Beneath you, the crystal clear water reveals a myriad of fishes and aquatic animals and plants. Some of the larger islands within the delta are rich with game, so stalking around these with a guide is fascinating.

Savuti
Savuti, in the heart of Chobe National Park, is one of Africa's most famous big game areas. At times it has amazing concentrations of game, whilst always remaining a beautiful place with an atmosphere all of its own. The key to its attraction is the mysterious Savuti Channel, which is often dry but sometimes, inexplicably, flows. Then it spills out from the southern end of the Linyanti swamps and, after passing through a gap in the Magwikwe Sand Ridge, starts to spread out across the Mababe Depression, forming the Savuti Marsh.

Savuti is a day's drive from either Kasane or Maun so most guests fly in to Savuti's airstrip. You can camp at the public campsite. There are also two new lodges here – Savute Elephant Camp and Savuti Safari Lodge. Both concentrate on fly-in guests and don't normally accept passing visitors.

THE ECLIPSE ZONE
There are two very different possibilities in Botswana. One is to venture into the wild areas of Chobe and the Linyanti, where you'll either have to join a safari run

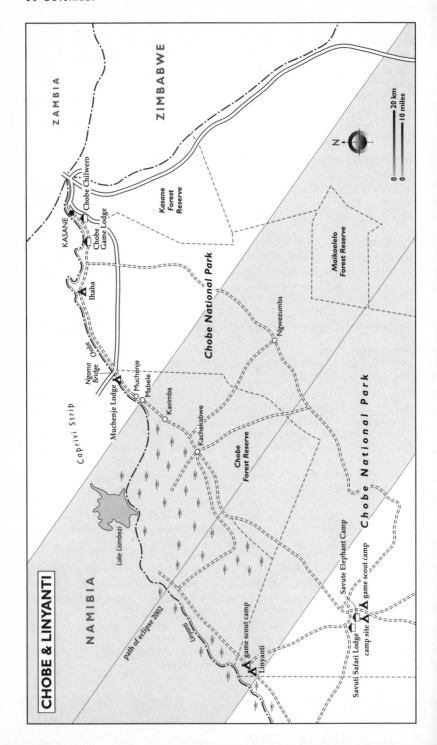

by local guides, or drive yourself in a fully equipped 4WD. In the latter case, you'll need far more detailed instructions than are given here.

The other option is much simpler: to observe the eclipse on or around the good Kasane–Nata road, which you can easily reach by car, hitchhiking or public transport.

Chobe National Park/west Linyanti area

Within Chobe, none of the main campsites is in the band of totality except for the little-used Linyanti site, which is just on the southern edge of the eclipse path. That would certainly be my first choice – though from there I might try to venture northeast, out of the park towards Lake Liambezi (dry since 1985). There are many small villages in this isolated area, very few of which ever see any visitors. The locals will probably assume that you're lost.

Within the park itself, if you take the route from Kasane to Savuti Campsite (both of which are outside totality), then one promising area is Ngwezumba Pans. About 100km south of the Chobe River, this is a complex of large pans surrounded by grassland plains and mopane woodlands. There are well over a dozen individual pans and all hold water after the rains. This makes them a natural focus during the first few months of the year, when the animals tend to stay away from the permanent waters of the Linyanti and Chobe rivers.

The area is notable for its oribi antelope, perhaps the only place in Botswana where they occur naturally. These small, elegant grazing antelope are orange-red above and white underneath. They are usually seen in pairs, or small groups, feeding in the open grasslands during the morning or late afternoon. If startled they will often emit a shrill whistle before bounding off with a jerky motion.

Getting there and away

For this area you'll need a well-equipped 4WD and a driver capable of using it. If there have already been substantial rains then you should be careful if you venture east of the Linyanti campsite. If you get the vehicle stuck in mud there will be no passers-by to help you.

Where to stay
Linyanti campsite
Beside the reed-lined channel of the Linyanti, in a corner of the Chobe National Park, is a small campsite on the very edge of the zone of totality. It overlooks the Linyanti River as it passes through the Linyanti Swamps, and is a magnet for game during the dry season. However, reaching it is difficult. There are two alternatives, both sandy and strictly for well-equipped 4WDs. For directions ask the national park's game scouts in Savuti.

Ngwezumba Pans
If this area is open then there will probably be two places to stay: the Tjinga (alias 'Tshinga' and 'Tchinga') and Nogatsaa campsites. You'll need to ask the game scouts at either park entry gate for the latest information.

Nogatsaa, the more northerly site, is situated by Nogatsaa Dam and has toilets and cold showers. The game-viewing hide, which overlooks the dam, is invariably deserted so spend the late afternoon just sitting and watching the game coming to bathe and drink.

Tjinga is about 21km south of Nogatsaa, and has no facilities other than a water tank with a temperamental mechanical pump.

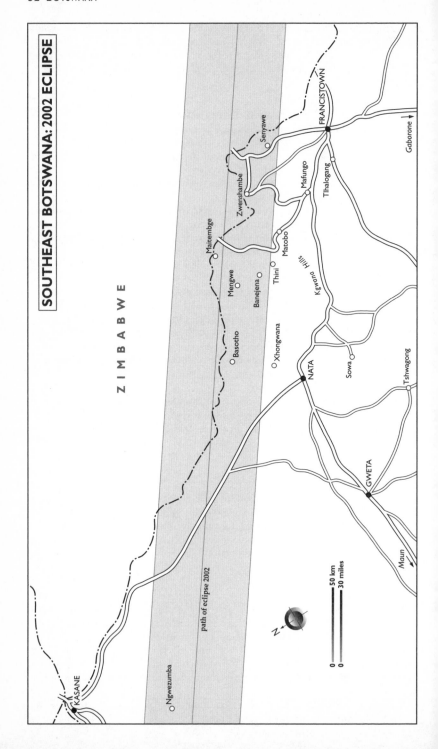

SOUTHEAST BOTSWANA: 2002 ECLIPSE

Where to watch the eclipse
The land is very flat around here. You can always stand on top of your vehicle.

East Botswana: Nata–Kasane Road
The easiest area of totality to reach in Botswana must be where it crosses the main Nata–Kasane road. It's a fairly open landscape with some large ranches. The road is relatively raised, and so may be the best site from which to watch the eclipse. However, to ensure you get in position sufficiently early for the eclipse, it would be foolish to rely on hitchhiking or a bus on the day. Either drive up on the day or arrive the day before and camp beside the road – well away from the traffic.

East Botswana: north of Francistown
Trickier to access, certainly more offbeat, is the area north of Francistown near the Zimbabwean border, around the villages of Zwenshambe and Maitembge. Getting here will be more difficult than reaching the centre-line of the eclipse along the main Nata–Kasane road, so allow plenty of time. You'd be best to bring your own vehicle.

The countryside is undulating, with occasional rivers and streams, signalling that you've left flat Kalahari sands behind – and that you should be able to find a vantage point from which to watch the eclipse.

As with any border area, approach this with caution. Botswana used to have refugee camps (for Zimbabweans) in this region, so it can be sensitive. Visitors should consider dropping into local police posts on their route, just to let the police know about them. Asking, naively, for directions or 'if it's safe to proceed nearer the border' are easy ways to do this. Show them this book, and you'll probably end up with a fascinated, if incredulous, audience.

FURTHER READING FROM BRADT
Africa by Road, Charlie Shackell and Illya Bracht
Botswana: Okavango, Kalahari, Chobe, Chris McIntyre (due summer 2001)
East and Southern Africa: The Backpacker's Manual, Philip Briggs
Southern Africa by Rail, Paul Ash

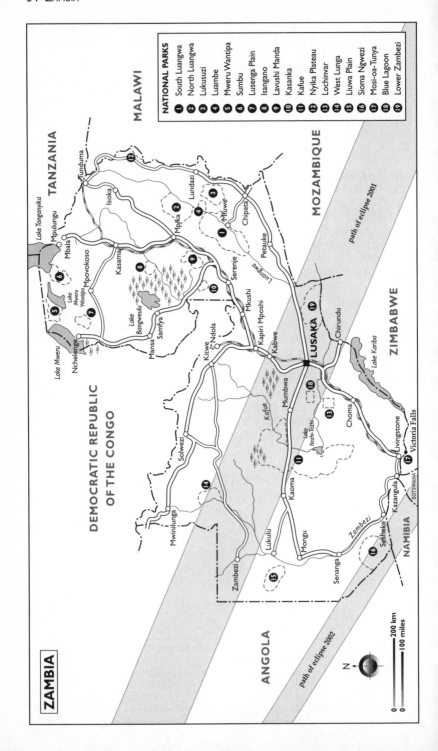

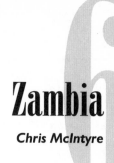

Zambia

Chris McIntyre

Visiting the eclipse areas

OVERVIEW

Last total solar eclipse: May 1919
Next total solar eclipse after 2002: August 2046

The 2001 eclipse neatly bisects Zambia and blankets the capital city, Lusaka. For visitors seeking the longest possible land-based duration Zambia is the best option after Angola, with totality lasting 4 minutes on the Angolan border and 3 minutes 27 seconds on the Lower Zambezi River.

Most of Zambia is a high, undulating plateau. Only a few rift valleys lie below 500m. There is a low chance (10–20%) of cloud in the west with a 20–30% chance in central Zambia. Given these factors, and that the eclipse is in the early afternoon, the scene is set for a superb occasion.

The path of totality lies over several national parks, including the north of Kafue National Park and all of Zambia's Lower Zambezi Valley, including the Lower Zambezi National Park. Because the eclipse passes over so much of the country, these parks should be spared crowds.

The main problem, nevertheless, will be lack of accommodation. Most of the lodges and camps in the parks take small numbers of people, often on exclusive safaris. There are not even the campsites found in Zimbabwe, or the network of good rural roads or communications.

So eclipse-chasers in Zambia have limited options. You can stay in or around Lusaka (perhaps camping); secure one of the few places still available on small, upmarket trips; or hire a self-sufficient 4WD vehicle in which you can drive yourself. However, the latter is a recipe for disaster if you haven't driven around Africa before.

Alternatively, take 2–3 days to head up through the Copperbelt and west, aiming to reach the undeveloped Kabompo or Zambezi areas which promise super views.

For the 2002 eclipse, the possibilities are more limited. Cloud cover is highly likely. Totality passes over the far southwest of Zambia, including part of the Sioma Ngwezi National Park. All of this area is adjacent to the Angolan border so guns are common. Visitors would require at least a three-vehicle convoy, and probably also an armed army escort. For the latest eclipse information on Zambia consult the Bradt website: www.bradt-travelguides.com.

The country telephone code is 260.

ORGANISED TOURS

See *Planning and Preparation*, page 20, for specialist eclipse companies. Beware of booking trips with operators new to Zambia, and check that tour operators have firm bookings by asking them to name their camps. Good specialist safari companies to Zambia running eclipse trips include:

UK

Abercrombie & Kent Sloane Square House, Holbein Place, London SW1W 8NS; tel: 020 7730 9600; fax: 020 7730 9376; email: info@abercrombiekent.co.uk

Art of Travel 21 The Bakehouse, 119 Altenberg Gardens, London SW11 1JQ; tel: 020 7738 2038; fax: 020 7738 1893; email: safari@artoftravel.co.uk. No trips for 2001; tailor-made for 2002.

Cazenove & Lloyd 3 Alice Court, 116 Putney Bridge Rd, London SW15 2NQ; tel: 020 8875 9666; fax: 020 8875 9444; email: enquiries@caz-loyd.com. Tailor-made trips for 2002.

Grenadier Safaris 11/12 West Stockwell St, Colchester CO1 1HN; tel: 01206 549585; fax: 01206 561337; email: james@grenadir.demon.co.uk. Tailor-made trips for 2002.

Okavango Tours and Safaris Marlborough House, 298 Regents Park Rd, London N3 2TJ; tel: 020 8343 3283; fax: 020 8343 3287; email: info@okavango.com. Eclipse-viewing from Busanga Plains plus safari in South Luanga. Cost: £2,484 per person sharing.

Rainbow Tours 64 Essex Rd, London, N1 8LR; tel: 020 7226 1004; fax: 020 7226 2621; email: info@rainbowtours.co.uk; web: www.rainbowtours.co.uk. A 10-day tour including Victoria Falls and Lake Kariba, viewing the 2001 eclipse from a canoe safari on the Lower Zambezi.

Sunvil Discovery Upper Square, Old Isleworth, Middlesex TW7 7BJ; tel: 020 8232 9777; fax: 020 8568 8330; email: africa@sunvil.co.uk; web: www.sunvil.co.uk/africa. The author runs this company, and has 5 eclipse trips to Zambia. These include a week at Kingfisher Camp (Lower Zambezi) for up to 6 people (£2,541 each); 2 13-night trips for up to 8 people to Victoria Falls, Kariba, Kafue and Lower Zambezi (£3,134 each); and a 15-night trip with canoe safari and a view of the eclipse from the Taj Pamodzi in Lusaka (£3,035 each).

Talking Travel Manor Barn, Wylye Rd, Hanging Langford, Salisbury SP3 4NW; tel/fax: 01722 790023; email: wildlife@dialstart.net; web: www. exploreafrica.org. Eclipse-viewing over the Zambezi Valley near Chirundu plus time in Matusadona and Elephant Point Lodge on Kariba. Talking Travel is not bonded, so you must organise your own flights. Cost: US$1,965 per person sharing. Proprietor also has excellent contacts with farmers in the Mavuradona area.

Truck Africa Tel: 020 7731 6142; web: www.truckafrica.com. Overland trip visiting Zimbabwe, Zambia and Botswana. Cost: £450 per person.

Wildlife Worldwide 170 Selsdon Rd, South Croydon CR2 6PJ; tel: 020 8667 9158; fax: 020 8667 1960; email: sales@wildlifeworldwide.com; web: www.wildlifeworldwide.com. Journey on the *Pride of Africa*, a steam-hauled luxury train, from Johannesburg to Lusaka via Victoria Falls, viewing the 2001 eclipse from a farm south of Lusaka. Cost: £3,175 per person. Other trips on application.

USA

Adventure Center 1311 63rd St, Suite 200, Emeryville, California 94608; tel: 510 654 1879; fax: 510 654 4200; email: sandy@adventure-center.com

David Anderson Safaris 4635 Via Vistosa, Santa Barbara, CA 93110; tel: 800 733 1789 or 805 967 1712; fax: 805 964 8285

Australia

The Classic Safari Company Town Hall House, Level 11/456 Kent St, Sydney NSW 2000; tel: 1 800 351 088 or 2 9264 5710; fax: 2 9267 3047; email: tracey@africatravel.com.au

African Wildlife Safaris 1st Floor, 259 Coventry St, South Melbourne, Victoria 3205; tel: 3 9696 2899; fax: 3 9696 4937; email: office@africasafaris.com.au

NATIONAL PARK ACCOMMODATION

To camp in a remote park with your own vehicle, book in advance with the Zambia Wildlife Authority (ZWA, formerly ZWPS) in Chilanga, about 20km south of

Lusaka. Send written requests to the Chief Warden, P Bag 1, Chilanga, though telephoning (1 278366) or calling in person is more effective. The next best option is the regional ZWA offices – easier than negotiating with the scouts on the gate. Generally these are in the main towns near the parks, some signposted ZWPS.

GETTING AROUND
By air
Most air charter companies are high quality and should be booked through experienced Zambia tour operators. Expect a five-seater to cost around US$1.10 per km including any mileage to and from its base. Small carriers include:

Airwaves Air Charters Tel: 1 223952/224334; cell: 752304/755640; fax: 223504
Avocet Air Charters Tel: 1 233422 (airport) or 264866 (after hours); cell: 702056; fax: 229261/2
Eastern Air c/o Steve Blagus Travel, Nkwazi Rd, PO Box 31530; tel: 1 227739/40 or 227285; fax: 223724; tlx: ZA 43320. Regular shuttle flights between some of the more outlying areas.
Proflight PO Box 30536, Lusaka; tel:1 264439 or 263686 or 263687; airport tel: 271437; fax: 222888/262379. Flies from Lusaka to Mfuwe and Livingstone.
Stabo Air Charters Tel: 1 235976 (24-hour); cell: 771822; fax: 233481
Staravia PO Box 34273, Lusaka; tel: 1 291962; airport tel: 1 271332/3
Zambian Airways (formerly Roan Air) PO Box 310277, Lusaka International Airport; tel: 1 271066 or 271230; tlx: ZA 40410. Regular hops to and from the Copperbelt, with flights up to Mfuwe (and from Lusaka to Mfuwe) during the dry season.

By rail
The ordinary trains are slow and have a limited network. TAZARA trains run on a reliable international system between Kapiri Mposhi and Dar es Salaam in Tanzania.

By bus
Zambia's local buses are cheap and frequent. There are also 'postbuses', which take mailbags and passengers between main town post offices. These have fixed schedules; book in advance.

There is usually no public transport into the national parks so visitors rely on light aircraft to fly to remote camps.

By taxi
Taxis are common and convenient in Lusaka, Livingstone and the main towns of the Copperbelt. Elsewhere they are uncommon. Agree the rate before getting into the vehicle.

Driving
Most major arteries and roads in the cities are tarred, alternating unpredictably from silky smooth to dangerously pot-holed. Elswhere, roads are often unsurfaced and usually badly maintained. A tough 4WD with high ground clearance is essential. Travel away from the tar roads is very difficult during the rains.

Hitchhiking
Hitchhiking is practical and lifts are normally paid for, but getting a good lift, even on main routes, can take six or eight hours. Always carry a few litres of water and some food with you.

Unfortunately, drinking and driving is common. Notwithstanding this, Zambia is generally a safe place to hitchhike for a robust male traveller or a couple travelling together, but not for single women, or even two women travelling together.

By bicycle and on foot

Distances in Zambia are often long and the population is sparsely scattered so walkers and cyclists will find fewer stops than elsewhere in Africa. But cycling is practical if you carry all your food, water and camping equipment.

The 2001 eclipse

OVERVIEW

The centre-line enters Zambia northwest of the town of Zambezi where eclipse-chasers will need a fully equipped 4WD and a sense of adventure. It then passes over the Busanga Plains in northern Kafue National Park. This is a prime location among superb game on expansive plains, but the plains may prove tricky to reach if the rains have been abnormally late, and accommodation is very limited. There are virtually no campsites and camping is forbidden elsewhere in the park.

The centre-line then passes just north of the cotton-milling town of Mumbwa (the Moon's shadow will cover the largely unvisited Blue Lagoon National Park, and a lot of undistinguished bush), before crossing the Great North Road about 40km north of Lusaka.

The shadow will also cover the major towns of Kabwe and Kafue and, because of ease of access, this is probably where most eclipse-watchers will congregate.

Further southeast, the line passes over the Great East Road about 50km from Lusaka, which will probably be much less busy than the best points on the Great North Road, and hence a good bet for travellers relying on local transport.

After this, the Moon's shadow drops from the escarpment and into the Lower Zambezi Valley. A spot on the escarpment could be spectacular as you could watch the darkness pass into the heart of the Lower Zambezi National Park.

Most of the best lodges and camps in the Lower Zambezi National Park are full. You may be able to drive into the park to camp, but it's unlikely. Some of the wiser tour operators are organising trips that fly into the Lower Zambezi for the day from a safari in South Luangwa or elsewhere.

Excellent, detailed maps covering the whole of Zambia can be bought cheaply from the government map office at the Ministry of Lands in Mulungushi House, Lusaka, by the corner of Independence Avenue and Nationalist Road.

PRE- AND POST-ECLIPSE EXCURSIONS
Victoria Falls

With an average of 550 million litres of water cascading each day over a slab of rock, Victoria Falls is a 'must see' for many people. It is now also the adventure capital of Southern Africa – you can whitewater raft, canoe, bungee-jump, abseil, river-board and microlight.

The Luangwa Valley

East of Lusaka, the Luangwa Valley is top of the list for big-game enthusiasts – a rift in the earth the size of Switzerland. At its centre, the tropical Luangwa River meanders along sinuous curves in the valley's soft, volcanic mud.

Kasanka, Bangweulu and Shiwa N'gandu

After the rains, Bangweulu is a water wilderness the size of Botswana's Okavango Delta, with its own endemic species of antelope, the black lechwe, and breeding pairs of one of Africa's strangest rarities: the shoebill stork.

Nearby Kasanka is a jewel of a reserve, where several excellent small camps are bases for exploring on foot, by canoe or by vehicle. The more adventurous might head for the manor house and estate at Shiwa N'gandu, subject of Christina Lamb's compelling book, *The Africa House*.

ECLIPSE CENTRES: LUSAKA AND ENVIRONS
The eclipse zone
Lusaka is just south of the centre-line and well within the 100% zone. It is relatively easy to access and probably has more accommodation for visitors than the rest of the country put together. Even if most of this appears to be booked there are bound to be temporary campsites springing up on its edges, or people opening their houses to paying guests.

Most groups of serious astronomers are planning to head north, to around where the eclipse centre-line is due to cut the Great North Road. However, the whole area around Lusaka, from north of Kabwe to south of Kafue town, will be in shadow.

Pre- and post-eclipse excursions
The best place to spend some time near Lusaka is probably Lechwe Lodge (see page 66), near the town of Kafue.

Lusaka
Lusaka is not high on Zambia's list of attractions. Its wide, tree-lined boulevards can be pleasant but the traffic is chaotic and many of the suburbs are sprawling and poor.

In my experience, the city's bad reputation for crime is exaggerated, but walking around at night is stupid while, during the day, pickpockets may strike.

Lusaka's focus is the axis of Cairo Road, which runs roughly north–south. Parallel and to the west is Chachacha road – a terminus for numerous local minibuses. Cairo Road is the city's commercial and shopping centre.

About 2km to the east is the larger 'Government Area', linked to Cairo Road by Independence Avenue. Here you will find the big international-standard hotels and government departments.

Getting there and away
By bus
The Intercity bus terminal is on the western side of Dedan Kimathi Road. For Kitwe there are numerous departures, mostly in the morning and early afternoon; for Kapiri Mposhi, departures throughout the day; for Mongu, one in the early morning, and another in the afternoon.

Postbuses must be booked at their depot, behind the main post office off Cairo Road and Dar es Salaam Place. Book three days before departure. Tickets can also be booked at the local post offices where the buses stop.

By train
Express trains to Livingstone leave at 19.30 every Monday, Wednesday and Friday, taking about 12 hours. Slower trains leave every morning.

Where to stay
International hotels
Most of the organised eclipse tours will stay here; although all are booked, there are likely to be cancellations.

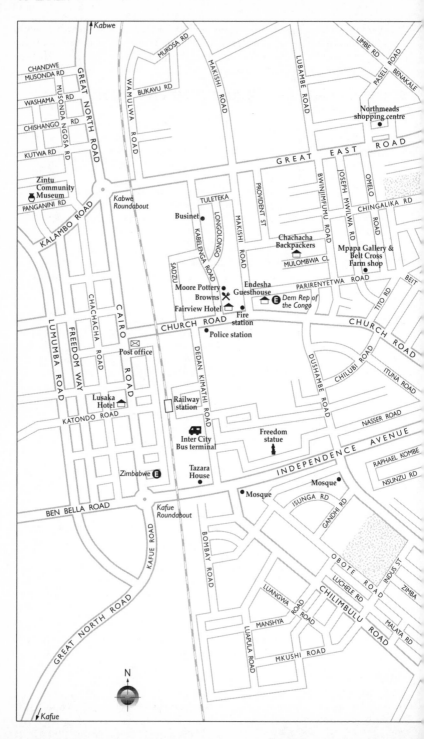

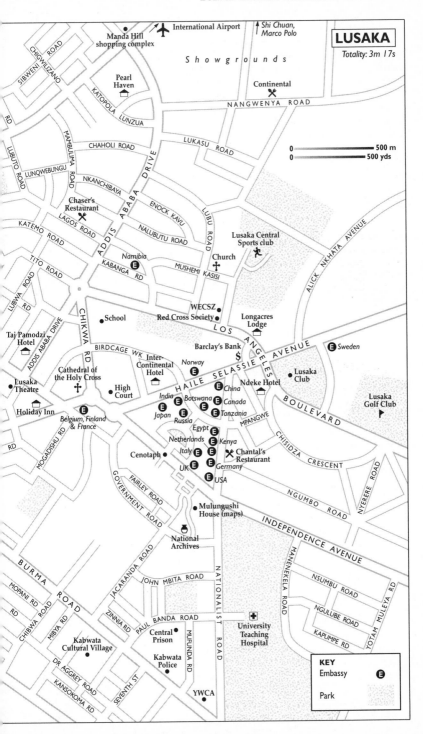

Hotel Intercontinental Haile Selassie Av, PO Box 32201; tel: 250600/1 or 250148; fax: 251880. Lusaka's most imposing hotel US$130 single, US$150 double.

Holiday Inn Garden Court PO Box 30666; tel: 251666; fax: 253529; tlx: ZA 42510. On the corner of Independence Avenue and Church Road. US$140 single, US$160 double.

Taj Pamodzi Hotel PO Box 35450; tel: 254455; fax: 224005 or 250995; tlx: ZA 44720 PAMHO; email: pamodzi@zamnet.zm. Opposite the Holiday Inn, at the corner of Church Road and Addis Ababa Drive, the Pamodzi is one of the city's best locations for eclipse-watching – tall with many balconies. The higher of the Pamodzi's 9 floors have some fine views across the city. US$130 single, US$150 double.

Lodges outside town
Greener, more relaxing and even more full are Lusaka's lodges:

Chaminuka Lodge PO Box 35370, Lusaka; tel: 233303/4; fax: 233305. Chaminuka is about a 30-minute drive north of the international airport. It stands atop a small rise overlooking the Chitoka Lake. A short drive from the lodge, Chaminuka Bushcamp is a lot more basic; it has a raised lookout mound. US$600/$400 for a twin/single.

Chisamba Safari Lodge PO Box 51018, Lusaka; tel: 704600–3; fax: 704800/221175. Occupies a very good position but is booked by TravelQuest (see *Planning and Preparation* page 20). Take the Great North Road for about 38km, turn right and follow the signs for a further 7km. US$160 double/twin, US$128 single.

Lilayi Lodge PO Box 30093; tel: 279022/5; fax: 279026; tlx: ZA 40536 LILAYI. Lilayi stands in a lovely game area about a 20-minute drive from Lusaka on the Kafue Road. Fully booked; US$80/$120 standard/deluxe single, US$90/130 double.

Budget hotels
Most visitors prefer the city's smaller guesthouses to budget hotels because they are often friendlier. But here is a selection:

Andrews Motel PO Box 30475; tel: 272101/2 or 273535; fax: 274798 or 272532. About 8km from the Independence Avenue roundabout on the Kafue Road. There's a campsite beside it. Kw85,000/US$34 per twin; Kw130,000/US$52 for a family room for 4.

Hillview Hotel Makeni PO Box 30815; tel: 278554; fax: 229074. About 15km from the city: take the Kafue road and turn right shortly after Andrews Motel. The Hillview has an airy, almost colonial atmosphere. Kw70–90,000 double.

Kafue Road Garden Hotel Kafue Road, PO Box 30815; tel: 274646/7; fax: 233264. On the edge of town, opposite the Castle Shopping Centre and fuel station, this has quite pleasant rooms set in its own gardens. US$45 double, US$30 single.

Small guesthouses
Gringos Plot 214B, Zambezi Rd (corner of Lukanga), Roma, P Bag E353; tel: 295190/292984. Lovely garden at the back. Kw60,000 deluxe double, Kw45,000 twin double.

Jul's Guesthouse Plot 5508 Lusiwasi Rd (off Libala Rd), Kalundu, PO Box 32863, Lusaka; tel: 1 292979/293972; fax: 291246. In a quiet, residential area. US$40 per person sharing, US$80 single.

Laughing Waters Lodge Mungwi Road (after Zambian Breweries Plc), Lusaka West; tel: 227546; fax: 224829; email: lwlodge@zamnet.zm. 10km north of Lusaka, set in a small game area, where ostriches roam. US$70–80 per person for executive chalets.

Palmwood Lodge Chudleigh, PO Box 35256, Lusaka; tel/fax: 286570

Vineyard Guest House Mumana Rd, Chilwa Mabwe, PO Box 34993; tel: 292361; fax: 291204. One of Lusaka's older guesthouses, the Vineyard has a good reputation. Once inside its high walls you'll find carefully tended green lawns and an outside sitting area. Kw44–77,000 per room.

Hostels and camping

If you're visiting on a tight budget then one of the backpackers' dorms in the centre of town is a possibility. The alternatives are some of the pleasant camping sites on the edge of town.

Chachacha Backpackers' 161 Mulombwa Close; tel: 222257. Off Bwinjimfumo Road, it is the liveliest place in Lusaka for independent backpackers. US$3 per person camping, US$6 for a dorm bed.

Eureka PO Box 30370; tel/fax: 272351 or tel: 278110. Lusaka's best campsite is on a private farm on the eastern side of Kafue Road, about 10km from the Independence Avenue roundabout. US$5 per person per night camping (half that for overlanders or backpackers).

Fringilla B&B Tel/fax: 611199; fax: 611213. Situated about 50km north of Lusaka on the Great North Road, Fringilla is a superb spot for watching the eclipse. Separate from the main house is a shady campsite with facilities. US$35 twin/double, US$28 single, US$48 for a family room. Camping is US$4 per tent, and the huts are US$9.

Pioneer Campsite PO Box CH29, Lusaka; cell: 1 771936; email: pioneer@zamnet.zm. Another well-located 26-acre site, about a 20-minute drive from the centre of Lusaka (out on the Great East Road, turn right 3km past the airport turn-off and follow the signs). US$5 camping per person, US$8 for a dorm bed, US$20 for a 2-bed chalet.

Where to watch the eclipse

Within Lusaka itself, the higher buildings are probably going to be the best places. Outside the city, the keenest of eclipse-chasers will probably be found around the points where the Great North Road and the Great East Road are bisected by the eclipse's centre-line. That's about 40km north and 50km east, respectively. Fringila Farm and Chisamba would be particularly good out-of-town spots from which to watch the eclipse.

Blue Lagoon National Park
Getting there and away

Blue Lagoon, on the north side of the Kafue River, is not well signposted. From Lusaka take the Great West Road, turn left about 28km after leaving Cairo Road, opposite a small shop called Bancroft Supermarket. This track will lead you to the national park's scout camp at the gate. You will then need to be guided on to another road to get into the park.

From the west, pass through Mumbwa and take the first right turn after an Agip garage near Nangoma, around 81km east of Kafue's Nalusanga Gate. In less than 1km, turn right at the crossroads. Continuing for 9km brings you to Myooye village, where you should take the left fork that passes the clinic on the right-hand side.

Follow this track for 31km to a T-junction, ignoring smaller side tracks. (If the group of huts on the left, halfway along this road, has a flag flying, it means that the Tonga chief who lives here is in residence.) At this T-junction turn right. Continue for 22km, first ignoring a right-hand turn, then passing the first gate and finally reaching the scout post.

Where to stay

There is no organised camp here so bring supplies. There is no shortage of spectacular sites.

Where to watch the eclipse

This park is dominated by the Kafue flats, which are flooded in the rainy season. A causeway extends for about 5km giving a wonderful view of the stunning birdlife.

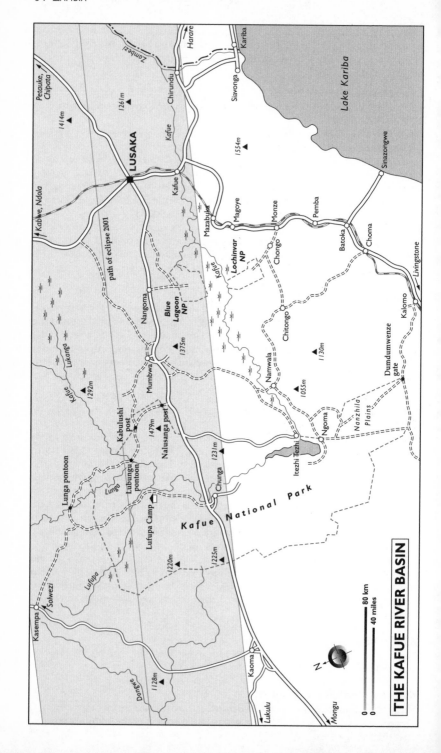

THE KAFUE RIVER BASIN

This will be one of the best eclipse-viewing places in the park and you may be able to see the effect of the darkness on the animals and birds.

Kabwe

This pleasant town is about 130km north of Lusaka, built on the old colonial model with pleasantly wide streets. Kabwe is easily reached from Lusaka on any bus or train heading north towards the Copperbelt towns – Ndola, Kitwe, Mufulira, Luanshya and even Kapiri Mposhi.

Where to stay

Elephant's Head Hotel PO Box 80410, Kabwe; tel: 222521/2/3. On the corner of Freedom Way and Buntungwa Street, on the southern side of town, this is Kabwe's main hotel. Kw100,000 per twin.

Hotel Horizon Tel: 223398; fax: 221019. On the corner of Independence Avenue and Buntungwa Street. Kw70,000 per twin.

Where to watch the eclipse

Kabwe is towards the northern edge of the eclipse zone and has little in the way of spectacular scenery, so head south towards the centre line.

Kafue area

This small town is close to the Norwegian-built hydro-electric dam on the Kafue River. Tours of the plant are possible if arranged with ZESCO (Zambia Electricity Supply Corporation), which even has its own small lodge for visitors. Kafue is easily reached from Lusaka on any bus to Livingstone or Chirundu/Harare.

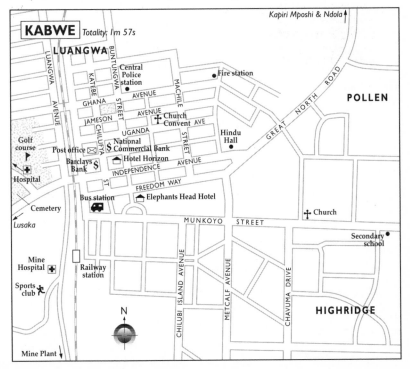

Where to stay

River Motel PO Box 373, Kafue; tel: 32 30992. Kw35,000 twin room, Kw40,000 chalet.
Lechwe Lodge PO Box 37940, Lusaka; tel: 32 30128; fax: 32 30707; cell:1 704803; email:
kflechwe@zamnet.zm. This is fully booked for the day or two around the eclipse, but
would be a prime spot during the rest of June. There are many activities. High viewing
platforms near the river should prove promising places for viewing the eclipse. US$120 per
person inclusive.
Camp Pretorius PO Box 30093, Lusaka. About halfway between Chirundu and Lusaka, it
has a simple waterfront campsite. Turn northeast towards the Kafue Gorge Power Station,
leaving the Lusaka–Cirundu road about 10km after the Livingstone turn-off. Signposts will
lead you to the camp after about 20km. US$5 per person per night camping.

Where to watch the eclipse

There's a good vantage point on the main road overlooking Kafue town, though
most watchers would probably prefer to be either out in the bush at somewhere
like Lechwe Lodge – or to drive north of Lusaka to be nearer to the centre-line. If
you can get permission from ZESCO, then the large Kafue Dam might be a fun
observation spot.

ECLIPSE CENTRES: THE WEST
Overview

Western Zambia is very much the 'wild west' of the country. It is filled with mostly
small, rural towns with lots of scattered villages and the occasional mission station.
It's a practical destination only for backpackers with a lot of time and stamina, or
those with their own fully equipped, self-sufficient 4WD vehicles. Even then, it's
difficult to get around.

Apart from the main roads from Lusaka to Mongu and Lukulu, most of the
area's gravel roads occasionally degenerate into deep sand. Thus they require a
4WD even in the dry season, and the worst of them will require almost constant
low-range driving through long sections of Kalahari sand.

Gateway towns
Mongu

On the edge of the Barotseland floodplains, Mongu is the provincial centre for
western Zambia but too far south to be in the total eclipse zone. It is linked to
Lusaka by a tar road so it is well supplied.

Getting there and away

Mongu is served by Eastern Air – on Tuesdays and Sundays from Lusaka and every
Tuesday from Livingstone. Several buses link Lusaka to Mongu daily. There is also
a postbus.

If you want to head north to Lukulu and beyond, then by far the best route is
from just after the Kaoma turn-off from the Lusaka–Mongu road. This is an all-
weather road. However, if you are starting from Mongu, then there are two other
more direct possibilities. Both will depend on how much the land has dried out
after the rains.

One starts by heading west from Mongu towards Kalabo. Several kilometres
before the Sandaula pontoon over the Zambezi, at Lealui, a road turns off north.
This passes the Barotseland Fishing Tours and Safaris Camp, then the Libonda
pontoon, and continues towards Lukulu on the eastern bank of the Zambezi.
Nearer to Lukulu it passes Tiger Camp and Bahati Lodge, before finally reaching
Lukulu after about 120km.

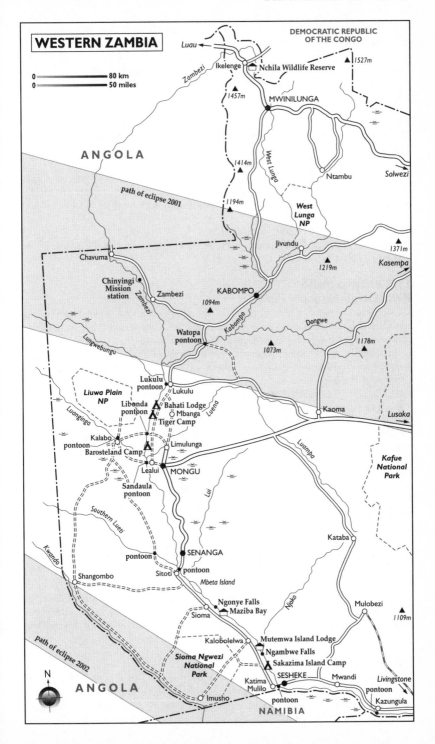

The alternative, which is easier, is to go from Limulunga towards Mbanga. For this you should cross the dambo at the end of the Limulunga Road, and then ask for the road to Mbanga. This is a bush track through small villages across the floodplain. If you are heading for Tiger Camp then pick up a guide at Mbanga, who will show you the camp. Otherwise continue through Mbanga in the same direction to reach Lukulu.

Where to stay
There are several small hotels in Mongu, and all are very basic. Because of the town's bad reputation for crime you should take maximum precautions against theft.

Try the **Ngulu Hotel**, a few km south of where the Lusaka road meets the main street, or **Lyamba Hotel** (PO Box 910193; tel: 7 221271/138) near the boat terminal. Given the problems of theft around Mongu, any campsite should be chosen with care. Consider the compound at Limulunga.

Pre- and post-eclipse excursions
Liuwa Plain National Park is south of the 100% eclipse zone, but still worth a visit if you've at least two self-contained vehicles.

The eclipse zone
West Lunga National Park
This covers 1,684km² of forests, dambos, open grasslands and papyrus swamps. It is bordered by the Kabompo River to the south (adjacent to which are most of the park's swamps) and by the West Lunga River to the west.

The totality zone just touches the southern tip of the park but West Lunga requires an expedition to explore it. Check with the National Parks and Wildlife Service for the latest news and go with at least two vehicles for safety: there are no camps here, or commercial operators, or even scouts inside the park.

Despite persistent local poaching, a reliable source reported sightings of buffalo, impala, puku and warthog in the park recently. It is also thought to harbour elephant, lion, leopard, hippopotamus and a wide range of antelope. All the park's game, however, is skittish and scarce.

Getting there and away
It is easiest to approach from the Copperbelt or by skirting Kafue National Park's eastern boundary and proceeding through Kasempa. Approaching from Mongu is very time consuming – a good 4WD is essential even in the dry season.

From the Copperbelt take the tar road through Kitwe and Chingola to Solwezi, from where it turns south until crossing the Mutanda River at Mwelemu. Take the road to the south, towards Kabompo and Kasempa. After almost 90km the road is joined from the east by an alternative road from Kitwe.

About 16km later there is a road left to Kasempa, and one right to Kabompo. Take the road to the right. After 140km there is a signpost to turn right to the small village of Jivundu, which is on the south bank of the Kabompo River. The park is on the north bank and there is a pontoon to take you across.

Where to stay
In mid-1999 the 'road' into the park was overgrown and required clearing to make it passable. To penetrate deeply into the park, it might be best to leave your vehicle at Jivundu and take a guide from there to walk with you for a few days.

Zambezi town

Those who want to maximise length of totality and chance of good weather will probably want to come here – provided they are self-contained.

Zambezi is a small town with a few very basic shops, a mission and a small local market. There is one simple hotel here, the **Zambezi Motel** (tel: 8 371123; around US$12 per night) and an even more basic government resthouse (around US$5 per night). Zambezi has one, unreliable fuel station.

Because tourists are rare, and the border with Angola is a sensitive one, travellers going west or north from Zambezi should report to the local police – just to let them know of their presence. Perhaps inquiring 'if it is safe to proceed' is the easiest approach.

Getting there and away

The road from Kabompo, which is usually known as the M8, is remarkably good. From Lukulu follow the road north towards Watopa Pontoon about 70km away (1½ hours' drive). It's on the left, just after you enter the two-shop town of Watopa. Look out for the 'God's Word Grocery' and note that the pontoon (or ferry) is incorrectly marked on the ITM map of Zambia. From here it is about 20km north to the junction with the road from Kabompo to Zambezi and, turning left, it is a further 75km to Zambezi.

This good M8 road continues to the Angolan border, at Chavuma.

Where to watch the eclipse

One obvious location beside the Zambezi and close to the centre-line is the Chinyingi Mission. This is about a third of the way from Zambezi to Chavuma, just after the Makondu River.

The mission, run by helpful and jovial Capuchin brothers, is on the east side of the river. It is perhaps most famous for the Chinyingi suspension bridge – one of only four to span the Zambezi anywhere along its length.

Kabompo

Very close to the centre-line, Kabompo is a small, rural town on the good M8 road – but is otherwise fairly undistinguished. Most eclipse travellers will probably end up camping in the bush, having first asked the permission of the local village headman.

ECLIPSE CENTRES: KAFUE NATIONAL PARK
Overview

This is one of the world's largest parks, covering about 22,400km² (about the size of Wales or Massachusetts). Its geography varies considerably.

Totality passes over its northern half, with the centre-line around the southern edge of the renowned Busanga Plains. This is probably the best location if you want to watch the wildlife.

Unfortunately, Kafue has very few lodges and camps and even fewer campsites. Everything in the northern side is full – including several temporary bushcamps planned by local operators.

It may be possible to drive in for the day, but it is about two hours from the gate to Lufupa, and then about another three to the Busanga Plains. If the rains are late then the roads further north will be difficult – so take two vehicles.

Gateway towns

Most people approach Kafue from Lusaka, as Mumbwa has little to recommend it for visitors.

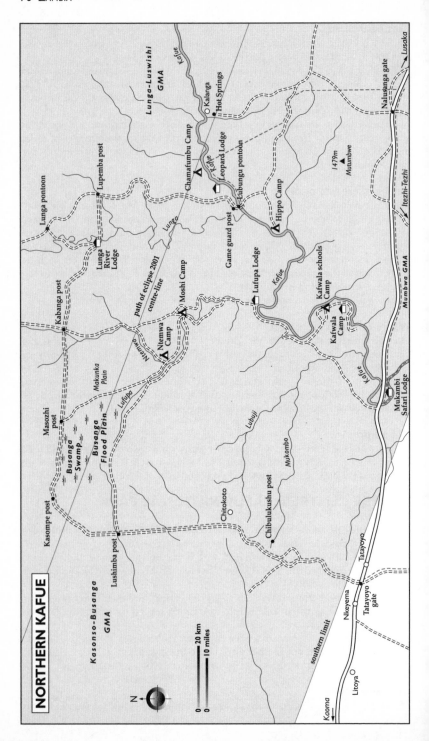

NORTHERN KAFUE

Mumbwa

Three hours' drive from Lusaka (148km), on the Great West Road to Mongu, a large modern factory looms next to the road. Orderly warehouses stand behind well-watered lawns. This hive of activity is perhaps the country's biggest cotton ginnery.

A few kilometres west is a turning off the road to the north, which leads after 5km to the thriving township of Mumbwa. There are petrol stations, a Barclays bank and many small local shops.

All buses between Lusaka and Mongu stop here. **La Hacienda Hotel** is the only place to stay.

Pre- and post-eclipse excursions

Kafue National Park is so big that a visit to northern Kafue for the eclipse could easily be followed by a few days safari in the south – say the Nanzhila Plains area.

The eclipse zone
The Busanga Plains

The northern section of the park is a slightly undulating plateau veined by rivers – the Lufupa, the Lunga, the Ntemwa, the Mukombo, the Mukunashi, and the Lubuji – which are all tributaries of the main Kafue River. The permanent waters of this are wide, deep and slow-flowing, to the obvious pleasure of large numbers of hippo and crocodile. Its gently curving banks are overhung by tall, shady hardwoods, and the occasional islands in the stream are favourite feeding places for elephant and buffalo. In short, it is a typically beautiful large African river.

The Lufupa is probably the most important of the Kafue's tributaries. It enters the park from the north, and immediately feeds into a permanent wetland in the far north of the park: the Busanga Swamps. In the wet season these waters flood out over a much larger area, the Busanga Plains, before finally draining back into the river.

The area is perfect for huge herds of water-loving lechwe and puku, which are joined, as the waters recede at the end of the wet season, by large numbers of zebra, wildebeest, and other plains grazers.

Getting there and away

With a couple of 4WDs and experienced drivers, you will find that Kafue is a magical wilderness with lots of empty space and a few decent tracks through it. But for most visitors transfer in to the park will be organised by their tour operator.

By air

There are several airstrips dotted around the park. There are no scheduled flights into the park, but Lunga River Lodge runs charter flights between the lodge and Lusaka, Livingstone and Mfuwe (for South Luangwa). Other destinations are possible on request.

Visitors to Chilongozi's Busanga camp normally arrive by air, whilst those visiting Lufupa and Shumba are generally driven in from Lusaka.

Driving

There are reasonable gravel roads from either Kitwe (via Ingwe) in the Copperbelt, or Solwezi (via Mwelemu) in the north, to Kasempa – which is just 50km north of the park. From here gravel roads lead southwest towards Kaoma and southeast towards Mumbwa. No fuel and only minimal supplies are available at Kasempa. If you are coming from the main Lusaka–Mongu road, Mumbwa has the last fuel station before you reach the park. If you are driving into the north of the park, to Lufupa or Kafwala, turn north off the main road at the scout gate beside the west bank of the Kafue River.

Where to stay

Camping is usually restricted to recognised sites, and is not allowed on the Busanga Plains. The full range of camps in the north of Kafue is listed here, but many are already full.

Lufupa Lodge Busanga Trails, PO Box 37538, Lusaka. Within Zambia contact via Steve Blagus in Lusaka; outside Zambia contact Sunvil Discovery in the UK, tel: 020 8232 9777; fax: 020 8568 8330; email: africa@sunvil.co.uk. US$1,450 per person for 7 nights inclusive.

Shumba Bushcamp Book as part of a trip to Lufupa Lodge. There is some doubt about whether it will be dry enough to reach by June 21.

Lunga River Lodge African Experience, PO Box 30106, Lusaka. Satphone: 873 762 093 985; email: safariafrica@experience.co.za. US$280/390 per person per night sharing/single.

Busanga Bushcamp Contact via Lunga River Lodge, of which it is a satellite, standing on the Busanga Plains. US$320/450 inclusive per person per night sharing/single.

Busanga Plains Tented Camp Contact via Chilongozi Safaris, P Bag 286x, Ridgeway, Lusaka; tel: 1 265814; fax:1 262291. This is a small, seasonal bushcamp. US$250 per person sharing per night, inclusive.

Hippo Camp Lubungu Wildlife Safaris, PO Box 30796, Lusaka; tel: 1 242083/244285; fax: 1 243032. Sited on an anomalous patch of private land within the national park, perfect for the eclipse, very close to the centre-line – although there aren't the open plains of Busanga. Simple accommodation US$40 per person sharing, self-catering.

Chamafumbu Camp Contact via Pioneer Campsite, Lusaka. (See page 63.) On the north bank of the Kafue River, about 8km east of Leopard Lodge, after the river leaves the park, this is a small and very simple fishing camp. (It's marked as Mbizi on some maps.) For the self-sufficient who fancy seeing the eclipse from deep in the bush.

Ntemwa Camp Contact via Chilongozi, P Bag 286x, Ridgeway, Lusaka; tel: 1 265814; fax: 1 262291; email: info@chilongozi.com. 105km north of the main bridge over the Kafue, Ntemwa has a beautiful situation overlooking a watercourse just south of the Busanga Plains. It's perfect for the eclipse ... if Chilongozi can build it and have it running in time.

Moshi Camp Contact Star of Africa, P Bag 6, Hillside, Zimbabwe; tel: (263) 9 41225 or 41715 or 41837; fax: (263) 9 229909. Moshi is slightly south of Ntemwa, about 90km north of the bridge, and in another perfect location. It has been derelict and was recently bought by Star of Africa, which hopes to have it up and running in time.

Kafwala Camp Wildlife and Environmental Conservation Society of Zambia. Book through the WECSZ branch in Kabwe – PO Box 80623, Kabwe; tel: 5 223467 or 224600; fax: 5 224859. On the bank of the Kafue about 700m below the start of the Kafwala Rapids, northeast of the main bridge over the Kafue, it is one of the few official camps where camping may be allowed. Access is usually restricted to members of the WECSZ, and it must be booked in advance, though it's easy to join and the society does a lot of good. Around US$15–20 per person per day.

There are no **campsites** in the park but camping can usually be arranged at Lufupa and Kafwala. There is absolutely no camping allowed on the Busanga Plains.

Where to watch the eclipse

Anywhere in northern Kafue should have a super view of the event. The south side of the Busanga Plains lies under the eclipse's centre-line, and is flat and open enough to be spectacular – but sometimes floods can prevent entry until early July.

ECLIPSE CENTRES: THE LOWER ZAMBEZI
Overview
Like most of the Kafue National Park, the Lower Zambezi National Park is really a place for self-sufficient travellers or visitors on organised trips. For backpackers it's not easy to reach. However, the neighbouring Chiawa Game Management Area, and the area around the border town of Chirundu, are more easily accessible.

Gateway towns
Chirundu
The busy border post is just on the southwestern extreme of the zone of totality. This is a promising place to look for a lift but it has the slightly seedy, unsafe feel typical of a town where many people come and go, but few stay.

About 2–300m north of the border at Chirundu is a road signposted northeast to Chiawa and Masstock Farms; this is the road to both Gwabi Lodge and the Lower Zambezi National Park.

Where to stay
Nyambandwe Motel PO Box 37160, Lusaka; tel: 1 515084/515088. Few stay here by design. US$20 double, US$15 single.
Gwabi Lodge PO Box 30813, Lusaka; tel: 1 515078. Set in green lawns about 12km from Chirundu, and 3km up from the confluence of the Kafue and Zambezi rivers. Well prepared for campers and budget travellers. US$65 per person per night including dinner. Camping US$6 per person.
St Nectarios Lodge PO Box 30815, Lusaka; tel: 1 251734; fax: 1 233264. On the Zambezi, about 1km from its confluence with the Kafue. About Kw50–75,000/US$20–25 per room, including breakfast.

The eclipse zone
The most accessible thoroughfare in the Lower Zambezi area is the river itself, and you can be sure of considerable floating traffic during the eclipse. The centre-line passes right through the heart of the national park, close to Jeki Airstrip. The zone of totality will cover the Zambezi from Chirundu to east of the Mozambique border.

Chiawa Game Management Area (GMA)
This lies between privately owned land to the east of the Kafue River, and the Lower Zambezi National Park. The best game is in the national park, but densities are increasing in the GMA and there are now several lodges.

LOWER ZAMBEZI – THE HARD WAY
Masochists might like to know that there's a much more difficult approach to the park, via the Great East Road. You'll certainly need permission from the national parks office in Chilanga to attempt this route. The road starts just beyond the national park's boundary (as indicated by a tsetse fly barrier) and after about 22km leads to the park gate and nearby scout's camp. You'll need to collect a guide from here if you wish to continue.

The road heads for Chakwenga, about 60km inside the park, and then drops over the escarpment, becoming steep and overgrown. This isn't an easy option at all, but might afford some superb spots overlooking the escarpment from which to watch the eclipse. The road eventually leads down into the main game-viewing area on the valley floor.

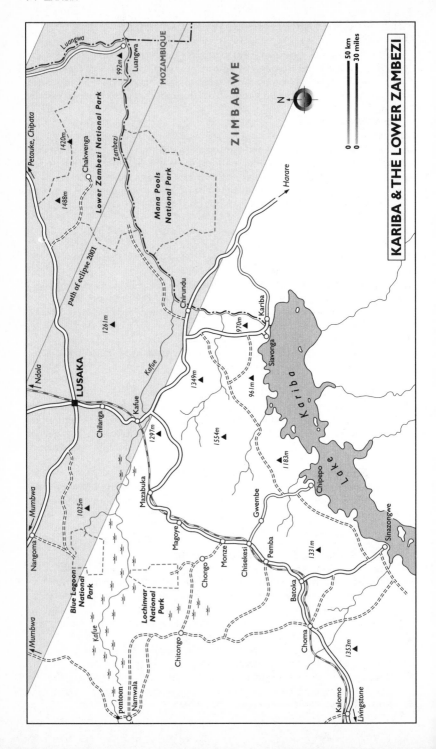

KARIBA & THE LOWER ZAMBEZI

Getting there and away

There is no public transport into the GMA and hitchhiking is virtually impossible. If you stay at one of the private camps you will be transferred there from Lusaka by road or private plane.

Alternatively, take a canoe safari, staying in temporary 'fly' camps each night. These generally start at either Kariba or Chirundu, and at the end you'll be transferred by road from the valley.

The last option is for the adventurous and well-equipped – to drive in with their own vehicles, and all their own supplies and camping equipment. The roads into the park need 4WD vehicles (ideally two) but are not difficult in the dry season. Get detailed maps of the whole valley before you leave Lusaka, and pack a compass. It would be wise to get a permit before you arrive from the national parks office in Lusaka or Chilanga. Take the turning from the main road just before Chirundu and follow the signs to Gwabi Lodge. Where the sign points left, indicating the lodge is 2km ahead, continue straight ahead to reach the pontoon that crosses the Kafue River. Then stick close to the river on the main track.

Where to stay
Private camps and lodges in the GMA
All the lodges are a high standard. Most prices include all meals and activities.

Kiambi Camp Karibu Safaris, PO Box 35196, Northway 4065, Durban, South Africa; tel: (27) 31 563 9774; fax: (27) 31 563 1957. Kiambi can be used only as part of a 6-night Karibu safari through the valley. US$1,500 per person sharing.

Kayila Lodge Safari Par Excellence, Harare, Zimbabwe; tel: (263) 4 700911/2. Kayila is solidly built and set among baobabs on a small rise beside the river. US$240 per person (US$195 before June 15) inclusive.

Royal Zambezi Lodge PO Box 31455, Lusaka; tel: 1 223952/224334; fax: 1 223504; cell: 752304. Comfortable Meru-style tents. Also runs a small self-catering camp a few kilometres downriver which is likely to offer camping during the eclipse. US$185 per person sharing, inclusive.

Kiubo Camp Contact via Karibu, above. The second of Karibu's permanent camps in the Lower Zambezi, Kiubo stands at a point where the escarpment is close to the river, making a lovely backdrop, and some excellent sites from which to observe the eclipse. Rates: see Kiambi Camp, above.

Private camps and lodges in the national park
Most prices include all meals and activities. Some include park fees.

Chiawa Camp G&G Safaris, PO Box 30972, Lusaka; tel: 1 261588; fax: 1 262683; email: chiacamp@zamnet.zm. Chiawa is a small, friendly camp set beneath a grove of mahogany trees, about 8km (30-minute drive) within the national park. Fully booked. Try Sunvil Discovery (see page 56) for last-minute cancellations. US$295/415 per person sharing/single, inclusive.

Sausage Tree Tongabezi, P Bag 31, Livingstone; tel: Livingstone 3 323235, fax: 3 323224, email: tonga@zamnet.zm. Sausage Tree is one of the few camps which hasn't yet sold out. It is set in a beautiful position inside the Lower Zambezi National Park, with a lovely backwater, the Chifungulu Channel. Eclipse rates: US$15,000 per person sharing/single for the eclipse period, including flight transfers to/from Livingstone or Lusaka.

Mushika Camp Safari Expeditions (Zambia) Ltd, PO Box 71542, Lusaka; tel/fax: 1 640542/617552; email: safex@zamnet.zm. Brand new camp.

Mwambashi River Lodge Safari Par Excellence, Harare, Zimbabwe; tel: (263) 4 700911/2. US$240 per person.

Kulefu Camp Contact via Kiambi and Karibu. Deep within the Lower Zambezi National Park.

Kingfisher Camp PO Box 36600, Lusaka. Between the Lower Zambezi National Park and the Luangwa River, set in a narrow neck of land 10–15km wide, close to the dramatic Mpata Gorge. It is 30 minutes by boat from the village of Luangwa, reached from the Great East Road. Book for the eclipse through Sunvil Discovery (see page 56).

Where to watch the eclipse

Being on the river during the eclipse could be magical. You'd have a dramatic view of the darkness coming over the Zambian escarpment, then reaching the Zimbabwean side. However, no boat would be stable enough for those with telescopes or cameras. Anchoring near a shallow sandbar and standing on that would be more solid and probably more memorable ... but would you see a crocodile approaching in the brief darkness?

On shore, overlooking the river from a high bank, would be a good bet. Many of the lodges have super positions in this respect. Or perhaps out game-viewing, to watch the reaction of the animals. Or perhaps walking, with an armed guide, up one of the foothills of the escarpment, to gain a view of the river and the whole valley.

The 2002 eclipse

OVERVIEW

Viewing the 2002 eclipse in Zambia is going to be difficult. The zone of totality passes over the far southwest of Zambia, including part of the Sioma Ngwezi National Park. However, all of this area is adjacent to the Angolan border and there are no proper roads. Guns and refugees are common – a combination that bodes ill for those driving a vehicle or carrying a backpack worth many times the local annual wage. It would be prudent to approach the Kwando River area in a convoy of vehicles, ideally with an armed army escort.

Getting there and away
Driving

One possibility for the 2002 eclipse would be to stay in the Livingstone area, visiting the falls, and then head into Namibia or Botswana for the eclipse itself. Livingstone's Nakatindi Road continues past the lodges by the river and, after about 60km, to Kazungula – where Namibia, Botswana, Zimbabwe and Zambia all meet at a notional point. Here you can continue your bumpy way northwest within Zambia to Sesheke. This distance from Kazungula to Sesheke is about 130km, and the road has been in a bad state of repair for years. It is slow and uncomfortable. At Sesheke, you can cross the Zambezi by ferry and drive into Namibia at Katima Mulilo. If you have a South African registered vehicle then you may also need to obtain police clearance at Katima Mulilo to take the vehicle out of Namibia. This is a deterrent to car thieves.

The alternative at Kazungula is to turn south on to a large ferry across the Zambezi, entering Botswana near Kasane. If you're driving in to Botswana then you must purchase road insurance, for about 20 Botswana pula or 25 South African rand (US$ or UK£ are not accepted), on entry.

Even if you're ultimately aiming for Namibia, this may be a better, less bumpy option. Then you drive around Kasane on the excellent tar road, past the small airport and the gate into Chobe National Park, to the Namibian border at Ngoma. At Ngoma, you'll cross the Chobe River into Namibia, and continue north on a good, partially tarred gravel road to Katima Mulilo.

Getting from Zambia to Botswana or Namibia without your own vehicle can be done as well. Hitchhiking from Livingstone to Victoria Falls, in Zimbabwe, is simple enough. Getting from there into Botswana is trickier, but still possible. Best to take a taxi the few kilometres out of Victoria Falls on the road to Bulawayo, to the Kazungula turn-off, and then hitch west into Botswana at that junction.

Alternatively, most of the transfer companies in Victoria Falls run scheduled transfers for about US$50 per person; they will pick you up from a hotel in the Falls, and drop you off in Kasane, or vice versa.

Getting to Namibia is harder as the Sesheke road is difficult to hitch on – and yet it is much shorter than going via the Victoria Falls, and Kasane. Either way it may take a few days and a lot of patience. However, first check to see if there are any buses heading west from Livingstone to Sesheke. If the road hasn't yet been rained upon then you may be lucky as buses do run occasionally in the dry season.

FURTHER READING FROM BRADT

Africa by Road, Charlie Shackell and Illya Bracht
East and Southern Africa: The Backpacker's Manual, Philip Briggs
Southern Africa by Rail, Paul Ash
Zambia: The Bradt Travel Guide, Chris McIntyre

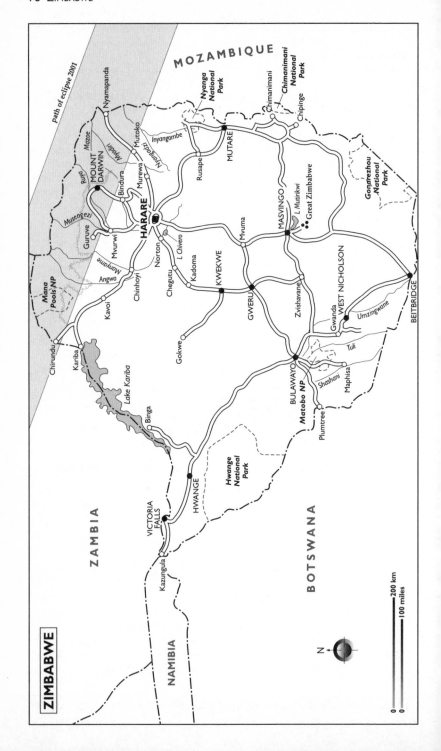

Zimbabwe

Matthew Bokach

Visiting the eclipse areas
OVERVIEW
Last total solar eclipse: August 1886
Next total solar eclipse after 2002: June 2095

Of all the countries over which the eclipses are passing, Zimbabwe probably has the widest range of tourist opportunities. Its infrastructure and tourism industry are second in this region only to those of South Africa. Zimbabwe has a well-developed national parks estate with the largest herd of elephants in the world and easy access to endangered species such as both black and white rhinoceros; there is even the possibility of seeing painted hunting dogs.

The two paths of totality are passing over some Zimbabwean hotspots. In 2001 the full eclipse will pass over Mana Pools, a world heritage site, and the Mavuradona Wilderness in the north. In 2002 it will be the turn of the Matobo Hills in the south, known worldwide for their beauty.

The Zimbabwe tourism machine has thousands of places available on a wide array of organised trips, tours and festivals. Car hire is easy and camping sites are plentiful. Zimbabwe's extensive public transport system will enable those without cars to penetrate deep into communal areas where they can share the experience with rural Zimbabweans who do not even know what an eclipse is. The options for independent travellers, therefore, are wide.

At the time of going to press, Zimbabwe's tourist industry has collapsed. Whether this is temporary or more long-term cannot be predicted at present, so travellers should check in advance. In practical terms, all of the bed space within the 2001 path of totality, whether a hotel room in Kariba town or a campsite in the Mavuradona Wilderness, is fully booked. However, many of these bookings do not reflect flesh-and-blood clients, but zealous tour operators setting up package deals. It is quite likely that the operators will fail to fill all these spaces, and so they may become available again. Mania about 2002 will probably not begin until after the June 2001 eclipse but Bulawayo is predicted to be one of the most popular spots from which to base a trip for the 2002 African eclipse.

The 2001 eclipse falls during the dry winter months, which run from May to October and are comfortable for travelling. The 2002 eclipse falls when the country is green because of the rain, but the price paid for this is a greater chance of cloudy skies.

For updated Zimbabwe eclipse information you can try the Harare-based Astronomical Society of Southern Africa (web: www.geocities.com/zimastro) as well as the Bradt website: www. bradt-travelguides.com. Zimbabwe's international telephone code is 263.

ORGANISED TOURS
UK

Africa Travel Centre (see page 103) 12-day trip viewing eclipse in Mavuradona National Park. Cost: from £2,075, excluding flights.

Bukima Expeditions 15 Bedford Rd, Great Barford MK44 3JD; tel: 01234 871329; fax: 01234 871886; email: bukima@compuserve.com; web: www.bukima.com. A 2-week Victoria Falls–Harare trip, viewing 2001 eclipse from Zimbabwe, site to be confirmed. Cost excluding flights: £240 + US$180 local payment.

Grenadier Safaris 11–12 West Stockwell St, Colchester CO1 1HN; tel: 01206 549585; fax: 01206 561337. An 8- or 9-night tour around Zimbabwe, viewing the 2001 eclipse from the Lower Zambezi valley. Cost: £2,500-3,000 per person.

Rainbow Tours 64 Essex Rd, London; tel: 020 7226 1004; fax: 020 7226 2621; email: info@rainbowtours.co.uk; web: www.rainbowtours.co.uk. 10 days including canoe safari, viewing eclipse from banks of Zambezi.

Safari Consultants Orchard House, Upper Rd, Little Cornard, Suffolk CO10 0NZ; tel: 01787 228494; fax: 01787 228096; email: bill.safcon@pop3.hiway.co.uk. 12 nights in Zimbabwe including canoeing trail. Cost: £3,215 per person. Also, 9-night Zimbabwe adventure trip including canoeing, £1,825 per person.

Sunvil Discovery Upper Square, Old Isleworth, Middlesex TW7 7BJ; tel: 020 8232 9777; fax: 020 8568 8330; email: africa@sunvil.co.uk; web: www.sunvil.co.uk/africa. Sunvil's Falcon B trip (max 10 people) has 3 nights at Kwetsani in the Okavango, 3 in Victoria Falls, and 4 in Hwange – with a flight into Mana Pools and a riverside picnic for the eclipse. Cost: £3,830 per person sharing.

Truck Africa Hurlingham Studios, Ranelagh Gardens, London SW6 3PA; tel: 020 7731 6142; fax: 020 7371 7445; email: sales@truckafrica.com; web: www.truckafrica.com. A 22-day, overland safari through Zimbabwe, Zambia and Botswana, viewing the 2001 eclipse from Eureka campsite in Lusaka, Zambia. Cost: £700 including kitty, excluding flights.

Zimbabwe

There is a dizzying number of canoe safaris, walking safaris, festivals and day-trips from Harare and Kariba for 2001. Plans for 2002 are in the pipeline from a few of the operators listed below (for more on 2002 contact the Bulawayo Publicity Association, see page 93). Prices are for one person assuming double occupancy. For general tour information try the following websites:

www.africaguide.com/country/zimbab/safaris.htm
www.samara.co.zw/samara/links.cfm (follow the link to tourism)
www.vicfalls.com
www.zimbabwe.net (follow the link to tourism)

General eclipse trips and safaris

Explorers Tours, Spears Travel and Total Solar Eclipse (see *Planning and Preparation*, page 20) are all eclipse-chasing companies offering trips to Zimbabwe.

Carew Safaris P Bag 295A, Harare; tel/fax: 58 551; email: carew@carewsafaris.com; web: www.zimbabwe.net/tourism/companies/carew/2001. A well-established company in Mavuradona Wilderness area, offering a 4-night Tingwa Valley safari involving hiking and horse riding for US$300 per night. Alternatively, spend 2 or 3 nights in its Zambezi tented village with talks and exhibits thrown in, for US$250 per night. May offer elephant-back safaris.

Goliath Safaris PO Box CH294, Chisipite, Harare; tel: 4 739836/7/8; fax: 4 708843; email: goliath@internet.co.zw. Three-night camping safari on the shores of the Zambezi within Mana Pools National Park for US$693.

Green Route PO Box 488, Harare; tel: 4 708737/8; fax: 4 733068; email: HayleyId@greenroute.co.zw. Offers a 2-country, deluxe trip including eclipse-viewing in Guruve and time in Botswana and at the Victoria Falls for US$2,300, if you apply as a group of 15–30, or US$1,800 for a group of 40–150.

Sky Safaris Tel: 4 728493/4; email: eclipse@skysaf.co.zw; web: www.lionroars.com/ECLIPSE/EclipsePackages.htm. Many eclipse tours, including day-trips from Harare and longer journeys, the latter including a 3-day expedition in Doma safari area on the escarpment. The firm is advised by the Astronomical Society of Southern Africa.

Sunset Tours Tel: 4 795386/7; fax: 4 723146 or 4 795868; email: DarleneHa@zimsun.co.zw. Offers a day-trip from Harare to the Zambezi valley near Muzarabani for US$128 as well as longer packages. Some 5% of proceeds will be donated to the Astronomical Society of Southern Africa.

UTc PO Box 2914, Harare; tel: 4 770623/4/5; email: utc@utczim.com. The largest and best-organised Zimbabwe tour operator is offering a day-trip from Harare for US$230 and a 3-night trip including city tour of Harare for US$459. UTc has also booked spaces on many of its competitors' packages.

Wildlife Expeditions Tel: 4 722804 or 91 339696; fax: 4 335341; email: wildlife@icon.co.zw. Three nights at the Nyatana Wildlife Reserve festival on Nyatana Island in the Mazoe River (which flows through northeast and north-central Zimbabwe). Some 1,000 people are expected to be there for entertainment, elephant-back safaris, game walks, canoeing and cultural tours. Some proceeds from the cost, which is US$675–1,350, will be donated to local rural district councils. Also, 3 nights with 20–50 others at the firm's Phindundu camp in the Chitake Wilderness on the edge of the Zambezi escarpment for US$600. Possible camps in Umfurdzi Wilderness area.

Zambezi Safari and Travel Company PO Box 158, Kariba; tel: 61 2532/3351/3215/3361 or 11 603388; fax: 61 2291; email: info@zambezi.com; web: www.zambezi.com. Offering a day-trip from Kariba to Tamarind Camp in Zambia, where the eclipse centre-line meets the Zambezi opposite Mana Pools. The trip costs US$200 with an optional stay in a Kariba hotel for an extra US$55. Also, a 9-day tour including the eclipse, Victoria Falls and Matusadona National Park for US$2,495. Other options are fully booked at time of going to press.

Canoe safaris

The crocodiles and hippos will not know what has hit them in June 2001 when the Zambezi suddenly becomes covered with canoes carrying people from all over the world. Canoe safaris are standard fare for the Zimbabwean tourism industry, so you may find a good deal by shopping around.

Buffalo Safaris PO Box 10G, Gawa, Kariba; tel: 61 3041/2/3; fax: 61 2827; email: buffalo@internet.co.zw. Or book through Safaris Incorporated, tel: 4 728255/6 or 11 204209; fax 4 729932/729457; email: safaris@harare.iafrica.com. This umbrella tour operator offers canoe trips on Lake Kariba.

Goliath Safaris (for contact details see above). Offers a 4-night safari between Mana Pools and Kanyemba for US$575; and a 3-night safari between Chirundu and Mana Pools for US$478. Clients are expected to paddle themselves and set up their own tents.

River Horse Safaris Tel: 61 2944/2447/2345; fax: 61 2422; email: riverhse@icon.co.zw 2- or 3-night safaris in 18ft Canadian canoes starting at US$395.

Air safaris

An aircraft seems an exotic way of viewing an eclipse but you will miss a lot of the eclipse atmosphere from the air, so only consider it in cloudy conditions. Even then, light planes cannot always get above the clouds.

There are many air hire companies based in Victoria Falls, which may offer trips for both eclipses. For their numbers contact the Victoria Falls Publicity Association (tel: 13 4202).

Cross Country Air Safaris may be an option if all the Zimbabwean suggestions have been exhausted (see *South Africa*, page 103).
EcoLogical Tours PO Box 4043 Bulawayo; tel: 9 61189/69559; tel/fax: 9 540590; email: cbristow@acacia.samara.co.zw. A small air safari company based in Bulawayo, in the Bulawayo Centre mall, just off the corner of Main Street and 9th Avenue.
United Air Services PO Box 93, Kariba; tel: 61 2305/2277; fax: 61 2498; email: karibaops@pci.co.zw. Harare office tel: 4 302076/9 or 11 205108; fax 4 304871; email: betty@hunting.co.zw. Victoria Falls office tel: 13 4530 or 3383; fax 13 4220. An exclusive air charter company offering eclipse flights.

Rural homestays

Campfire (Communal Areas Management Programme for Indigenous Resources) is a nationwide organisation which attempts to link local development initiatives to sound environmental and conservation practices. It has encouraged rural district councils whose constituencies lie within the paths of totality to organise communities to host fee-paying eclipse tourists. Contact the project's manager at Campfire head office to find out how the scheme is going (tel: 4 747422/29/30; email: campfir@id.co.zw). Alternatively, contact the councils directly. The list below is west to east along the path of totality.

A RURAL ECLIPSE

At least two thirds of each path of totality falls within rural communal lands, most of which are just as scenically beautiful as the tourist areas. They are occupied by people who have borne direct and indirect costs to their livelihoods in the name of tourism. Land set aside for national parks and safari areas, and the ravages of wild animals on crops and domestic stock, are only the easiest examples to cite. The eclipses offer a unique opportunity to let the benefits of tourism reach otherwise untouched areas, and at the same time have a true cross-cultural experience. Imagine sitting by a cooking fire one evening, with a meal of stiff maize porridge, goat meat and perhaps even fried caterpillars, discussing the movements of the Sun, Earth and Moon with a local family via some teenage translator adept at English.

Such an adventure could look something like this: arrive in Zimbabwe a couple of days before the eclipse and hire a car. Drive to a rural communal area that lies within the path of totality and seek out a good eclipse-viewing site. Look for a nearby group of huts, or homestead, belonging to the local family and ask if you can stay there. Most rural Zimbabwean families would be overjoyed to host foreign tourists no matter what the occasion.

Even if there is no homestead nearby you will need permission from traditional chiefs before parking a car or pitching a tent. Ask around for the local 'kraal head' or 'headman'. Some kraal heads will be empowered to grant permission themselves, but most will have to take you to the chief. This could be quite a distance away and you may need to pay the kraal head's bus fare. The chief should grant permission easily without charge. Bear in mind that although you are not staying with a specific family, you are still going to attract a lot of attention from local folk, which should be one of the attractions of this option.

Hurungwe RDC (Karoi): 64 6881/2/3
Guruve RDC (Guruve): 58 319/219
Muzarabani RDC (Centenary): 57 229
Pfura RDC (Mt Darwin): 76 2883/2581
Rushinga RDC (Chimanda): 76 524
Chaminuka RDC (Shamva): 718 2800
UMP RDC (Murewa): 78 2591
Mudzi RDC (Mudzi): 72 2553

NATIONAL PARK ACCOMMODATION

Zimbabwe has an extensive and varied system of national parks, most of which are crawling with game and feature quite nice, cheap lodging. Lodging options vary from park to park, but usually consist of four-person (two-bedroom) lodges with en suite washing facilities, and two-person (one room) chalets with shared washing facilities. Both types of lodging also have stoves, refrigerators and some basic cookware; the lodges include an oven, all plates, dishes, silverware, etc. Towels and bedding are provided, as are mosquito nets in those parks where necessary. The lodges are US$15 a night, and the chalets are US$2.50. Because the demand for lodging usually far exceeds the capacity of the parks system as a whole, the Department of National Parks and Wildlife Management initially assigns spaces on a lottery system. Bookings for a given month are determined on the first day of that month the year before. So, to request a place in Matobo National Park for the December 2002 eclipse, your written request for lodging should be submitted to

If you stay at a homestead bear in mind that Zimbabwean hospitality knows no bounds, and sacrifices which would be seen as extreme in many European cultures are practically expected of a host. Family members may give up their beds. They may slaughter poultry or even small livestock in your honour, wash your outer garments and provide you with chairs while they sit on the ground. Not accepting such offers is tantamount to rejecting the family's hospitality as somehow inadequate.

In recompense, bring some food with you such as a 20kg bag of mealie meal, fresh fruit and vegetables, sweets for children and dried or tinned meat.

The following are useful points of etiquette:

• Do not purify water by filtering or chemically treating it in the family's presence – this introduces technologies to which they have not realistic access once you have left. Instead, check the family's source of drinking water. Water from a borehole is fine to drink, if a bit tasty at times, but surface water should be avoided. If the water source is questionable, ask them to boil it for you first. You could bring bottled water, which would be less inappropriate than treating ordinary water.

• Accept the fact that women have roles in traditional Zimbabwean culture that are deferential to men – and some families will extend the same expectation to female visitors.

• Expect to sleep in the same room as your partner only if you have let it be known that you are married.

• Do not hang your undergarments in a public place to dry after washing or give them to someone to wash.

• It is perfectly acceptable to offer to help wash up or pound the maize.

the Department before December 1 2001. Any spaces unfilled after the lottery are assigned on a first-come, first-served basis. To request lodging, send a letter to: **National Parks Central Booking Office**, PO Box CY140, Causeway, Harare; or send an email to: national_parks@tga.gov.zw. (Just to be safe, I recommend you send your request by mail.) You should include in your request how many people you wish accommodation for, what type of lodging is acceptable (best to be flexible here), and for which night(s) you want it. If writing to request lodging in multiple parks, it is best to send a separate letter for each park/month.

GETTING AROUND
By public transport
Transport is abundant, accessible, cheap and generally safe except after dark within Harare.

Transport within Harare and Bulawayo is by minivans known as *kombis* which run on set routes radiating from the central business districts. Almost any passer-by on the street can direct you to the correct rank for the place you want to visit.

Harare is the transportation hub for the north and east of the country, and Bulawayo for the south and west; there are few areas in the country one cannot access by taking a long-distance bus. There are two classes of long-distance buses: the newer, nicer Volvo buses which ply mainly tarred roads, and the older more stereotypical 'chicken buses'. To reach a remote, off-the-tar rural location, go with a 'chicken'. Long-distance journeys on public transport take time and involve unforeseen delays – and being late is not an option with the eclipse. Estimate how much time your trip will take, and plan on spending twice that amount. Leave the day before the eclipse if possible.

By car
Most main roads in Zimbabwe are excellent. All the major international car hire companies are represented in both Harare and Bulawayo: to beat the crowds, book before you leave your home country. Local car hire companies are cheaper. The surcharge for returning the vehicle to a different city can be as much as a day's rental. Because car hire for just a day works out quite expensive you may find that joining an organised day-trip to the eclipse is cheaper.

Hitchhiking
Getting a lift is usually pretty easy and safe. It is a good idea to establish a price before getting into the vehicle; free lifts are common, but should not be assumed. It is safer to hitch with a friend; there have been very isolated incidents of hitchhikers being hijacked by their 'benefactors' and robbed, especially leaving Harare. That said, I have been hitching in the country for almost four years and have had many of my most interesting conversations with Zimbabweans while getting a lift.

By bicycle and on foot
Although Harare and Bulawayo are too far from their respective eclipses for bicycle or hiking day-trips to be feasible, both regions offer excellent cycling and walking conditions. You can buy good-quality bicycles in Harare although they are pretty expensive even by foreign currency standards. It is best to take your own bicycle to Zimbabwe. Take spare parts as these are available only for certain models. You could either set out several days before the eclipse or transport the bicycle on Volvo or chicken buses. Local *kombis* are not likely to allow them.

The 2001 eclipse

OVERVIEW

June is a wonderful time to experience Zimbabwe: the weather is mild throughout, and the game-viewing is starting to be excellent as water holes dry up and leaves fall off the deciduous trees. Almost half the length of the Zambezi valley escarpment in Zimbabwe falls within the path of totality in 2001. So, one option is to pick a spot on the escarpment where visibility is over 100km and thrill to the spectacle of a lunar shadow falling over the world stretched out before you. Across the escarpment first contact will begin between 13.45 and 13.55, depending on where you are. The world-famous Mana Pools National Park, where first contact begins at 13.44, will be the other attraction. The usual draw of this remote corner of Zimbabwe is its abundant wildlife and the fact that you can walk freely and unaccompanied (at your own risk, of course) throughout it (although you do need a vehicle to enter the park and hitching is forbidden). Spend a couple of days in Mana and the sight of four dozen elephants charging down to the river for a drink will seem mundane. Now picture yourself floating down the Zambezi in a canoe, watching those same elephants abruptly stop dead as the sun disappears and the world is cast into twilight: what happens next? If you are one of the many people wondering just how African wildlife will react to an eclipse, then Mana is the place for you. Other places where you can take in wildlife and the eclipse simultaneously include a number of private lodges as well as some eclipse-specific events taking place in the many safari areas within the path of totality. Finally, the extensive communal areas in the eclipse path merit some mention – these are just as full of hills and valleys, and their denizens are much more in need of the cash which tourism brings to Zimbabwe than are the private safari operators.

GATEWAY CITY: HARARE

Zimbabwe's capital city will feel disturbingly familiar to most tourists from developed countries. Its daunting horizon, full of skyscrapers, is visible from the airport (about 15km away); its streets are normally clogged with vehicles; despite all the efforts of a loyal cadre of city council employees, the sidewalks are always blowing with trash. Nightlife here is fun and varied, there is an amazing array of dining and lodging options to suit all tastes and budgets, and it's only very specialised services that aren't on offer somewhere within the sprawling Harare urban area. Day-trips from Zimbabwe's capital city into the path of totality are not only feasible, they are being organised in their dozens by just as many safari and tour companies as have bases there. For further information try the helpful Harare Publicity Bureau on Unity Square just off 2nd Street (tel: 4 705085/6).

PRE- AND POST-ECLIPSE EXCURSIONS

If you have covered Kariba and Mana Pools in the course of your eclipse-viewing, you'll need some travel time to reach Zimbabwe's other big attractions, most of which lie either to the east or the west of the country. The gateway to the east is Mutare, a simple four-hour bus ride from Harare, or take the overnight train. From here, longer excursions to Nyanga and Chimanimani National Parks can be undertaken, or you can stick to the nearby Bvumba Botanical Gardens which has the reputation for being a birding hotspot. You'll need at least three days to see and enjoy either of the national parks properly.

The **Great Zimbabwe Ruins**, another world heritage site, make an easy day trip from Harare. A number of safari operators in Harare organise these, and it

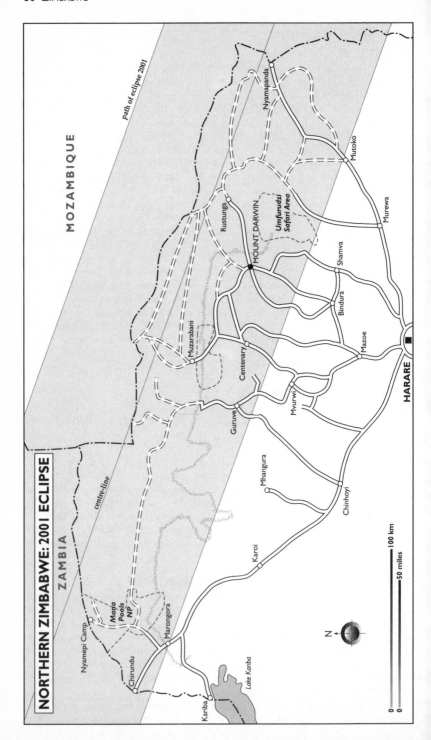

would be a great way to spend one of your last days in the country if time is tight. Alternatively, the nearby town of Masvingo is ideally located as a jumping-off point to go either east or west.

Of course, the two big attractions of Zimbabwe are the world-famous **Victoria Falls** and **Hwange National Park**. Enough superlatives have been committed to print elsewhere about these two places; just don't come to Zimbabwe without seeing them.

GETTING AROUND
By public transport

All buses leaving from Harare do so from the infamous Mbare bus terminus, in the high-density suburb of the same name. You can avoid this intimidating place, however, because long-distance buses going to just about anywhere within the path of totality can be boarded at two other sites around Harare. To catch public transport going to Mozambique, Malawi and the Tete Corridor (Murewa, Mutoko and Nyamapanda etc), first take a local *kombi* going to Highlands and ask to be dropped at the Grange. Buses to other sites in the path of totality leave from Rotten Row, just off the corner of Jason Moyo Avenue.

By car

To hire a vehicle from a small, independent company, contact the Harare Publicity Bureau (see above). The international car-hire firms Avis, Budget, Europcar and Hertz are all represented in Harare.

A variety of road maps is available at any bookstore, or visit the Surveyor General's map sales unit on Samora Machel Avenue just off the corner of Julius Nyerere Way.

There are only four double-lane tar roads leading north out of Harare into the path of totality so independent travellers should get out of town early on the morning of the eclipse. Better to sit at your eclipse-viewing site for a few extra hours than to be caught on the road in a traffic jam and miss totality.

From the Harare city centre, take Enterprise Road for Murewa, Mutoko or Nyamapanda; take Lomagundi Road (accessible by following L Takawaira north out the city centre until it comes to an end) for Karoi, Kariba and Mana Pools; and take Second Street for all other locations in the path of totality.

Hitchhiking

Try the following sites for finding lifts:

To Murewa, Mutoko, Nyamapanda: same place where one catches buses (see above).
To Karoi, Kariba, Mana Pools: catch a Greencroft *kombi* and alight at the Greencroft shopping centre. Alternatively, catch a Westgate *kombi* and drop off at Westgate shopping mall. If taking the latter option, ask the conductor to point out which bus shelter to wait at, as Westgate is a pretty big place.
All other locations: catch a Marlborough *kombi* and ask to be dropped at Golden Stairs road. Again, telling the conductor your plans will give him a clear idea where to drop you.

By bicycle and on foot

Northern Zimbabwe is particularly accessible by bike. There is an extensive network of tar and bike-able dust roads, and bicycles are common among locals. You should be relatively fit if planning to do this, as the areas in question are hilly, especially those closer to the Zambezi escarpment. However, although visitors may walk anywhere within Mana Pools, bicycles are not allowed in the park. Also, biking around Kariba is not advisable given the concentration of game in the area.

Those who want to combine some hiking with their eclipse would do well to choose the Mavuradona Wilderness (see below).

ECLIPSE CENTRES: NORTHWEST
Gateway towns
Kariba
Although Zimbabwe's premier resort town on the shore of Lake Kariba does not lie within the path of totality, it does offer an attractive option as a base for a day-trip up the escarpment or into Mana Pools. This is undoubtedly why tour operators have already block-booked all of the lodging available in Kariba. The Zambezi Safari and Travel Company (see listing above) is currently holding all the rooms at the **Kariba Breezes Hotel**, so bookings can be made through the company. That aside, because there are so many beds in Kariba it does seem unlikely that they will all have been claimed by the time of the eclipse. For the latest information on hotels and camping try the Kariba Publicity Association (tel: 61 2328/3213; email: kpa@samara.co.zw).

Karoi
This pleasant little town lies about halfway between Harare and Kariba and would make an excellent base for a day-trip into the path of totality. Try the **Twin River Inn** (PO Box 12, Karoi; tel: 64 6845; fax: 64 68456; email: twin@telco.co.zw).

Chinhoyi
This is the largest town on the A1 north of Harare, but an unexciting place. You can stay at the low-priced **Orange Grove Motel** (tel: 67 22785/2534/61; fax: 67 23095) in the town centre or try the Chinhoyi Caves National Park Campsite, just outside the caves. The **Caves Motel** is tel/fax: 67 223400.

Pre- and post-eclipse excursions
Lake Kariba is worth a visit, best seen from Kariba town, where there is a viewpoint over the 128m-high dam wall. The areas fringing the lake amount to one big wildlife sanctuary. Matusadona National Park occupies some of the lake's remoter shores. You can take a ferry across the lake. The **Kaburi Wilderness Area**, which practically borders Kariba town, lies between the lake shore and the Kariba–Makuti road. Walking is permitted there and the fees are a fraction of those charged by the national parks. There's a stream of plains animals crossing the floodplain in front of Kaburi campsite.

Those returning from the Kariba/Mana Pools area might like to check out the **Chinhoyi Caves National Monument**, located just outside the town of the same name. Here you can wander among some interesting caves and underground pools for a couple of hours.

Although the Hippo Pools campsite at the **Umfurudzi Safari Area** gets rave reviews from everyone who visits there, this is going to be one of the prime eclipse-viewing areas (see the listings for Wildlife Expeditions and UTc above; both companies have events planned here) and is likely still to be overloaded with people even after the eclipse.

The eclipse zone
Mana Pools National Park
The main focus of tourist activity for the 2001 eclipse will be the area around Mana Pools, where you can either stay or visit just for the day. Although it has

unquestionable appeal for its access to game, its suitability as an eclipse-viewing site may seem debatable: it is flat, low-lying and pretty heavily forested. However, the Sun will be quite high and well away from the horizon, reducing the impact of these factors.

There are currently no plans to restrict numbers of day visitors but this might change nearer the time. Therefore, it is not a bad idea to confirm details of park access and entry by phoning the warden (63 533).

The Wildlife Society of Zimbabwe has requested space in which to study the response of wild animals to the eclipse. At the time of writing, it was still unclear whether this would be granted and how it would affect others' access to the park.

Getting there and away
The nearest feasible bases for a day-trip to Mana Pools are Kariba or the small towns of Karoi and Chinhoyi. The trip from Harare takes about four hours by car to the park entrance, so this is also feasible but will not allow for much actual game-viewing. Anyone intending to enter the park, whether as a day visitor or an overnighter, must stop at Marangora and get an entry permit. You can then proceed down the escarpment to the entrance gate at the bottom, to hand in your permit and campsite details. From the gate, all visitors are required to drive to Nyamepi camp on the river, where the entry fees are paid. Get an early start so you have time to drive around the park and find an ideal vantage point.

Where to stay
National parks lodging in Mana Pools is already fully booked. Some of the private camps and lodges in the area are already full but you can check availability through their owner companies (see *Organised tours*).

Where to watch the eclipse
The landscape is higher and less forested further away from the river but it is also less accessible. Since being with lots of people (and animals) always makes for a good eclipse experience you may choose to head towards the river instead.

ECLIPSE CENTRES: NORTHEAST
Overview
The Zambezi escarpment is, I feel, the most promising place for viewing the eclipse. There are many roads heading north into this remote area where you will be very much an independent eclipse-chaser selecting your own site from many suitable places.

Gateway town: Bindura
This small town would make a good base for day-trips into the remote Mount Darwin area, and it has cheap hotels. There is the budget **Kimberley Reef Hotel** (PO Box 61, Bindura; tel: 71 6722; fax: 71 6708). The **Coach House Inn** is more upmarket (tel: 71 7507).

Pre- and post-eclipse excursions
Tengenenge Farm is the home of the sculptors' colony which spawned the world-famous Shona sculpture style of stonework. Tengenenge is just outside Guruve; however, those without their own transportation may find that getting there is not worth the effort, as it is a bit off the beaten track.

The eclipse zone
Mavuradona Wilderness
It is hard not to rave about the Mavuradona Wilderness as a potential eclipse-viewing site. It straddles the Zambezi escarpment, and includes at least two peaks – Eagle's Crag and Banirembizi – from which one can see Lake Cahora Bassa in Mozambique, about 100km in the distance. The landscape is beautifully forested, with gurgling mountain streams and scenic waterfalls galore. You will encounter a variety of wild game and birds while hiking on the many clearly marked trails.

A day-trip to the Mavuradona Wilderness base camp from Harare, followed by a vigorous hike to one of the peaks, should make for a memorable eclipse experience because of the vantage and the distance from the river, minimising the problem of clouds rising from the Zambezi.

Getting there and away
To reach the base camp, take any bus going to Muzarabani and alight at the 50.5km peg after Centenary. If driving, follow the signs to Centenary and then continue driving through town.

Where to stay
The bad news is that the Mavuradona base camp has already been completely booked by an American astronomical society. However, The Wildlife Society of Zimbabwe is planning to coordinate budget accommodation with local commercial farmers. Contact Mrs Irene Sharp (tel: 4 747859; email: zimwild@internet.co.zw).

Where to watch the eclipse
There is a wide range of choices but the two crags mentioned above will probably be the most dramatic places from which to watch.

Mount Darwin
Where to stay
The **Matambanadzo family** (tel: 11 205042; email: charlesmataz@hotmail.com) is offering to a maximum of 25 tourists the chance to use their rural homestead in Mount Darwin as an eclipse-viewing base, with accommodation in the house or in thatched mud rondavels and small cultural tours offered. Contact Charles Matambanadzo.

Guruve
Although Guruve is probably the least attractive of the communal areas over which the 2001 eclipse will be passing, there are plenty of small, rocky hills, known as *kopjes* (pronounced 'koppies'), scattered throughout the landscape which can be climbed in the absence of other options. The Guruve area is also home to a number of commercial farmers, at least some of whom are offering their farms as bases for day-trips, or even planning eclipse activities.

Getting there and away
Guruve is easily accessible from Harare, being only 150km north of the city.

Where to stay
Siyalima Farm (PO Box 290, Mvurwi; tel: 58 2357 or 91 354603; tel/fax: 58 535) can accommodate up to 12 guests in the farmhouse and a further 25 in simple grass chalets (cost: US$175-200). Siyalima (Ndebele for 'we are farming') should know of neighbouring farms offering similar schemes.

The other option is the very basic **Guruve Hotel** (tel: 58 256 or 58 561/2/3; US$10) which has 7 rooms with twin beds and shared bathing/toilet facilities. Its advantages are that it lies within the path of totality and is secure.

Where to watch the eclipse

Siyalima Farm lies near the edge of the path of totality. You can view the eclipse from one of three hills on the farm if you spend the night in farm accommodation (see above). The McGraths will hire a bus to provide transfers to and from Harare for large enough groups.

For day-trippers, the McGrath family will provide basic facilities for up to 100 people, with the understanding that these guests will actually view the eclipse from somewhere other than the farm.

Mutoko

This is the administrative seat of Mutoko District and lies on the edge of the path of totality. It is rocky and hilly without many trees. **Mutoko Luxury Lodges** (tel: 72 2809) has been block-booked by a tour operator but it is worth phoning in case places become available. The same applies to the **Chibanguza Hotel** in Murewa (tel: 78 2240), which lies about halfway between Harare and Mutoko.

The 2002 eclipse

OVERVIEW

Thank divine planning for the fact that a full solar eclipse will happen over the Matobo Hills, which are easily the highlight of the 2002 path of totality in Zimbabwe. This area, centrally located in the Zimbabwe portion of the path, has been ascribed spiritual significance by almost everyone who has seen it through recorded history. This includes the ancient Bushmen, whose cave paintings and archaeological remains are so numerous as to be uncountable within the hills. While the areas to the west and southeast of Matobo are less inspiring in terms of landscape, they do have the advantage at least of not being heavily forested.

The 2002 path, which will cross Zimbabwe in early morning, with first contact beginning just after 07.00, is restricted almost wholly to the province of Matabeleland South, one of the least developed parts of the country, and there are fewer organised tours and tourist-class lodging than for the 2001 eclipse. However, many 2001 operators are planning 2002 excursions, and there is a handful of private game lodges offering attractive activities either within or quite near the path of totality. The opportunity to share the eclipse with a rural community will be possible via any of the four rural district councils through which the eclipse is passing.

If there's anything disadvantageous about the 2002 eclipse, it's the timing: December is the middle of the rainy season in southern Africa, and there are chances that the eclipse could be obscured by clouds and/or precipitation just about anywhere within the path of totality. That said, the rains do not fall every day, or even most days, during the season, and there are just as many clear days as cloudy. In short, there are no guarantees for December 4 – but then what in life is ever guaranteed?

ORGANISED TOURS

Matabeleland South has a fairly sparse selection of tour operators and it is best to use the 2001 listing (see page 80). The closest operator to the path of totality is **EcoLogical Safaris** which organises air safaris, car hire, chartered safaris and hotels. The proprietor of EcoLogical also runs the Limpopo Valley Camp on

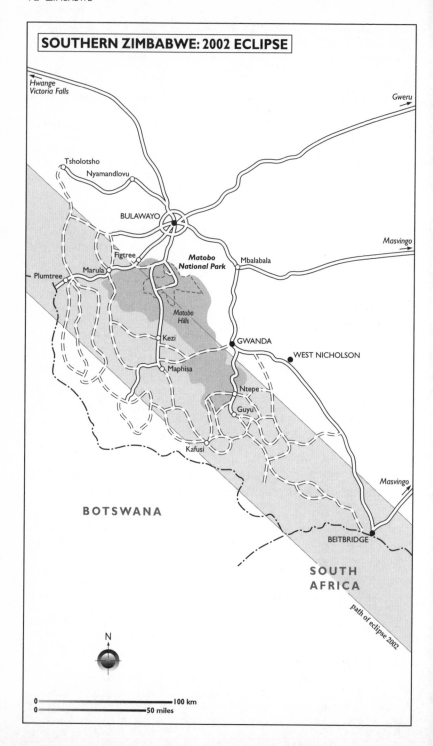

SOUTHERN ZIMBABWE: 2002 ECLIPSE

Hwange
Victoria Falls

Gweru

Tsholotsho
Nyamandlovu

BULAWAYO

Masvingo

Figtree

**Matobo
National Park**

Plumtree

Marula

Mbalabala

*Matobo
Hills*

Kezi

GWANDA

WEST NICHOLSON

Maphisa

Ntepe

Guyu

Kafusi

Masvingo

BOTSWANA

BEITBRIDGE

**SOUTH
AFRICA**

path of eclipse 2002

N

0 ——————— 100 km
0 ——————— 50 miles

Sentinel Ranch near the Thuli Circle safari area. It is just south of the path of totality, but could be used as a base camp for up to eight people in chalets.

Rural homestays
The most likely option is the Gwanda council. The full list (from west to east) is:

Bulilima-Mangwe (Plumtree) tel: 19 2382
Matobo (Matobo) tel: 82 354/62
Gwanda (Gwanda) tel: 84 2369/2312
Beitbridge (Beitbridge) tel: 86 2404/2508

Air safaris
EcoLogical Safaris organises air trips. **United Air Services** (see 2001 section above) is a larger, nationwide air charter company. There are many air companies at Victoria Falls who do custom air hire. Find them through the Victoria Falls Publicity Association (tel: 13 4202).

A few of the lodges below have light aircraft which will be available for hire by guests. These include Barberton Lodge and Camp Amalinda.

GATEWAY CITY: BULAWAYO
Zimbabwe's 'City of Kings' is easily the nicest in the country – even Zimbabweans from other parts of the country will agree that its laid-back pace, wide streets, and mostly old architecture all contribute to a relaxing atmosphere. It is Zimbabwe's second largest city and quite up to the challenge of accommodating the bulk of the southern African eclipse tourists in 2002. Because Bulawayo is the base for all tourist-oriented services for Matabeleland South – the province through which the eclipse is passing – you are likely (and recommended) to spend some time in the city. Bulawayo is also the most practical base for a day-trip down either the Matobo or Plumtree roads into the path of totality, and most of the tour operators in town will have put together such trips closer to the time.

The friendly source of all the information you could want about Bulawayo and its surrounds is the **Publicity Association** (tel: 9 60867/68; fax 9 72969; email: bulawayo@telconet.co.zw; web: www.arachnid.co.zw/Bulawayo). It is in the City Hall car park between Takawira and 8th Avenue, just off Silundika Street. Check *This Month* magazine, available at the publicity office, and also *The Chronicle* newspaper for the latest events, including eclipse-related ones.

GETTING AROUND
By public transport
All public transport to Matabeleland South (with the exception of *kombis* travelling down the Beitbridge road, see below) leaves Bulawayo from the Renkini Bus Terminus. This is located about a ten-minute walk west of the city centre along 6th Avenue extension. To travel anywhere in Matabeleland North (for example Hwange and Victoria Falls) the best option is to take a metered taxi to the Kukura Kurerwa (KK) bus garage and wait there for their next Volvo bus heading north. You can also take a *kombi* out to Entumbane bus terminus (from where all buses going north leave Bulawayo) but the crowds there are huge and it is some distance from the city centre.

Kombis heading down the Beitbridge road can be boarded in the parking lot across from the junction of Tongogara Street and Takawira. If you are not in a hurry, chicken buses heading to Gwanda and Beitbridge are fairly frequent and potentially more comfortable (depending on how full they are). If possible, avoid buses plying the route to Beitbridge via Zezani, as this involves quite a long distance on a poorly maintained dust road.

By car
The main international car hire chains (Budget, Hertz, Avis and Europcar) have branches in Bulawayo. A slightly cheaper alternative is the local Transit Car Hire (tel: 9 76495/394 or 11 201058; email: transit@acacia.samara.co.zw) which can be found on Mugabe between 8th and 9th avenues.

From Bulawayo city centre, take Robert Mugabe Street south out of town to reach Matobo and Maphisa; and Main Street south out of town to reach Plumtree or Marula; take LTakawira Avenue to the east out of town to reach Beitbridge, West Nicholson and Gwanda.

To reach locations in Matabeleland North from Bulawayo follow Main Street north from the city centre and follow the signs pointing to Victoria Falls.

Hitchhiking
To get a lift to Matobo or Maphisa, board a local *kombi* at the bus stop on Robert Mugabe Street just off the corner of 14th Avenue. Ask to be dropped where you can get lifts to Matobo. To catch a lift to Plumtree or Marula, board a *kombi* for Bellevue at the TM Hyper supermarket, on the corner of Fort Street and 11th Avenue. Alight at the Shell station about 2km out of town and then walk about 500m to the long-distance bus stop, from where you should be able to get a lift. Lifts to West Nicholson or Gwanda can be flagged down at the BP station on the corner of L Takawira Avenue and J Tongogara Street. Hitchhiking to Victoria Falls should be easy.

Do not hitch lifts to and from Beitbridge because of the occasional violent crime which spills over the border from South Africa.

By bicycle and on foot
Although Bulawayo is much closer to the 2002 path of totality than Harare is to the 2001 path, cycling to a viewing site from Bulawayo on the day of the eclipse is not feasible unless you set out quite early in the morning. At 60km down the Plumtree road from Bulawayo, the Marula area would be the closest (and flattest) area to aim for, for those who wanted to make the attempt. Depending on one's level of fitness (and sense of urgency), this would take at least three hours if not four. First contact in Plumtree is at 07.08, with mid-totality at 08.14.

The Matobo road offers some of the most beautiful scenery any cyclist could wish for. One possible way to enjoy the eclipse here would be to bike down to Maphisa (a good day's ride), spend the night there and then ride north on your bike back to Bulawayo, enjoying the eclipse along the way. Another excellent option that would offer intriguing landscapes and a taste of the rural life would be to bike or take a bus to Gwanda (see below) the day before the eclipse, spend the night there, then wake up fairly early in the morning and head south out of town, turning right down the (tarred) Fort Thuli road. With a departure time from Gwanda of about 04.00 and riding at a rate of 15km/hr, you'd be well within the southeastern edge of the Matobo Hills by the time of the eclipse. You could ride on tar as far as Guyu (about 70km out of Gwanda), then turn around and head back to Gwanda. (It is doubtful anyone could make the entire trip back to Bulawayo in one day.)

You could also cycle from Bulawayo the day before the eclipse to spend the night at the Rock Campsite in Marula (see below). Then you could continue your journey under the eclipse, in whichever direction suits you. Unfortunately, the best hiking area in Matabeleland South (the Toghwe Wilderness section of Matobo National Park) lies too far north of the path of totality to be a feasible base for an eclipse hike.

PRE- AND POST-ECLIPSE EXCURSIONS

You can easily spend days at **Victoria Falls** doing whitewater rafting, bungee jumping, game-viewing or just watching the water.

Those without the time to visit the **Great Zimbabwe Ruins** near Masvingo (about three hours from Bulawayo by private car, and a potential day-trip from Bulawayo if one gets an early start) should consider seeing the nearby **Khami Ruins**. While smaller, these are also a world heritage site and just as interesting. To reach them take 13th Avenue (not 11th, as signs and maps will lead you to believe) west out of Bulawayo for about 20km. The easiest way to get a lift is to catch a local *kombi* going to Nkulumane. These can be boarded at the large *kombi* terminus behind Lobengula Street between Takawira and 8th Avenues. Get off at the bus stop before the turning to the shopping centre, and then hitch from there.

If you have a morning to waste, there are few better places to spend it than the **Natural History Museum** (tel: 9 60045) in Centenary Park, a ten-minute walk from the city centre on Takawira. It has some of the most extensive natural history collections on the entire continent.

Finally, there's the **Chipangali Wildlife Orphanage** (tel: 9 72179/70764/ 46603), which began as a rehabilitation centre for injured wildlife and has evolved over the years into a glorified zoo. Chipangali is also the home of the recently opened Diana, Princess of Wales Educational Centre. Chipangali lies about 20km out of town along the Beitbridge road. If you do not have your own transportation, you can try for a lift at the BP station on Takawira and Tongogara or wait there for the next bus heading in that direction. There are a number of operators in Bulawayo who offer tours of these four places (and a few others); for details check at the publicity association.

ECLIPSE CENTRES: THE WEST
Overview

Although the region of the Victoria Falls and Hwange National Park initially looks a very promising venue, on closer examination there are several pitfalls. Firstly, the Falls do not lie within the path of totality. Secondly, only the remotest corner of the famous Hwange park lies in the eclipse path, making it inaccessible for all but the most determined of visitors.

However, as the Victoria Falls are one of the major highlights of a visit to Zimbabwe, you might want to do a combined Falls/eclipse holiday, using them as a base for a day-trip to Botswana to see totality. Several tour operators in the Falls already offer day-trips into Botswana to visit Chobe National Park, so packaged Falls/eclipse deals should also be available.

Gateway town: Victoria Falls

Mid-range lodging is sparse at the Falls, however, and cheap national parks lodging is available at nearby Zambezi National Park (book in the usual way) for those with their own transport. For details contact the Victoria Falls publicity association (tel: 13 4202). Getting from the Falls to the Botswana border is quite straightforward; simply drive south out of town and turn right at the sign for Kazungula border post. All you need is a valid passport. See *Botswana* (*Chapter 6*) for advice on where to go next.

Pre- and post-eclipse excursions

Matobo National Park is the big draw of the area. The name of this district comes from the Ndebele word for 'bald heads', no doubt a reference to the extensive bare granite *dwalas* which punctuate the landscape. Along with these are scattered piles of boulders, many of them precariously balanced and hence great photo subjects. The effect when seen from a high vantage point looks otherworldly, even without the shadow cast by a full solar eclipse. Cecil John Rhodes is buried within the park at World's View, which has an excellent panorama.

The eclipse zone
Hwange National Park

Before you jump at the idea of reliving your 2001 Mana Pools eclipse experience in this, Zimbabwe's premier game park, here is the bad news. Although Hwange is one of the largest game parks on the entire continent, the 2002 path of totality will pass over only its remote and virtually inaccessible southwest corner. You'll need planning, money and a lot of luck to view the eclipse from there.

Getting there and away

You could find a tour operator that is licensed to take tourists into national parks and organise a customised trip. A more practical option for combining the eclipse with some game-viewing in Hwange is to charter air transport and do a fly-in safari (See *Organised tours*).

Where to stay

The only overnight places from which you could feasibly get to the eclipse in time on the day are **Robins Camp**, which has chalets and lodges, or **Shumba Campsite**. To book either, submit a request to the national parks lottery, preferably before December 1 2001, when the lottery opens.

Where to watch the eclipse

Access to this area over ground is only possible with 4WD and some (potentially illegal) off-roading would probably be necessary to reach the path. To secure a 4WD vehicle, contact Eco-Logical Safaris (see *Organised tours*, above).

ECLIPSE CENTRES: MATOBO AREA
Overview

The Matobo National Park lies within the Matobo Hills but, sadly, is just outside totality. However, the hills themselves continue both south and east through the adjoining communal lands, and this is undoubtedly the best area in terms of geography for viewing the 2002 eclipse. There are places in Marula which will also be good eclipse-viewing choices.

The eclipse zone
Matobo Hills
Getting there

See *Getting around* on page 93.

Where to stay

There are a number of upscale game lodges within and around the national park that would make ideal bases for a trip into the path of totality (only 30–50km away) on the morning of the eclipse. The **Matobo Hills Lodge** (tel: 9 540944; fax: 9 229088; email: ttw@acacia.samara.co.zw; US$90–200 depending on number of meals and excursions) is run by the safari company **Touch the Wild**. It should run a day-trip to the eclipse. There is also **Camp Amalinda** (PO Box QP130, Queens Park, Bulawayo; tel: 9 43954/46443; fax: 9 46436; email: amalinda@acacia.samara.co.zw; US$110 full board or US$215 including activities such as an eclipse day-trip). It provides what is probably the most luxurious base in the Matobo area for a morning excursion into the path of totality. It is 44.5km from Bulawayo, and consists of lodges built of natural materials – four of them having been carved out of boulders. All have a panorama over the Matobo Hills. There is a private airstrip 1km away. The aircraft is available for hire at a steep US$250 per hour. Amalinda is also one of three lodges mentioned in this chapter to offer elephant-back rides, at US$50 per person. Other activities include game drives or horse riding, and cultural visits.

A good option for mid-range travellers who still want some comforts is the **Matobo Ingwe Lodge** (PO Box 8279, Belmont, Bulawayo; tel: 83 8233; tel/fax: 83 8217; email: ingwe@acacia.samara.co.zw; web: www.arachnid.co.zw/ingwe) which is only 34.5km out of Bulawayo (and hence the furthest of these from the path of totality). Accommodation is in thatched rondavels (US$43) or camping (US$3) per person (cooking gear required for self-caterers). The management has indicated it would be willing to take guests to the path of totality on the morning of the eclipse, and then on their standard game drive afterwards.

You could also try **The Farmhouse** (PO Box 9111, Hillside, Bulawayo; tel: 9 65499/70008 or 838 2506; US$60) which lies 48km from Bulawayo.

Independent travellers – with or without cars – would do well to try for a place at **Maleme Rest Camp** in the park. Once the Rock Campsite in Marula (see below) is full it will be the most attractive option for campers. Bookings are through national parks. To check for places nearer the date try the provincial National Parks office in Bulawayo (tel: 9 63646/61018) whose entrance is on the corner of 11th Avenue and Chitepo Street. Accommodation is in chalets. The camp itself is quite attractively nestled among huge boulders crawling with lizards, dassies and baboons – don't leave your windows open.

Matobo National Park also has campsites at the following dams: Maleme, Mtshelele, Toghwana and Mesilume, as well as at the Arboretum. By far the largest and most accessible of these is the **Maleme site**; it is the only feasible option for anyone on foot due to its location near the tar road. (Bear in mind the national park itself isn't within the path of totality; would-be eclipse viewers who are on foot will be relying on lifts and/or public transport to travel further down the road on the morning of the eclipse.) Camping at any of these costs US$8 per person per night, and it is usually not necessary to pre-book, but check with the provincial office (number above) in case of eclipse mania. An overnight entry into the national park is US$20 per person for non-residents; this permit is good for up to seven days.

The Maleme turn-off from the main road is well signposted, and it is usually easy to get a lift for most of the 7km to Maleme Dam. You can also walk there, with excellent chances of seeing klipspringers, sable, zebra, wildebeest and impala on the way. It will undoubtedly be easy to get a lift into the path of totality from here on the morning of the eclipse.

Where to watch the eclipse
The hills are forested but absolutely full of huge *dwalas* which will make for excellent eclipse-viewing.

Maphisa
Continuing south from the Matobo area, you soon leave the boundaries of the national park and enter communal lands. The hills become shorter, less common,

and less rocky until the effect is much less stunning than the area left behind. After crossing a few rivers and driving through Kezi you reach the small town of Maphisa. This is the administrative seat of Matobo district, but consists of little more than some shops, the administrative offices, and a single hotel. Still, it lies right near the centre of the path of totality, and would make a great base from which to venture out to a pre-determined spot on the morning of the eclipse.

Where to stay
One gets the impression that the mid-range **Maphisa Omadu Hotel** (PO Maphisa; tel: 82 325/375; US$8–22) doesn't see many foreign tourists though it does have a casino, full bar, restaurant, swimming pool and attractive thatched-roof rondavels.

Where to watch the eclipse
The highest point around Maphisa itself is the top of the hill at the 110.5km peg on the tar road, but this site has a lot of trees to the east that would be likely to block viewing. There is an attractive *dwala* to the west of the road near the 102km peg, which would probably offer excellent viewing, but since this is in the communal area it is important to secure permission from the local leadership before you watch.

Marula
Roughly halfway between Bulawayo and Plumtree, the Marula region is made up mainly of privately owned farms and game ranches. The landscape is a transition between the flat Kalahari plain to the west and the Matobo hills to the east: mostly flat but with some *kopjes* and *dwalas*, which could make good viewing sites.

Where to stay
The **Shashani Valley Lodge** (tel: 9 70728 or 91 301785; fax: 9 70728; email: pumula@acacia.samara.co.zw; US$150) is 59km from Bulawayo along the Plumtree road on a privately owned game ranch and is among the most attractive options within the path of totality. Not only is it perfectly situated overlooking the Shashani Valley, it is also the only lodge offering elephant rides within the path of totality (although Amalinda in Matobo and Sondelani in West Nicholson are both close). They also offer rock-climbing and a variety of other activities within the Matobo Hills. Run by the same people as Shashani is the **Rock Campsite**, just another 1km down the Plumtree Road. This is the only established campsite within the path of totality – if you are a backpacker intending to see the eclipse, it is probably a good idea to put this book down right now and book a place (US$5 with own equipment, US$25 in furnished 'tent under thatch' chalets).

Malalangwe Lodge (PO Box 2723, Bulawayo; tel: 19 3129; fax: 19 3183; email: stonehil@acacia.samara.co.zw; US$180) is part of the Stone Hills Wildlife Sanctuary and Research Centre and offers presentations, cultural trips and participation in biological research within the sanctuary. The lodge itself is set on top of a high hill with excellent viewing. Profits made on the lodging go toward the upkeep and management of the sanctuary. There is also a bush camp on the property that can accommodate up to 12 people.

Plumtree
The small town of Plumtree serves as Zimbabwe's southern border post with Botswana, although the border itself is another 10km down the road. There is not much to inspire one to linger, and the surrounding area is mostly flat and

featureless. As the private lodges in Matobo and Marula get booked up, this would probably be the next best choice as a base for eclipse viewing. By far the more basic of Plumtree's two hotels is the **Plumtree Hotel** located in the town centre (tel: 019 2226 or 019 2392). Much more upscale is the mid-range **Omadu Lodge Plumtree** (tel: 19 2227/56 ; fax: 19 3308), located about 2km past the town centre on the main tar road, which offers standard rooms and thatched rondavels. Unlike their counterparts in Maphisa, the friendly staff have a lot of experience dealing with international tourists due to the proximity of the border post. The management has indicated that it would be willing to set up organised viewing of the eclipse if there's enough demand, so be sure to mention this if booking a place here.

ECLIPSE CENTRES: GWANDA AND THE SOUTH
Gateway towns
Gwanda
While Gwanda does have a bit of a 'blink and you'll miss it' aura, it is actually the administrative seat for Matabeleland South province, and the high density neighbourhoods to the east of the tar road have exploded in the last couple of years as the town council struggles to provide enough housing and basic services for the growing population. Although the town itself is not in the path of totality, it would make a good base for a morning drive into the communal areas, which host the western boundary of the Matobo Hills.

There is only one lodging option, the two-star **Gwanda Hotel** (PO Box 235, Gwanda; tel: 84 2476/2751/3221). Be warned: some so-called hotels in Gwanda are hourly-rate specials where your safety would be less than guaranteed.

West Nicholson
This small mining town about 40km south of Gwanda is unnoteworthy but there are two luxury game lodges in its vicinity. Both are just above the path of totality, but you could easily persuade the managers of either to offer trips into totality. The **Barberton Lodge** (tel: 9 72870 or 11 211854; fax: 9 72870; email: barber@acacia.samara.co.zw; US$120–160) offers accommodation in stone and thatch chalets or in a bush camp of reed chalets. It is on a private game ranch with rhinos; all the expected activities are on offer. In addition, the lodge has a three-seater plane and private airstrip, so three visitors will get to enjoy what is probably the cheapest way of viewing the eclipse from the air at US$80 per hour. Even nicer – and correspondingly even pricier – than Barberton is **Sondelani Lodge** (PO Box 1472, Bulawayo; tel: 9 61347; fax: 9 64997; email: sondela@telconet.co.zw; US$230 including transfers, game drives and bar). This is set on a privately owned game ranch, also with rhinos and over 300 species of bird. Elephant rides are offered.

Pre- and post-eclipse excursions
For an interesting day-trip from Beitbridge, or a break in the long, boring drive between Beitbridge and Bulawayo, try **Sondelani Lodge** (see above) which offers many of its services, such as game drives and elephant rides, to day visitors.

The eclipse zone
South of Gwanda
The area due south of Gwanda along the Fort Thuli road (turn west about 7km south of Gwanda town) is as scenic as Matobo, and will probably have fewer visitors. Those who wish to have a rural eclipse experience would do well to check with the Gwanda rural district council (see above) as there are plans for homestays.

Beitbridge

Like its counterpart on the western border, Beitbridge does not inspire one to stay any longer than border-crossing formalities require. The landscape is mostly flat and featureless, set as it is within the Limpopo River valley, and the town has very little to offer tourists. However, there are a few high hills near the town which could serve as good eclipse-viewing locations (first contact starts 07.11), so you could do worse.

Where to stay

As this is the only border post between Zimbabwe and South Africa there is a lot of lodging available, most of it quite pleasant. As the limited lodging in the northwest gets booked up, staying in Beitbridge will become the only option for formal accommodation. The nearest car hire and entertainment (barring the casinos at two of the hotels) are both in Messina, across the border. Messina also has many more dining options that Beitbridge. The middle-range **Holiday Inn Express** (PO Box 371, Beitbridge; tel: 86 3001/5 or 86 3201/2; fax: 86 3375; email: hiebeit@hiebeit.zimsun.co.zw; US$47 per room) is tried and true – and the largest hotel within the 2002 path of totality. Management has indicated it would be willing to organise something for the morning of the eclipse if enough interest exists, so be sure to mention that you are coming for the eclipse if booking here. Failing that, there is always the roof of the hotel for a viewing point. Just as good as the Holiday Inn and a bit cheaper is the **Beitbridge Inn** (PO Box 82, Beitbridge; tel/fax: 86 2214; US$18). There is a good view to the southeast from the 2nd floor but this is probably not the best option in the area for viewing the eclipse. A step down in both price and luxury is the **Limpopo Lodge** (PO Box 375, Beitbridge; tel: 86 3330/1; US$8–11) which should have newly built chalets ready for the time of the eclipse. A limited number of campsites is available there for US$2.50 per tent – this is probably the only organised option for camping in the Beitbridge area. There is also the budget **Peter's Hotel** (tel: 86 2309; fax: 86 2321; US$11) whose proprietor, Willie Peterson, is willing to recommend eclipse-viewing points, including a hill outside town.

To eat, it is best to cross to Messina but you could try the Nevada Spur restaurant at the top of the range or the Last and First Beit Restaurant for a budget meal. There are also a couple of fast-food restaurants.

FURTHER READING FROM BRADT

Africa by Road, Charlie Shackell and Illya Bracht
East and Southern Africa: The Backpacker's Manual, Philip Briggs
Southern Africa by Rail, Paul Ash

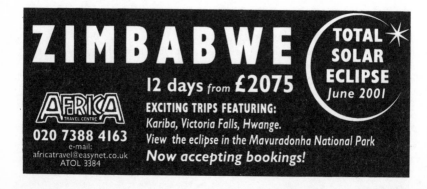

South Africa

Philip Briggs

Visiting the eclipse areas
OVERVIEW
Last total solar eclipse: October 1940
Next total solar eclipse: November 2030

South Africa lies too far south to fall into the path of totality for the eclipse in 2001, but the northeastern corner of the country will do so in 2002, most alluringly a substantial portion of the renowned Kruger National Park. Boasting far and away the largest and most sophisticated tourist infrastructure of countries covered in this guide, South Africa is of particular interest to those who want to combine an eclipse trip with a more general holiday – though as Sod's Law would have it, the path of totality through South Africa lies in a part of Northern Province where genuine tourist-class facilities are limited and organised tours virtually non-existent.

The far northeast of South Africa is relatively dry, with some areas experiencing an average annual rainfall of as low as 250mm. The eclipse does fall during the rainy summer months, but the normal weather pattern from November to March tends to be hot, clear days broken up by abrupt afternoon storms every few days. The prognosis for viewing the eclipse under a clear sky in the early morning is therefore better than at first appears from the cloud-cover statistics, which indicate an average chance of cloud of 40%. If you have a car and can move around on the morning of the eclipse, this figure drops substantially.

Concrete plans for the 2002 eclipse in South Africa are likely only to take shape after the 2001 eclipse so for detailed information nearer the event consult the numbers below or the Bradt website, on www.bradt-travelguides.com. Whatever happens, international flights may be heavily booked months in advance because the eclipse occurs during what is already peak tourist season.

The ideal place in South Africa will be the Kruger Park, for which reason this chapter concentrates heavily on possibilities within this superb tract of semi-wilderness. Be warned, however, that bed space within the park is restricted, as are day-entry permits, so without advance booking you'll almost certainly have to look at other options. Within the path of totality, these amount to Messina and the low-key and relatively unknown Nwanedi and Honnet game reserves, none of which is liberally endowed with accommodation options.

For independent travellers with access to vehicles, day-trips are a possibility, and the towns of Phalaborwa, Louis Trichardt and Pietersburg all lie close enough to the path of totality for you to be able to drive there in daylight hours. For those looking at organised day trips, Johannesburg or Pretoria seem the most likely candidates. Both of these cities boast a mind-boggling selection of tourist-class hotels, are serviced by the region's largest international airport, and lie four to five hours' drive south of the path of totality.

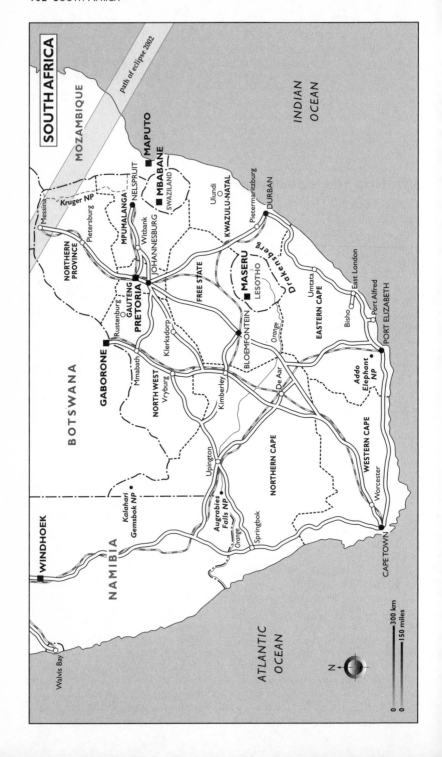

The part of Northern Province country from where the eclipse can be viewed is a relatively uniform tract of archetypically African savannah or bushveld. A notable feature of the region, particularly around Messina, is its gigantic baobab trees, which look as if they have been planted upside-down. The region is pretty flat, and the vegetation is generally not very thick or tall (except for the baobab trees and along perennial rivers). You should nevertheless avoid valleys or depressions to be sure of an unimpeded sighting.

Several different linguistic or ethnic groupings live in this part of Northern Province, among them the Venda, Pedi (or northern Sotho), Tsonga and Shangaan. Dutch settlers moved into the area to escape British rule in the Cape at the end of the so-called Great Trek of the 1830s and 1840s, and many towns in the region – notably Louis Trichardt and Pietersburg – are named after trek leaders. The relatively small proportion of people of European descent who live in Northern Province practically all speak Afrikaans (a derivative of Dutch) as a first language, though most also speak reasonably fluent English. Unusually, a smattering of Afrikaans will be the most useful language when dealing with Africans in this part of the country, since very few speak any English, but almost everybody can speak a bit of Afrikaans whatever their home tongue.

South Africa is not the destination for those who want a remote, rural eclipse experience because of the crime problem. The country telephone code is 27.

ORGANISED TOURS
Many of the eclipse-chasing companies will have plans for 2002 (see *Planning and Preparation*, page 20).

UK
Africa Travel Centre 21 Leigh St, London WC1H 9QX; tel 020 7387 1211; fax: 020 7383 7512; email: chris@africatravel.co.uk ; web: www.africatravel.co.uk . A 9-night South Africa tour viewing the 2002 eclipse from Messina. Cost: £1,695 per person. Can tailor-make small group trips.
Rainbow Tours 64 Essex Rd, London, N1 8LR; tel: 020 7226 1004; fax: 020 7226 2621; email: info@rainbowtours.co.uk; web: www.rainbowtours.co.uk. 2002 trip planned.

South Africa
For day tours out of Johannesburg and Pretoria, a useful contact is the **Info Africa** office in Pretoria (tel: 21 660 0880; fax: 21 654 4042; email: info@infoafrica.co.za). Many tours end up listed on the website of an organisation called **Computicket** (branches in most shopping malls in South Africa; tel: 11 445 8445; fax: 11 444 7606; web: www.computicket.com). The best way to find out about budget camping tours put together mainly for backpackers is by word of mouth – if you are travelling around South Africa before the eclipse. Otherwise, useful contacts include the **Baz Bus** (see below) or **Africa Travel Centre** (tel: 21 424 1035/7; web: www.abisa.co.za) which lists every feasible budget tour in southern Africa.

GETTING AROUND
By air
Cross Country Air Safaris (PO Box 95282, Waterkloof, 0145, South Africa; tel: 12 346 3740; fax: 12 346 3473; email: crossco@icon.co.za; web: www.airsafaris.co.za) is a Pretoria-based company which specialises in customised air safaris throughout southern Africa. It is located sufficiently close to the 2002 path of totality to be a good option. Rates will be roughly $460–505 per travelling day, which includes flight, accommodation, full board and game drives at selected lodges (if booking a combination lodging/air safari package). Camping rates are cheaper

By public transport

Messina lies on the N1 between Johannesburg and Beitbridge, the only trunk road between South Africa and Zimbabwe, traversed daily by numerous local minibuses, as well as coach operators such as Greyhound, Intercape and Translux, all of which can be booked through Computicket (see above).

The **Baz Bus** (tel: 21 439 2323; fax: 21 439 2343; email: info@bazbus.com; web: www.bazbus.com) is a popular backpackers' service covering a number of routes in southern Africa. It currently does the run between Johannesburg and Zimbabwe via Messina four times per week in either direction, and will pick up travellers at the hostel of their choice in either Johannesburg or Pretoria. No public transport runs into the Kruger National Park and, while a high proportion of organised tours to South Africa do pass through, most stick rigidly to the large camps in the far south, since they lie close to Johannesburg and provide a springboard for travel on to Durban. A very few organised tours might stray as far north as Letaba Camp, but even these do not normally drive further north to the area that will be in the path of totality. In other words, you can forget about seeing the full eclipse on any organised tour of the Kruger Park that hasn't specifically been designed for the occasion.

By car

Assuming that you have already made appropriate chalet or camping reservations, a private car would be the ideal way of getting to the northern Kruger Park. It would also allow you to drive up to the Messina area to view the eclipse without having to find accommodation within the path of totality. For those who do not have access to a private vehicle, there are numerous car rental companies operating out of Johannesburg, including international agencies such as Avis, Hertz and Budget and many (generally cheaper) local firms. Another self-drive possibility would be to fly or drive up to Phalaborwa, a large town fringing the entrance gate to the Kruger National Park with the same name, and hire a car to drive into the Kruger Park as a day-trip.

By bicycle and on foot

Neither of the obvious eclipse-viewing centres lends itself to a bicycle trip or visits on foot. Cycling and walking are forbidden within the Kruger Park, while Messina is a sizeable town easily reached by motorised public transport.

GATEWAY TOWNS
Johannesburg and Pretoria

These are, respectively, the largest city in South Africa and the country's capital. Plenty of local eclipse enthusiasts are likely to use them as bases, setting off at around 02.00 to cover the roughly 500km stretch of the N1 in time to see the full eclipse. For tourists, the main advantage of doing this will be that both cities have sufficient accommodation at all budget levels. The one downside, of course, is that it would mean driving for a couple of hours before sunrise – though the road itself is excellent, it holds no horrors in the form of stray animals and (other eclipse enthusiasts aside) the traffic should be very light during the wee small hours.

Johannesburg and Pretoria are likely to be the starting points for organised day trips or short overnight trips to Messina. Contact local tour operators and possibly backpacker hostels in and around Johannesburg. You could club together with others to arrange a day-trip to Messina with any local tour operator – there would be something to be said for going with a driver who is experienced in local conditions and knows the way.

Backpackers arriving at the airport will find a 'backpackers' info' stand in the arrivals hall which will organise a bed or room in (and free lift to) any of the two dozen or more hostels scattered around the cities. For advance information, take a look at the **Africa Travel Centre** website (see above) which lists most reputable hostels countrywide.

If you want to make your own hotel bookings, the options are endless, but the website of the **Protea Hotel Group** (tel: 11 419 8800; fax: 11 419 8200; email: uwelcome@protea-hotels.co.za; web: www.protea-hotels.co.za) is a good place to start, with 17 reliable and reasonably priced mid-range hotels in the Johannesburg and Pretoria area alone and another 60 countrywide. Hotel and guesthouse bookings all around South Africa can be made through **Computicket** (see above).

PRE- AND POST-ECLIPSE EXCURSIONS
Messina environs
The area is steeped in history, with perhaps the most intriguing site being the little-visited **Mapungubwe Hill** on the banks of the Limpopo 75km northwest of Messina. The extensive stone ruins on this hill, occupied between around AD950 and AD1200, were the precursor of the even more impressive stone city of Great Zimbabwe in the country of the same name, and several artefacts uncovered at the site – including a pair of golden rhinos – indicate it had strong trade links with the Swahili merchants of the Indian Ocean coast.

South through Kruger
Once the eclipse is over, you could stay on in Kruger for a few days, slowly working your way south to enjoy the marvellous game-viewing en route. The Kruger is one of the best places in Africa to see the so-called Big Five: elephant and buffalo are common throughout the park, while lion, leopard and rhino are most densely concentrated in areas south of Satara. Other common large mammals include zebra, giraffe, warthog, baboon, vervet monkey and a number of antelope, most visibly impala, wildebeest, greater kudu and waterbuck.

THE ECLIPSE CENTRES
Kruger National Park
Kruger is the largest game reserve in South Africa, covering an area of 1,948,528ha (larger than Belgium and roughly the size of Wales) and measuring around 500km from north to south. It is also one of the very best reserves on the continent, with more mammal species recorded than in any other African national park, as well as over 500 species of bird and a huge variety of plants and smaller animals. The path of totality will run through a substantial portion of the northern Kruger, with first contact just after 07.10. This area is not as developed for tourism as the southern half of the park, nor as good for general game-viewing. Having said that, the north of the park still has a good range of affordable overnight facilities and a richly varied fauna, and its mood is generally far more unspoilt.

Assuming that the weather co-operates, the Kruger Park must rank close to being the ideal place in Africa from which to view the eclipse in 2002. Not only does it offer an almost pristine terrestrial environment but it will also be fascinating to see how the wildlife reacts to the sudden darkening of the sun.

Unless the normal restrictions on numbers of day visitors are lifted for the occasion (unlikely), those who do manage to get to the Kruger Park for the eclipse can expect to view it in a reasonably uncrowded atmosphere. The converse of this, of course, is that those who don't reserve a room or campsite or day permit well in advance will be disappointed should they just turn up on the day.

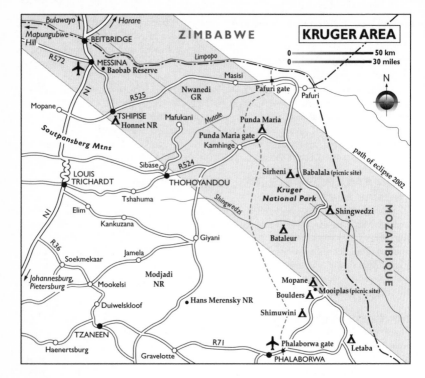

Where to stay

Every camp in the Kruger Park has its own character but the main factor in choosing your camp should be location relative to the path of totality. There are almost 900 beds and 100 camping stands within the eclipse path. You could also stay at a more southerly camp and drive north on the morning of the eclipse; or stay outside the park in Phalaborwa and enter for the day.

All camps offer accommodation and some also offer stands where you can pitch your own tents, though the standard varies. Most camps have a few two- or three-bed units, supplemented by cottages and chalets sleeping up to six people. Camp gates open at 04.30, an hour before park entrance gates open.

By African standards, the Kruger Park remains relatively inexpensive. An entrance fee equivalent to around US$10 is charged for two people and a vehicle, no matter whether they stay in the park for an hour or for two weeks. The cheapest option is to camp, which costs around US$10–15 per stand depending on how many people occupy it. A room for two will typically work out at between US$30 and US$50.

Day passes, accommodation and camping within the Kruger Park should be reserved through the National Parks Board offices in Pretoria or Cape Town (South African National Parks, PO Box 787, Pretoria, 0001; tel: 12 343 1991; fax: 12 343 0905; email: reservations@parks-sa.co.za). Reservations can also be made through Computicket.

A full list of the accommodation options and prices at each camp can be obtained from them. Bookings are passed to the individual camps only the day before the one for which the booking was made, so there is no point in contacting the camps except at short notice. Although the camps to the north of Letaba are infrequently visited by international tourists, it is reasonable to assume that they will be booked solid well in advance.

With the exception of Balule, Bataleur and Sirheni (see below), all the camps have restaurants serving unremarkable but inexpensive snacks and meals, as well as small shops stocking frozen meat, tinned foodstuffs, firewood, soft drinks and alcohol. All accommodation units and camping stands in the park have private standing barbecues (most accommodation units also have a fridge), and visitors to camps without shops can easily stock up at one of the larger camps.

Camps within the path of totality

Five camps lie in the total eclipse path. Apart from the two picnic sites mentioned above, these are the only places where visitors are allowed to leave their vehicles, and are thus the best places from which to view the eclipse as well as the only places in which to stay.

Shingwedzi Camp (79 units/292 beds/50 camping stands) is a personal favourite and should be the best location since it lies practically at the centre of the line of totality, which means the full eclipse will endure for longer than a minute. It has facilities for day visitors.

The bird hide a short distance south of Shingwedzi could be even more stunning but it is not very big and would not offer much of a view should you be trapped at the back. The nearby Kanniedood Dam offers excellent game-viewing and birding. Those staying at **Punda Maria** (23 units/54 beds/48 stands), which is another personal favourite, could view the eclipse from the camp itself. It has an intimate atmosphere and lies close to the central path of the eclipse, with first contact beginning at 07.12 and totality lasting 1 minute 20 seconds. There is some excellent game-viewing along the Pafuri River to its north. There are facilities for day visitors.

Sirheni (15 units/70 beds/no camping stands) is not open to day trippers. It has a fine central location and an intimate atmosphere. **Bataleur** (7 units/35 beds) lies midway between the central line and the southern limit of the path of totality. It is within easy driving distance of Shingwedzi. Like Sirheni, it is pleasantly small and not open to day-trippers.

Mopane Camp (106 units/320 beds) lies just within the southern fringe of the path of totality, which means the full eclipse will be very brief, so people staying here might consider driving the roughly 70km north to Shingwedzi (there is nowhere between these two camps where one may leave the vehicle). Mopane is a relatively modern camp, and more spaciously laid out than most, though I have always found it somewhat sterile and feel that the surrounding area is rather unrewarding for game-viewing.

Camps outside the path of totality

Bearing in mind that the speed limit within the park is 50km/h, that one would want to reach the path of totality before first contact at 07.10, and that elephants may sometimes enforce their right of way, there are four camps from which one could reliably reach the most southerly point from which the full eclipse will be visible (Mooiplaas picnic site). These add another 370 accommodation units with a total of around 1,000 beds, and another 100 camping stands.

Letaba (95 units/320 beds/30 stands) is the closest at a distance of 35km, and regarded by many as the best camp in the park, with an excellent location fringing the seasonal Letaba River. From here you could conceivably drive the extra 70km to reach Shingwedzi at the heart of totality.

Olifants Camp (108 units/290 beds), has an even better setting, on a rise overlooking the perennial Olifants River, but at a distance of 85km it is further from the line of totality and the only camp of the four not to offer camping stands.

Nearby **Balule** (5 units/15 beds /10 stands) is the smallest, most low-key camp in the park, lying 89 km from totality. It has a genuine bush atmosphere that makes it another personal favourite.

The most southerly spot possible is 125km away at **Satara** (162 units/406 beds/60 stands). This is the second-largest camp in the park, though singularly grim. It is, however, in a prime location where lion and cheetah are regularly encountered.

Staying outside Kruger

Phalaborwa is the only substantial town from which one could enter Kruger on a day-trip. The Phalaborwa Gate, which lies on the outskirts of town, opens at 05.30 in December. From there it is a 60km drive to Mooiplaas Picnic Site, which can easily be covered before the eclipse starts at approximately 07.10. Essentially a mining town, Phalaborwa does boast a dozen or so moderately priced hotels and guesthouses predominantly geared to travelling South African businessmen. The largest and probably the best hotel is the 55-room **Impala Protea Inn** (tel: 015 24 85681; fax: 01524 85234). Avis and a few other car rental firms have offices at the airport. You could also stay at **Elephant Walk** (30 Anna Scheepers Av; tel/fax: 015 781 2758; email: elephant.walk@nix.co.za) – a backpackers' hostel which could also be a useful source of advice. Accommodation costs about R50 (approx US$8) per person, camping R25 (approx US$4), free pick-up from anywhere in town. The hostel offers a Kruger Park Day Trip for about US$40.

The helpful **Turnkey Tours** (tel: 015 781 6770; fax: 015 781 5235), which effectively serves as the Phalaborwa tourist office, is the best source of current details of other accommodation options, car hire, flights and coach services. Its office is close to the Kruger National Park entrance gate, which forms the eastern boundary of the town centre.

Where to watch the eclipse

Apart from the camps that lie within totality (see below) there are also two designated picnic sites, both with toilets, barbecue stands, shady seating areas, and a limited selection of cold drinks for sale.

Mooiplaas picnic site lies a few kilometres south of Mopane Camp within the southern fringe of the path of totality. Babalala picnic site lies along the tar road towards Shingwedzi close to the central line of the path of totality.

No special permit is required to visit camps or picnic sites once you are in the park. Just drive in and park.

Messina

One suspects that this sleepy provincial town 16km south of the Zimbabwe border crossing at Beitbridge won't quite know what has hit it come December 4 2002. In ordinary circumstances, Messina is the sort of South African everytown that one would drive through, perhaps stopping to buy a cold drink or fill up with petrol, and barely remember what it looked like a day later.

Unremarkable as it may be, Messina will be the obvious urban focus for viewing the eclipse, with first contact at 07.11. It is linked to Johannesburg and Pretoria by the excellent N2 trunk road and a plethora of minibuses and coaches. It is also blessed with good amenities in the form of restaurants and shops. To find out about special eclipse arrangements closer to the event contact the tourist office on 015 534 0211.

Where to stay
In Messina town
The town has rather limited accommodation facilities. South Africa being the well-regulated country it is, I wouldn't like to bank on the council welcoming free campers with open arms.

The largest hotel in Messina is the 42-room **Impala Lily Motel** (tel/fax: 015 534 0127), an unpretentious, moderately priced affair with swimming pool, air-conditioning, a fair restaurant and well-wooded gardens. The only other hotel proper is the smaller **Limpopo River Lodge** (tel/fax: 015 534 0204), though the tourist office can provide current details of the few small private guesthouses that are scattered around town, and will also take bookings for the attractively shady **municipal campsite**.

Outside Messina
It will certainly be possible to visit Messina as a day-trip in time to see the eclipse, provided that you have private transport. You would have 2½ hours of daylight to get there in time. Working on the local speed limit of 120km/h, this would make the towns of Louis Trichardt (95km south along the N1) and Pietersburg (210km) feasible points from which to drive to Messina for the day. These are two of the largest towns in Northern Province, and between them they must have about ten times the bed space of Messina.

By far the largest hotel in this part of the world is the **Pietersburg Holiday Inn Garden Court** (tel: 015 291 2030; fax: 015 291 3150) which has 178 air-conditioned rooms and good facilities including a swimming pool. Larger hotels in and around Louis Trichardt include **Clouds End** (tel: 015 516 9621; fax: 015 516 9787), **Bergwater** (tel/fax: 015 516 0262) and **Mountain View** (tel/fax: 015 516 9631). But there are plenty of options, and the respective tourist offices will be able to provide current details; contact the Louis Trichardt Publicity Association (tel: 015 516 0040) or Pietersburg Publicity Association (tel: 015 295 3025). By tourist-class standards, accommodation in this part of South Africa is uniformly inexpensive, and at none of the above places are you likely to pay anything close to US$100 for a double room (unless special rates are charged for the eclipse). There is, however, little in the way of campsites or backpacker accommodation in either town.

Where to watch the eclipse
The attractive Messina Baobab Reserve a short distance from the town centre might make a more harmonious viewing point than the town itself. To add an extra seven seconds to the length of totality you could consider nipping over the Zimbabwean border to Beitbridge, which should not be a problem if you have a multiple entry visa. But be warned: the Zimbabwean border officials at Beitbridge are among the most difficult I have come across in Africa.

There is a garage/restaurant complex at the border and regular minibuses run from Messina up to the South African side, about 20 minutes' drive.

Other eclipse-viewing sites
Aside from Messina and the northern Kruger Park, there are few places where you'd realistically want to find yourself on the day of the eclipse. No other settlement that could by any stretch of the imagination be called a town lies within the path of totality; the closest is Thohoyandou, former capital of the Venda homeland, which falls just south of the path, and has fewer tourist facilities than Messina, Pietersburg or Louis Trichardt.

Two small game reserves lie within the path of totality to the southeast of Messina. The more central of these is the **Nwanedi Game Reserve** (tel: 015 593 9703) which was formerly a national park administered by the government of the defunct homeland of Venda, and harbours a good range of large mammals including cheetah, rhino, giraffe and various antelope. Facilities include a few self-catering huts and a small campsite. This should be an excellent target for self-drive tourists who don't mind cooking for themselves, though advance booking will almost certainly be necessary.

Closer to the southern edge of the path of totality, but with better facilities, the **Honnet Nature Reserve** harbours a variety of antelope and other harmless large mammals. The main tourist focus here is the inexpensive **Tshipise Aventura Resort** (tel: 012 428 7600; fax: 012 428 7649; email: info@aventura.co.za) on the northern border of the reserve, which offers 100-odd self-catering units and has a large campsite and restaurant. Accommodation works out at around US$40 for a double and camping at US$8 per site plus US$3 per person. There is also an overnight hiking trail with a 12-bed hut in the reserve.

A final possibility is **Mapungubwe Hill** (see page 105), which lies 75km from Messina West off the Pontdrift road and which you would have to visit as a day-trip. The combination of high elevation above a river and the atmospheric ruins certainly sounds compelling. If you think of heading out this way, the tourist office in Messina can offer advice.

FURTHER READING FROM BRADT

Africa by Road, Charlie Shackell and Illya Bracht
East and Southern Africa: The Backpacker's Manual, Philip Briggs
Guide to South Africa, Philip Briggs
South Africa: The Bradt Budget Guide, Paul Ash (due summer 2001)
Southern Africa by Rail, Paul Ash

Mozambique
Mike Slater

Visiting the eclipse areas
OVERVIEW
Last total solar eclipse: May 1919
Next total solar eclipse after 2002: August 2046

Mozambique was for 300 years a colony of Portugal. More recently the country has recovered remarkably well from a civil war which lasted decades, ending only in 1992. Unfortunately, it is still reeling from the effects of disastrous floods that killed scores and left hundreds of thousands homeless along the valleys of the Limpopo and Save rivers during early 2000.

As a result of this recent history the tourism sector, although growing exponentially, is quite unsophisticated and undeveloped when compared with neighbouring countries such as Zimbabwe and South Africa. Eclipse-chasers who travel to Mozambique for either the 2001 or the 2002 celestial event should be prepared to 'rough it' to a certain degree. Unless you are booked into one of the best hotels available (some of which will be built after this guide has gone to press) you should not expect facilities even approaching tourist standard. Adventurous travellers, however, will be able to view the 2001 eclipse from locations as exciting and unusual as a 3.7km bridge over the Zambezi at Sena, or from a beach on an isolated island in the heart of the Zambezi delta near Chinde.

There is likely to be no official response to either eclipse, and no formal recognition from the government tourist sector of their significance. By contrast, the private tour operators and lodge owners I have spoken to are enthusiastic about the eclipses and many will be able to lay on packages and excursions on request.

I suspect that for most tourists the easiest way to see the 2001 eclipse will be to head out from Harare, in Zimbabwe, or Blantyre, in Malawi, spending one or two nights in Mozambique before returning. For the 2002 eclipse, visitors can include the event in a longer tour of the southern Mozambique coastline which is well serviced by comfortable beach lodges.

The 2001 eclipse occurs at the beginning of the best season for visiting Mozambique, when temperatures are low and there is little rain. However, for those who want to combine their trip with birdwatching, the 2002 eclipse could not fall at a better time, in the middle of the rainy season. The big risk is cloud.

Please note that by law all adults in Mozambique must carry identification at all times. It is not often asked for, except perhaps if you are wandering around Maputo at night. But if you cannot produce it, you may have to 'bail' yourself out of a night in jail by paying a 'fine'.

Camping is fine in Mozambique. In rural areas, always ask to see the chief (*regulo*) and explain or show what you intend to do and why. Do not camp away from locals for fear of landmines and opportunist thieves waiting for the

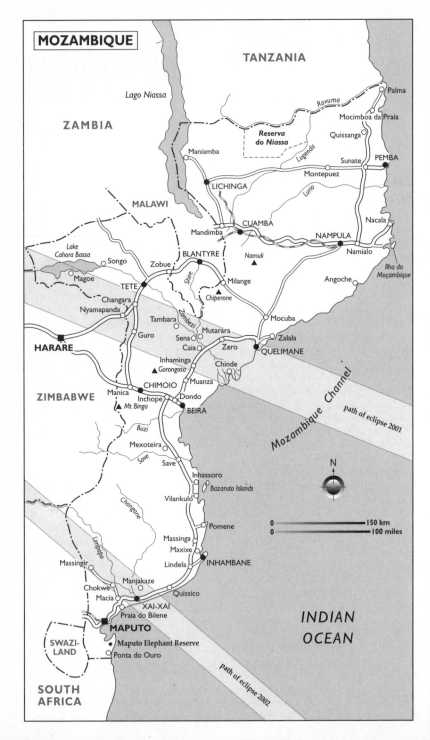

WHAT I WILL DO FOR THE 2002 ECLIPSE

I will be driving my 78 Kombi around. It's fitted for camping so that is what I'll do mostly. En route from Joburg I'll stay over in Barberton (turn right at Nelspruit) and then take the Bulembu/Piggs Peak route into Swaziland where I'll stay awhile at the Hlane Game Reserve just before the Lomahasha/Namaacha border. My first night in Mozambique will be at Fatima's Backpackers in the heart of Maputo, one of my favourite cities, after which I will head to Marracuene, park my bus and take a boat transfer up the Incomati River to the Incomati River Camp where I'll eat crab curry and watch the river for a few days. From there it's just an hour to Casa Lisa where I'll philosophise with Liz and Paul about this eclipse thing and carry on up to Bilene to check in for a little bit of luxury at Praia do Sol.

From Bilene it's just a couple of hours up across the Limpopo to Xai-Xai town and nearby Praia do Xai-Xai where I'll check in to the brand new and quite expensive and extravagant Xai-Xai Beach Hotel which is so close to the sand that if you fall off your bar stool, you're there. On the big day I'll charter a boat from the nearby fishing camp and instead of heading out to sea, we'll head up the Limpopo. Using a Global Positioning System receiver, we'll anchor exactly on the centre-line close to Chibuto with our bottle (or six) of Moët handy, get plastered, fall out of the boat and miss the moment.

moment when you are away gazing at the Sun. Great places to camp are next to the traditional wood-and-thatch churches (*egresas*) which have reed-fence enclosures behind them (one is a pit toilet and the other a place to wash). If you hang around there, the elders or *secretario* will soon arrive and make you feel very welcome.

For more information on Mozambique you can try the website www.bootsnall.com, and the Bradt website, for updated eclipse information, on www.bradt-travelguides.com. Mozambique's international telephone code is 258.

ORGANISED TOURS

The following companies should offer tours for both eclipses. For operators specialising only in one eclipse see the relevant section below.

UK

Rainbow Tours 64 Essex Rd, London N1 8LR; tel: 020 7226 1004; fax: 020 7226 2621; email: info@rainbowtours.co.uk ; web: www.rainbowtours.co.uk . 18-day camping safari through South Africa, Mozambique, Zambia and Botswana, viewing the 2001 eclipse from Changara in Mozambique. Cost: £1,645 per person. Also, 16-night tour of Malawi and Mozambique, viewing eclipse from near Tete. Provisional cost: £2,795 per person. Trip planned for 2002.

South Africa

Mozambique Travel Services Johannesburg; tel/fax: (27) 11 659 1766; email: moztrav@mweb.co.za
Mozambique Connection Johannesburg; tel: (27) 11 803 4185; fax: (27) 11 803 3861; web: www.mozambiqueconnection.co.za
Serendipity Leisure Cruises Johannesburg; tel/fax: (27) 11 678 0831; email: slcruise@mweb.co.za. This firm will run eclipse trips on chartered yachts.

Starlight Cruises tel: (27) 11 807 5111; web: www.starlight.co.za. This firm operates a 21,000-ton cruise ship, the *Monterey*, in the Mozambique Channel, and has indicated that special eclipse departures are likely.

Unusual Destinations Johannesburg; tel/fax: (27) 11 706 1991; fax: (27) 11 463 1469; web: www.unusualdestinations.com

Zimbabwe

MOZAIC Harare, Zimbabwe; tel/fax: (263) 4 301 164; email: traveller@primenetzw.com; web:www.icon.co.zw/mozaic

Finally, I am a specialist tour guide to unexplored parts of Mozambique. I charge a basic rate of US$30 per hour to put together information regarding specific trips people want to undertake independently, or US$150 per day plus expenses to accompany a trip. My contact details are: tel: (27) 11 482 6795; fax: (27) 11 482 6795; email: mozman@my-deja.com; web: www.mozguide.com.

GETTING AROUND

By air

Linhas Aereas de Mocambique (LAM) (tel: 1 42 3355; web: www.lam.co.mz) is the Maputo-based Mozambican domestic and international airline. It flies from Maputo to Quelimane and Tete, and to Harare via Beira. It recently introduced a youth fare (for under-26-year-olds) which offers a discount of 40%. Always confirm internal flights at least twice, especially the day before: the airline tends to follow a 'first come, first served' rule regardless of who has paid for tickets and who has not. Schedules change about three times a year.

By public transport

Public transport varies widely across the country, affected by such matters as the quality of roads. There is regular transport to major towns in the south from Maputo, and transport is also frequent along the Tete Corridor in the west. Breakdowns are frequent everywhere.

By car

The roads in Mozambique are highly variable, from those barely negotiable with a 4WD to well-maintained tarmac. Overgrown tracks not used by the locals should be avoided because of landmines. Always ask the local *regulo* (traditional chief) or *secretario* (government administrator) to find someone to accompany you in very remote areas. You will be expected to feed him and pay him about US$10 per day, as well as tipping the *regulo*.

Driving at night is very dangerous because of trucks without lights, especially the ones that break down – or park – in the middle of the road. Drunks are another road obstacle – they tend to jump out bravely in front of vehicles at the last minute.

There are car hire firms in Maputo but there are none in the region of the 2001 eclipse. To take a car into Mozambique from a neighbouring country you must be in possession of the original and notarised copies of registration papers, as well as your driver's licence (international recommended, not obligatory). At the border (whether Nyamapanda/Cuchumano from Zimbabwe or Mwanza/Zobue from Malawi or Lebombo/Ressano Garcia from South Africa) you will have to pay a tax of around US$10 per person, as well as US$20 per vehicle for a temporary import permit (TIP) and 3rd-party insurance (*seguros*) for around US$20. Insist that you buy all of these as, if you cannot produce proper documentation at police checkpoints, you could be heavily fined.

However, never hand over the originals of any of the documents as officials might not return them without a bribe.

Hitchhiking

Normally, hitchhikers are expected to pay, so ask how much it is before you get in. An exception is along the Tete Corridor route where you may pick up a free lift with South African tourists. Try not to hitch after midday as many drivers will be drunk.

By bicycle and on foot

Mozambique is a fairly cycle-friendly country and many people use bicycles to travel long distances. However, one aspect is definitely not cycle-friendly – the (probably often inebriated) truck and bus drivers who steer their monstrous machines with scant consideration for other road users. I have cycled these roads and found people living along them provided me with everything I needed – at the cost of smiles and handshakes. But I had sometimes to pull right off the road when trucks and buses approached from the rear.

It is not practical or advisable to walk long distances in Mozambique because of the huge tracts of emptiness between towns, as well as a real threat of landmines 'off the beaten track'.

The 2001 eclipse
OVERVIEW

The eclipse bisects Mozambique's central regions – the provinces of Manica, Tete, Sofala and Zambezia.

Manica and Tete are landlocked while Sofala and Zambezia have a 600km coastline split by the 130km-wide delta at the mouth of the mighty Zambezi River. Here Mozambique, which is generally a long and thin country, suddenly bulges westwards, meeting Zambia some 1,200km from the Mozambique Channel. Tete province is dominated by the 250km-long Lake Cahora Bassa formed behind a dam wall 160m high, across the Zambezi River at Songo.

The 2001 route does not fall anywhere near the traditional tourist destinations within Mozambique. This is a poor, undeveloped region compared with the south, although it is correspondingly more friendly. If visiting this area go well-equipped, with a tent and sleeping bags. You can buy food. This is such a difficult region for travelling that, unless doing a straightforward jaunt in your own car along the Tete Corridor, you should allow plenty of time to get to your viewing site and try to arrive the day before.

First contact enters the far northwestern corner of Mozambique, at 13.47, at Zumbo, the largest village (population about 20,000) in an area where vehicle access other than via Zambia is almost impossible, even in a 4WD. The centre of the shadow will then move along the Mozambique/Zimbabwe frontier, passing over the southernmost reaches of Lake Cahora Bassa near Mucumbura, before vaguely following the Zambezi down to its delta at Chinde, where it will arrive at 14.00.

The period June–November is the driest part of the year throughout Mozambique, so this eclipse will not be obliterated by a tropical cyclone, or have the road to the centre-line swamped by a flash flood the day before or after.

Unfortunately this does not mean that skies will be cloudless. Rising thermals of air over the warm land will still bear enough moisture to produce widespread high-altitude riffles of fair-weather cumulus cloud. To minimise the chance of clumps of condensed water vapour ruining your big day, get as close to the sea as you can, or even get out over the waves in a suitable boat (see *Organised tours*). Note too that the 2,000km² lake, Cahora Bassa, is like an 'inland sea' which will also have a cooling (and therefore clearing) influence on the skies above.

June–September is the cooler season in Mozambique and temperatures can drop to around 10°C at night, rising to above 30°C during the day along the coast. Coastal areas, such as Chinde, do benefit from the cooling effects of onshore breezes and during evenings and mornings they are visited by a cool, creepy, fine mist which the locals call *kassi-kassi* as it is accompanied by a slight breeze which rustles the fronds of the coconut palms.

The staple diet of the inland tribes (Ama-Shona and Tchena) is a porridge called *ncima* made from pulverised maize kernels. Closer to the coastline most people (Macua and Chuabo tribes) obtain their protein from the fish they catch in their huge sea-going dugout canoes known in the Chuabo language as *ingalaoa*. They also eat a lot of *mu-kwane*, a dish made from coconut mixed with the leaves of the *mandioca* (cassava) plant.

ORGANISED TOURS

Even though there may be few tourist facilities in the area, and certainly no operators permanently based in either Tete or Quelimane, there should be the odd tour put on by a specialist travel agency or tour operator such as those listed above. Try **Unusual Destinations** (see above) which will be leading an eclipse trip to Quelimane.

GATEWAY CITIES

Neither Tete nor Quelimane is easily accessible from Mozambique's capital city, Maputo, other than by air. So, unless you are planning to look around the southeastern shores of the Mozambican Channel (which has superb beaches), common sense dictates that you use either Harare (Zimbabwe) or Blantyre (Malawi) as your springboard to the heart of Mozambique.

Harare

This would be a good base for those who want to see the eclipse in the remoteness of Mozambique but would prefer the logistically easier and more comfortable option of spending the rest of their trip in Zimbabwe. The Mozambique visa office in Harare is at the embassy (152 Herbert Chitepo Avenue; tel: (263) 4 790 837; fax: (263) 4 732 898) which has a reputation for being very disorganised – so travellers should not expect to get a visa in one day although it is officially possible. Visa charges decline depending on how long you are prepared to wait. Best to ask for a 30-day tourist visa (US$10–20). A transit visa, although cheaper, is valid for only two days, which will not be enough, and the fine for overstaying is US$100 per day.

Harare has numerous car-hire companies, some of which allow their vehicles over the border and offer reliable 4WD pick-ups for those heading to the Sena Bridge via Tete. An excellent firm is MOZAIC, a Harare-based Mozambique specialist (see *Organised tours*, above). If you are driving over the border into Mozambique do not forget the essential motoring documents (see *Getting around*). For more information on Harare, see *Zimbabwe*, page 85.

Blantyre

Blantyre could be a useful base for getting to the Tete Corridor to view the eclipse. Alternatively you could head southeast from Blantyre to reach Quelimane and view the eclipse from the coast. To obtain Mozambique visas yourself in Malawi go to Limbe (next to Blantyre). The visa office – friendly and well-organised – lies on the Masauko Chipembere (formerly Kamuzu) Highway (Nunes Building, next to Maselema post office; tel: (265) 64 3189).

However, you could also try Doogles Lodge (tel: (265) 621128; email: doogles@malawi.net) which is just behind the Stage-Coach bus station and has staff well used to dealing with the vagaries of getting into Mozambique. Some may find Doogles a tad impersonal, but its staff have a thorough knowledge of the needs of all types of traveller in this area of Africa.

Blantyre is not well served by car hire and many companies may not be insured for Mozambique, so their vehicles cannot be taken over the border.

GETTING AROUND
By air
Both Quelimane and Tete are served by LAM from Maputo, each flight being about US$300 return. There are six flights a week to Quelimane and three a week to Tete. There are charter flights between Quelimane and Chinde (see below).

By public transport
There is plenty of public transport along the main Tete Corridor between Zimbabwe, Tete and Malawi. Known as the 'gun run' until the civil war ended in 1992, it has become one of the principal routes through Africa.

There is also public transport to Quelimane from Blantyre and Nampula. And there is regular public transport from Quelimane to Caia in the form of trucks, taxis, pick-ups and the odd bus (though they are uncomfortable and susceptible to breakdown).

By car
Cuchumano (on the Zimbabwe border), Changara and Tete are linked by the tarmac road from both Harare and Blantyre. It is generally well maintained (but badly pot-holed along some stretches between Cuchumano and Zobue).

The 300km-long, and very lonely, link from Zambia via Cassacatiza is an outside option if you happen to be in that area, but the surface is in poor condition and a 4WD vehicle is recommended.

You cannot hire cars in Tete or Quelimane but you may be able to commandeer a sedan, more used to making the run between Quelimane and the airport, for a long-distance drive to Caia.

By bicycle and on foot
Feel free to walk across well-trodden areas such as Sena Bridge, or to wander around Chinde (no cars anyway), but do not under any circumstances go into areas not used by the local people as this is almost certainly due to the presence of landmines and unexploded ammunition.

By boat
Quelimane is not accessible by the liners that serve the eastern shores of Africa because it is one of Africa's few true river ports, lying 7km from the coast. There is, however, an irregular service between Beira and Quelimane run by AMI or Mocarga (both on Avenue Poder Popular, Beira). There are also coastal trawlers which do the Quelimane–Chinde run on an irregular basis. Travellers with more time on their hands than cash might arrive in the area a few days early in order to negotiate such a passage.

The barges that once linked Tete with villages as far downstream as Chinde no longer operate because of the past civil strife and the silting up of the lower reaches of the Zambezi.

ECLIPSE CENTRES: THE WEST
Overview
The west includes both the most accessible and the most inaccessible eclipse-viewing centres. The Tete Corridor is a good road that actually bisects the centreline. For those who want a more challenging trip there are the rewards of Lake Cahora Bassa.

Gateway town: Tete
Tete, along with Quelimane, will provide the accommodation for most of the Mozambique sky-gazers. Tete is the land of the *embondeiro* (baobab), a bizarre, almost fairytale tree with its bulbous, grey, elephantine trunk and girth of up to 50m. Located at a point where people have been crossing the mighty Zambezi River for thousands of years, Tete town is a typical 'bridge settlement'. Although an important town from a historical point of view, it is rather dreary, dry and dusty. It lies on the banks of one of the world's greatest rivers but is by no means picturesque. For much of the last century, a vehicle ferry linked Tete (and therefore Zimbabwe) to Malawi and the rest of Africa, but in 1960 an impressive 800m-long suspension bridge replaced the barge.

Tete has fuel stations, supermarkets, hotels, restaurants, banks, international public telephones, a hospital (only for real emergencies) and vehicle spares.

Where to stay
Coming from Changara you will drop down almost to river level as you arrive on the outskirts of Tete and, just around a long left bend, you will see **Motel Tete** (tel: 52 22 345; fax: 52 22 625; US$60 double) just off the Estrada Nacional 103. This is the newest and possibly nicest place to stay in Tete at present because of its air-conditioned en-suite double rooms overlooking the 'Old Man' Zambezi River just a stone's throw away. At seven storeys, **Hotel Zambeze** (tel: 52 23003) in the middle of town is easily the tallest building in Tete, but while the views from its rooftop terrace may be impressive, the level of service usually is not. Better bets are **Pensão Central** (tel: 52 22 523; US$20 double) next to the Governor's Quarter, and **Pensão Alves** (Avenida 25 de Junho; tel: 52 22523; US$20 double). Both have air-conditioned rooms. Campers can head for the **Complexo A Piscina** (tel: 52 24021; US$20 double), which has a (usually fetid) swimming pool, air-conditioned double rooms and grassed areas where you can pitch your tent. A Piscina is tucked away next to the bridge, on the downstream side. For eating, I have enjoyed excellent breakfasts at **Motel Tete**, delicious lunches at **Restaurant Freitas** (next to A Piscina) and great evening meals at the **Pensão Central**. Prices are in the US$2–10 range. I have been told that Jemba, on the waterfront upstream from the bridge, and Pastelaria Confiancia (a bakery) on Avenida 25 de Junho are also well worth a look-in.

Pre- and post-eclipse excursions
Around Lake Cahora Bassa
A visit to the spectacular **dam site** is well worthwhile. To get a permit call at the HCB (Hidro-electrica Cahora Bassa) office in Avenue 25 de Junho in Cahora Bassa. If you want to get to the lake without a permit and/or feel like hunting for tiger fish, go to the boom below the road up to Songo and ask for the Ugezi Lodge

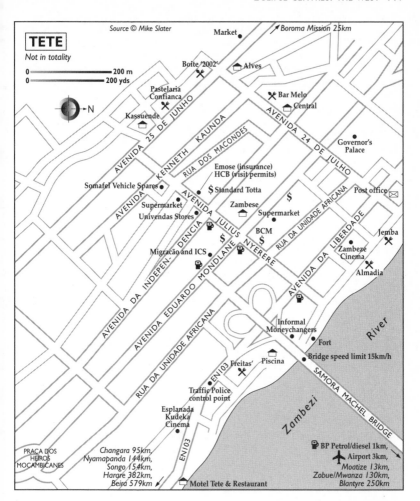

TETE
Not in totality

Source © Mike Slater

(tel: 152 297 3401; fax: 152 297 3402; US$80 per person). It has fully equipped, safari-style tents.

From Tete

A pleasant trip is to take a 4WD (or hitchhike from beyond the *mercado*) up to the old **Boroma Mission**.

You reach it by going up Avenida Julius Nyerere, turning right at the T-junction into 25 de Junho, going out past the hospital and turning left before the turning to an airfield. Then carry on for about 40km.

The eclipse zone
Lake Cahora Bassa

About half of this 250km-long lake lies under the total shadow zone but, compared with other eclipse lakes such as Kariba in Zimbabwe, Cahora Bassa is almost devoid of tourist facilities. The only real options are a couple of fishing lodges from which you could make a foray to the eclipse path for a really isolated viewing. You could also try the first spot in Mozambique to be overshadowed – the remote hamlet of Zumbo in the extreme northwest corner of Tete province. Zumbo's inaccessibility and lack of creature comforts may exclude it from being a popular spot but, as it overlooks the headwaters of one of the world's greatest artificial lakes, the rewards may outweigh the effort of getting there.

Getting there and away
To get to Zumbo the only feasible route is from Zambia, so you will have to get a visa from the Mozambique embassy in Lusaka (Lufubu Road, Plot no 5627; tel: (260) 1 291 251; fax: (260) 1 290 411). This is smuggler territory and it is best not to go there without someone who is familiar with the area.

Don't even contemplate making it to Magoe, on the southern side of the lake, unless you have a 4WD vehicle. Take the Enterprise Road from Harare in the direction of Mutoko/Nyamapanda. After about 25km turn left to Shamva (signposted). Carry on for an hour or so through Shamva and Mt Darwin. About 15km from Mt Darwin on a good tarmac road, turn right on to gravel towards Mukumbura. Show your passport with visa at the border (08.00–16.00) and then carry on along a rough track for around 100km to Magoe. There, ask for directions to Johan Hougaard's camp at Magoe. Allow plenty of time – you want to be in place before first contact at 13.49.

Where to stay
Apart from camping, the only possibilities are the lodges at Magoe and Songo. At Magoe, Johan Hougaard (tel: (263) 4 40 9191) runs fishing rigs for kapenta (a sort of fresh-water sardine) and has set up a tented camp for fanatical fishermen seeking to do battle with the ferocious tiger fish. His tents (US$80 per person per day) have double beds, electricity and fans and there is a separate ablution block. Contact details for Songo are above (see *Pre- and post-eclipse excursions*).

Where to watch the eclipse
At Magoe and Songo you should be able to hire boats by prior arrangement to take you to a choice eclipse-viewing site. From Magoe, which lies on the edge of totality, you would need to boat west along the lake to be sure of being well in the path, perhaps then turning south to where the Musengezi River meets the lake, to be as near to the centre-line as possible. From Songo, well outside totality, you would need to travel at least 130km west along the lake to reach even the edge of the path of totality.

The Tete Corridor
Sadly the wide Zambezi at Tete is outside the path of totality so those in Tete will have to head in the direction of Changara on the big day. However, the Tete Corridor bisects the eclipse path and so there are many sites further to the west from which you could view the eclipse.

Getting there and away
If travelling from Tete, your only option is to take public transport in a westerly direction because there is no vehicle hire in that town. Journey times vary greatly, mainly because of frequent breakdowns. Tete to Nyamapanda should take two to three hours while Tete to Changara should take about two hours. At Changara you have the option of either turning right and carrying on for around 40km towards Zimbabwe, or turning left and carrying on for 40km towards Guro. Either way you will end up on a tarred road in the middle of the bush but, because the Nyamapanda road climbs up a small escarpment offering superior views, I recommend this choice.

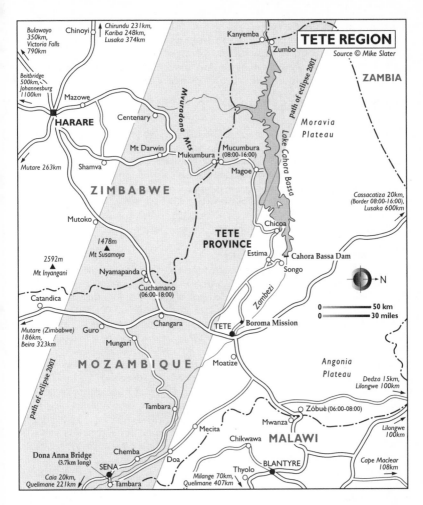

Coming from Zimbabwe you could drive, catch a lift or, if in a group, walk across the border and carry on for about an hour to the centre-line. Do not stray from the hard shoulder as this area was extensively mined. If petty paperwork at the Nyamapanda/Cuchumano frontier-post conspires to delay your entry into Mozambique from Zimbabwe, cast your eyes to the heavens for succour as you will be only a short distance from the centre-line anyway.

Where to stay

If you do not stay in Tete, Blantyre or Harare (see above) there are few alternatives except for near the border post between Mozambique and Zimbabwe. On the Mozambique side of the border, Cuchumano is little more than a customs and immigration post, a short row of government houses and a few informal roadside bars. Nyamapanda, just a few hundred metres away in Zimbabwe, is better developed and has a couple of service stations, restaurants (trucker stops) and a caravan and camping park which is about 10km out on the road towards Harare. This would make a good base for a walk, cycle or drive into Mozambique to the centre-line on the day.

Where to watch the eclipse

First contact hits Nyamapanda at 13.53 and totality lasts 3 minutes 15 seconds. Perhaps the best place to view on the Changara–Harare road is close to the Zimbabwe border on the Mozambique side, which has the benefits of height and being bang on the centre-line, 4km before Cuchumano.

ECLIPSE CENTRES: THE EAST
Overview

The east is, overall, even more inaccessible than the west but the determined will find themselves some spectacular eclipse-viewing sites. The coast, among the millions of regimented coconut palms on Chinde island, should be one of the remotest spots in the 2001 path. Its remoteness is rivalled only by the majestic Sena Dam further inland. The main town in the region is Quelimane which lies quite near the edge of totality, with a total eclipse of 1 minute 18 seconds, and will have one of the best chances of clear skies of all the Mozambique sites – cloud data show that skies will be clearest over coastal areas and probably completely cloudless over the sea.

Pre- and post-eclipse excursions

Praia do Zalala (Zalala beach), just 25km northeast of Quelimane (and outside the umbral path), is beautiful, scattered with statuesque, sea-going canoes. You can get there in your own car or on crowded public transport, in either case along a pot-holed road. You can stay at the Complexo Kassi-Kassi (tel: 4 212 302, fax: 4 213 599) which offers basic beach houses, camping sites, a reasonable restaurant (usually open only over weekends) and a sea breeze which can be a welcome relief from Quelimane's stifling concrete.

If you have a 4WD you could go to **Pebane** which has an excellent swimming and surfing beach (camp here after consultations with the *chefe*). You could take two days (800km) and drive to wonderful, undiscovered **Mozambique Island**. Head north via Mocuba to Alto Mólocuè (stay at Pensão Santa Antonio – en-suite rooms with fans for US$30). Turn east to Nampula and carry on via Monapo to the island (*ilha*) which is linked to the mainland at Lumbo by a causeway – so you can drive right on to it. The easiest place to stay is Hotel Omuhipiti (Pousada de Mozambique) which stands on the narrow neck of the 2km-long island, overlooking a small bay and the fortress. It has air conditioning and modern bathrooms. Enquire about Hotel Omuhipiti through Promotur in Maputo (fax: 1 43 0315) or by emailing the island museum's curator, James, on Ilha@teledata.mz.

The eclipse zone
Quelimane

Quelimane was a strategic location on a main channel of the Zambezi delta until the drought of the 1820s caused it to dry up. It was the gateway to the important trading settlements of the interior, and so attracted the attention of the Portuguese who occupied it during the 17th century. Today this little town is somewhat sweaty even during June, which is its coolest month. It has some interesting architecture, but attracts few tourists as it is not on the coast, and the seas off nearby Zalala beach are dirtied by the outflow of the muddy Zambezi.

Getting there and away

Quelimane is unlikely to be accessible from Beira by road. The swampy route via Dondo and Caia is often still impassable in June even in a 4WD. The best road route to Quelimane is unquestionably from Blantyre via an excellent, recently re-surfaced road to the Mulanje/Milange border and, from there, on a gravel road

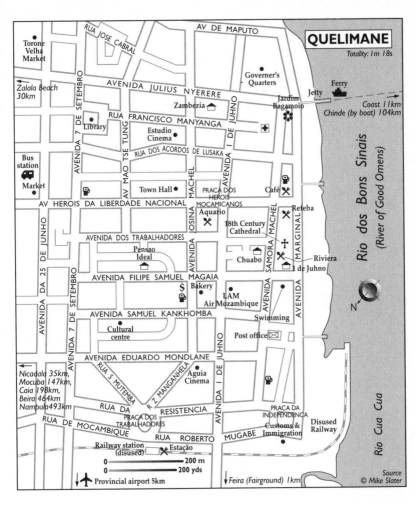

(very slippery when wet) to Mocuba, from where it is good tarmac to Quelimane. It is 189km (three hours) to Mocuba and 148km (two hours) to Quelimane.

Where to stay and eat

For what is really a very small and quite isolated town, accommodation options in Quelimane are surprisingly many and varied. Top of the heap is **Hotel Chuabo** (tel: 4 21 3181; US$100 per person), one street up from the river-road (Marginal). With its air-conditioned suites, expensive furniture and fittings and working lifts this hotel is incongruous in an otherwise quite unassuming array of lodging options. Next is the **Pensão Ideal** (tel: 4 21 2739; US$15 per person) which is well-managed, has air conditioning in some rooms, and offers excellent meals. Third choice and cheapest is the **Hotel Primeiro de Julho** (tel: 4 21 3067; $12 per person), close to the riverside end of Avenida Paulo Samuel Kankhomba (a two-minute walk from the Hotel Chuabo) which is clean and has friendly staff but no air conditioning. Rooms are equipped with fans, and washing water is supplied in buckets in the shared ablution facilities.

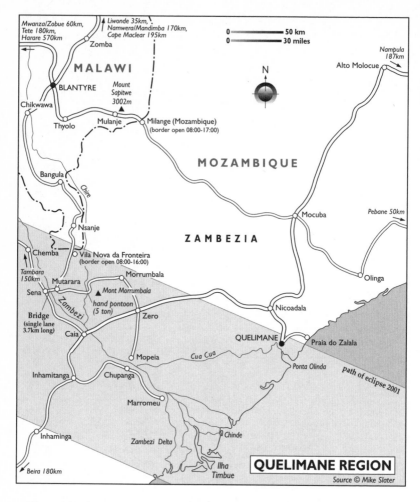

Mwanza/Zobue 60km,
Tete 180km,
Harare 570km

Liwonde 35km,
Namwera/Mandimba 170km,
Cape Maclear 195km

Zomba

0 ⟶ 50 km
0 ⟶ 30 miles

N

Nampula 187km

MALAWI

Alto Molocue

BLANTYRE

Mount Sapitwe 3002m

Chikwawa

Thyolo

Mulanje

Milange (Mozambique)
(border open 08:00-17:00)

MOZAMBIQUE

Bangula

Chire

Mocuba

Pebane 50km

Nsanje

ZAMBEZIA

Chemba

Vila Nova da Fronteira
(border open 08:00-16:00)

Olinga

Tambara 150km

Mutarara

Morrumbala

Sena

Zambezi

Mont Morrumbala
hand pontoon (5 ton)

Zero

Nicoadala

Bridge
(single lane 3.7km long)

Caia

QUELIMANE

Praia do Zalala

Inhamitanga

Chupanga

Mopeia

Cua Cua

Ponta Olinda

Path of eclipse 2001

Marromeu

Inhaminga

Zambezi Delta

Chinde

Beira 180km

Ilha Timbue

QUELIMANE REGION

Source © Mike Slater

You might also consider staying 25km away in Praia do Zalala (see above).

The hotels and *pensões* in Quelimane all have restaurants, but I can only really recommend the Pensão Ideal for consistently good food (best to send someone to order a few hours in advance). Another excellent, clean, if somewhat characterless option is Café Riviera under Hotel 1 de Junho on the corner of Avenida Samuel Magaia and Samora Machel. Riviera's food ranges from *lulas* (calamari-squid) and *camaroes* (prawns) to excellent *caril* (curries), but don't expect a beer or wine with your meal as this establishment is strictly Halal. Refeba, on the Marginal (river road) near the jetty, and Aquario, off the central square, are also worthwhile and the Mercado Central is dotted with stalls offering basic rice and fish or chicken at around US$2.

Where to watch the eclipse

The eclipse hits Quelimane at 14.01. Totality only lasts just over one minute so you may find it worth the effort to travel south, for example to Chinde (below), to increase the time. If you decide to view from Quelimane, try the airport (although the guard there may get a little jumpy if you start waving a camera around). You could also try the 37km road between Quelimane and Nicoadala, which passes through open fields and would give an unobstructed view.

Chinde

It is far better, if difficult, to travel from Quelimane to Chinde to view the eclipse. Chinde, an island in the heart of the expansive Zambezi delta, lies in the middle of dozens of glinting channels amidst millions of bowing coconut palms. The *administrador* of Chinde told me a few years ago that, due to wave and river erosion, his little village gets smaller every time it is flooded by the Zambezi or a tropical cyclone howls in from the east. In fact Chinde should be called Chinde II as the original Chinde, which was an important river port for the export of slaves, wood, ivory and sugar dating back to the 1700s, was claimed by the Indian Ocean breakers a century ago.

Getting there and away

Chinde lies 105km to the southwest of Quelimane and can be accessed only by boat or air charter. Flying to Chinde is worth it even if only for the opportunity to view the sinuous Zambezi delta from the air.

Book the SANAir flight well in advance. You will need to arrive in Quelimane at least one, but preferably two days before June 21 in order to confirm arrangements at the airport in person (mornings are best). Expect to pay around US$150 return (if the plane is full); the flight takes about 30 minutes. Fly-in shadow-seekers will probably have to return on the same day as, if you do not, your flight expenses will double.

The boat option is only for those with much time and little money, as the government ferry (enquire at the jetty near the Governor's Palace) is rusty, unreliable and often not working.

Chinde has almost no facilities for visitors so be self-sufficient (bring your own drinking water) and do not expect to be able to buy anything there except bananas, coconuts and papaya.

Where to stay

Today Chinde is quietly crumbling away, and all overnight visitors are strongly advised to expect to camp and to prepare accordingly (right down to drinking water) as no formal tourist facilities at all remain and there is no electricity. Go straight to the offices of the *administrador* and explain that you wish to be shown a place where *acampar* (camping) is permitted. He may suggest that you stay in his hot, concrete *casa visitar* (guesthouse), but politely indicate how much you like to live in your little tent – in that climate a tent in the sea breeze is far preferable.

Where to watch the eclipse

The coconut palms could obscure the view so the airstrip may be the best place to party.

Caia

Caia is a neat little town with great views of the Zambezi River and Mount Morrumbala. It has the big advantage of being almost exactly on the centre-line and sufficiently near the coast to have a better chance of clear skies than the west.

Getting there and away

To get to Caia from Quelimane you may be able to rent one of the airport sedans (about US$50 per day including driver but excluding fuel). Failing that, *chapas* (local truck taxis), and sometimes buses, leave from the Mercado Municipal (market), which is a 15-minute walk from Hotel Chuabo, every morning at around 05.00. They will get you to the ferry terminal, over the Zambezi from Caia, usually by midday. The ferry (which can take six cars or two large trucks) charges US$20 per car, and runs when full. To avoid waiting and to save money, you can always take one of the small, hand-powered boats and dugouts across the river and walk to Caia, which lies half an hour from the river's edge.

Where to watch the eclipse
The 2km tarmac airstrip adjacent to Caia may be the best viewpoint. Be friendly to any police or officials who approach you as they may not quite understand the purpose of your visit. See page 157 for eclipse-related vocabulary.

The Sena–Mutarara bridge
Getting there and where to stay
Perhaps due to its remote location in a bit of Mozambique that is almost inaccessible after a normal wet season, I should give this spot less prominence. True, the 60km goat track from Caia is not served by any form of local transport – it will be a jarring, seven-hour ride even in the best of 4WDs. And the 250km of rutted and muddy gravel from Tete via Mungari and Tambara will exclude all but the most fanatical. But the majestic Sena bridge is such a brilliant platform that I am sure some of you will be there.

It is three hours from Quelimane to Caia along a good road and then seven hours from Caia to Sena – so getting to Sena even from Caia is not a feasible day-trip. Anyone taking this option should leave at least two days in advance from Quelimane and stay the first night at Caia (or next to the road between Caia and Sena). There are truckers' eating places at the truckers' stop near the ferry terminal. You could camp next to the little airport building at Caia although there are no facilities there. The next day, drive right through Caia to reach the road up to Sena. This track does not offer views of the Zambezi as it follows the wrong side of the railway, which is raised a couple of metres above the flood plain.

At Sena, speak·to the village head (*chefe*) and ask to *acampar*, showing him your tents if necessary to avoid any misunderstanding.

Where to watch the eclipse
The railway bridge (converted for motor cars) is the longest in Africa. The middle of this awesome engineering feat may be just off the centre-line but the unique location and seminal view will more than compensate for this.

Note that if you meet another car going in the opposite direction on the bridge, one of you will have to reverse all the way back as there are no passing bays.

The 2002 eclipse
OVERVIEW
When the 2002 eclipse reaches the Mozambique coast it will pass over some of the country's most highly developed transport, communications and tourism infrastructure. Visitors will be able to choose from a wide variety of hotels, lodges, hostels and camping sites. One of the reasons why this part of the country is so accessible is that there are cheap, daily flights from Johannèsburg with South African Airlines and LAM, and many people fly via that city rather

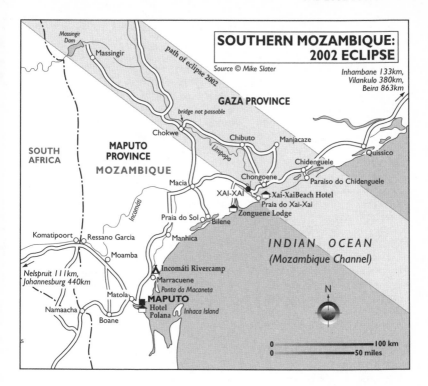

SOUTHERN MOZAMBIQUE: 2002 ECLIPSE

Source © Mike Slater

Inhambane 133km,
Vilankulo 380km,
Beira 863km

than directly to Maputo. Trains and buses also connect Johannesburg with Maputo.

The eclipse enters Mozambique with first contact just after 07.10, passing over the 700m-high Lebombo mountains on the South African border. After that it crosses sparsely populated thorn scrub (bushveld). This strip of Mozambique is dominated by Rudyard Kipling's 'great grey-green, greasy' Limpopo River (Rio Limpopo) and its wide, flat and almost featureless floodplain.

Only at the coast does the landscape change, endless open savannah being replaced by moist coastal forests and extensive plantations of cashew trees. Bordered in the southeast by a string of sparkling lagoons and a strip of seemingly endless golden beaches, this is one of the most beautiful sections of Mozambique's 2,700km long coastline. The eclipse runs out over the warm, azure waters of the Mozambique Channel, which separates southeast Africa from Madagascar, leaving the continent at 09.45 (fourth contact).

Mozambique is also privileged to host the longest period of totality on land for the 2002 eclipse. Totality will be at its longest at a point exactly halfway between Chongoene and Chidengiele on the road from Xai-Xai to Quissico.

Weather-wise, if the rains come early, December in southern Mozambique can be very wet, but historical data show that rain is usually confined to isolated afternoon thundershowers until well into January. The further from the coast one moves, the drier the climate. But in inland areas such as Massingir, slash and burn agriculture is common – the fires reaching a peak just before the January planting season. Smoke may get in your eyes if you choose this option. Onshore winds restrict the coast to a cool 25°C – up to ten degrees lower than inland areas – and the breezes will blow away any smoke that may waft up from the charcoal pits.

December is summer in southern Africa, and this is the main holiday period for South Africans, thousands of whom pack up their 4WDs, hitch up their ski-boats and head for the beautiful beaches south of the Save River. The busiest period at the Lembombo/Ressano Garcia border post is usually the day schools close and for a few days after, and then from January 2 in the opposite direction. If possible, avoid the border on the 'Maputo Corridor' for the first week of December (go via Swaziland). Many South Africans unfortunately do not respect local laws and sensibilities, so there can be a sort of undeclared 'war' going on during this period, one which usually leaves the Mozambican Traffic Police quite a few million meticais richer.

People in the floodplain area are mainly of the Changana tribe, which has a proud history of resistance to Portuguese colonial rule. It was their warrior-chief Gunghunhana (known as the Lion of Gaza) who was finally captured at Chaimate in 1895 and deported to the Azores where he died in 1906. More recently, thousands of men from these districts were recruited to work in the goldmines on the famous reef which runs under the Johannesburg area, and it was upon their sweat and souls that South Africa's relatively strong economy was built. It is not uncommon to hear South African tourists (of whom there could be quite a few during December) communicating with the camp or lodge staff in a simple language, a sort of bastardised mixture of Zulu, Changana and Afrikaans which was for many decades taught in South Africa's mines.

ORGANISED TOURS
Mozambique
I recommend the following:

Eurotravel Tel: 1 49 2446; fax: 1 49 4462; email: eutravel@joafal.uem.mz. Has a reputation for catering for the more budget traveller.
Incomati Safaris Email: incomati@virconn.com. The only full, Mozambique-based tour operator. It is putting together a package for the 2002 eclipse.
Mextur Tel: 1 42 8427; fax: 1 42 8420. Will arrange hotel bookings, car hire and internal flights.

South Africa
Many South African tour operators run overland routes into Mozambique. Some of the operators are listed at the top of the chapter. Others who run trips to the area of the 2002 eclipse include the following:

Drifters Tel: (27) 11 888 1160; fax: (27) 11 888 1020. An excellent budget operator specialising in overland tours to Mozambique, and may put on an eclipse special.
Karibu Safari Tel: (27) 31 563 9774; fax: (27) 31 563 1957; web:www.karibu.co.za. Offers an overland trip which crosses the eclipse path.
Mozambique Connection Tel: (27) 11 803 4185; fax (27) 11 803 3861, web: www.mozambiqueconnection.co.za. Experienced in all aspects of travel to and in Mozambique.
Mozambique Tours and Travel Tel: (27) 31 303 2190; fax: (27) 31 303 2396; web: www.mozambiquetravel.co.za
The Mozambique Travel Centre Tel/fax: (27) 11 701 3756 or 11 659 1766; email: moztrav@mweb.co.za

Finally, **Fatima's Backpackers**, a budget hostel in Maputo, may run minibus trips to the eclipse path.

GATEWAY CITIES
Johannesburg
To obtain a Mozambique visa in Johannesburg go to the Mozambique Consulate (18 Hurlingham Rd, Illovo – a leafy suburb near Rosebank; tel (27) 11 327 2938; fax: (27) 11 327 2945). Visas can be issued in one day (US$18 for 30-day single-entry) so long as your passport will have six-month validity from the date of leaving Mozambique and your application is in before 10.00. It is best to arrive at the consulate at 07.30 to be first in the queue. Visas are cheaper if you can wait a day or three.

You will then have to pay for the visa at any First National Bank (account details at consulate) and return in the afternoon at 14.00 to queue to collect. Due to chaotic queues close to year-end holidays, it may be best to use a visa service – contact Mozambique Connection (see above).

Harare
Harare could be a gateway to the 2002 eclipse as well as to 2001 (see above). The route from Harare to the eclipse path is generally very good though with some bad pot-holes for about 20km as you approach the Save River Bridge. The route is via Mutare, through Gondola and on to Beira. Most people taking this route spend the night at Casa Msika (tel: 51 22675; fax: 51 22701) which has an excellent restaurant, campsite and bungalows and is 117km along the road from Mutare to Beira. Otherwise there is at present nowhere else to stay and camping along the main road is not advisable because of incidents of banditry.

Maputo
The capital city of Mozambique, Maputo (formerly Lourenço Marques), is a busy, beautiful blend of Portuguese town-planning and architecture surrounded by the chaotic, vibrant *bairros* filled with the noise and music of traditional and adopted cultures. Since 1994, when Mozambique experienced its first democratic elections, growth in this part of the country has been phenomenal (10% per annum) and nowhere is this more evident than in Maputo city where new hotels are still being thrown up almost every month.

The town is a major port serving South Africa's industrial and commercial heartland around Johannesburg. Maputo's population is around two million and a short walk down Avenida Julius Nyerere will not only introduce you to an array of comfortable hotels and great restaurants but will reveal in the faces of the Maputenses a beautiful blend of peoples as diverse as the Portuguese, Brazilians, Tonga and Changana. Nightlife here swings to the rhythms of Latin America, and bounces to the beat and energy of African drums. Maputo is a friendly and safe city and you will find everything a tourist could desire here.

Those who plan to venture inland for the eclipse with their own transport – for example to Massingir – will be best to base themselves in Maputo. For those relying on public transport it is a different story. As the eclipse is so early (first contact begins between 07.13 and 07.17 depending on where you are) it will be nearly impossible to be in place ready for first contact without the risk of delay. If you are using public transport it is not a good idea to spend the night before the eclipse in places like Maputo outside the eclipse path – the hurry is silly, the road dark and dangerous (unlit vehicles, dazzled pedestrians, straying cows) and you may end up standing next to a broken-down bus instead of gazing up in wonderment.

Where to stay in Maputo
Backpackers and other budget varieties of independent traveller who want to spend US$10–30 per person per night should head either for **Fatima's Backpackers**

(1317 Av Mao Tse Tung; email: fatima@virconn.com), or for the **Costa do Sol** (tel: 1 45 0115; fax 1 45 0162) if you need a little more comfort and a safe place to park your car (never leave your vehicle unattended in Maputo).

People looking for beds in the intermediate range (US$40–100 per person) can check in at **Kaya Kwanga** near the beach (tel: 1 49 2215; fax: 1 49 2704) which is a great family spot, or **Villa Italia** (tel: 1 49 0701; fax: 1 49 0724), which has sea views.

If money is no object, look no further than the splendid, gracious, opulent, but strangely homely 5-star **Hotel Polana** (tel: 1 49 1001; fax: 1 49 1480; web: www.polana-hotel.com) where manager David Ankers is like everyone's daddy. This hotel not only has Africa's most beautiful swimming pool, but does not turn away lonesome mountain bikers covered in mud.

The **Hotel Cardoso** (tel: 1 49 1071; fax: 1 49 1804; email: hcardos@zebra.uem.mz) is almost as famous as the Polana.

If you want to stay outside Maputo there are several choices to the north. **Incomati River Camp** (email: incomati@virconn.com) is a pleasant place. You drive to Marracuene and park at the pontoon (*batelhão*) terminal from where you can take a transfer by boat.

Some 18km north of Marracuene on the EN1 is **Casa Lisa**, a campsite and chalets in the bush which caters for motorists who cannot get to or from their destination in one day. Great food and service. Tel: (27) 13 744 9412 and ask for 433 (radio phone).

Pre- and post-eclipse excursions
One of Africa's best wildlife areas, South Africa's **Kruger National Park**, is just a two-hour drive from Maputo. This is a must, either before or after the eclipse excursion. Many of the companies listed under *Organised tours* above offer tours to the Kruger Park out of Maputo, while most overland companies that include southern Mozambique in their itineraries also include a few days in Kruger.

The southern Mozambique coastline is still one of the world's most remote and unspoiled and yet it is dotted with a wide variety of upmarket lodges, simple family resorts and cosy camping sites.

GETTING AROUND
By air
There are no scheduled flights between Maputo and Xai-Xai, Chibuto or Massingir, but air charter is available from Maputo's international airport, with Sabin Air (tel: 1 46 5108); Trans Airways (tel: 1 46 5108; fax: 1 46 5011); and Metavia (tel: 1 46 5487).

By public transport
From Maputo there are buses (known as *autocarros* or *machimbombos*) leaving at least twice daily for Beira and all towns in between. Buses are operated mostly by Transportes Oliveiras (tel: 40 0475) and depart from near the big traffic circle (Praça) at the beginning (if you are entering Maputo) of Avenida 24 de Julho. Buses operated by Transportes Virginias (tel: 42 1271) leave from the Hotel Universo (1340 Avenida Karl Marx). Departure times for the express buses can be as early as 05.00, so make sure your transport from your lodgings to the terminus is reliable. From Maputo the bus ride to Xai-Xai normally takes around three and a half hours so it is not a feasible option for the morning of the eclipse.

By car
The national road (EN1) north of Maputo to Xai-Xai is usually well maintained and it takes about two and a half hours to get there. It straddles the path of totality, and

three good, all-weather branch roads lead from it to the towns of Chibuto (almost on the centre-line), Manjakaze and Chokwe. Small traditional mud-and-grass huts dot the sides of the roads, and there are basic roadside stalls offering cool drinks and beer every few kilometres so the lonesome wanderer need not go thirsty for far.

In Maputo there are at least three reputable **car-hire** companies, all of which offer 4WD vehicles and which I have personally found to be reliable and competitively priced. These are Europcar (tel: 1 49 7388; email: europcar@virconn.com;) Imperial (tel: 1 49 3543; fax: 49 3540) and Avis (tel: 1 46 5497; fax: 49 4498). It is advisable (but very expensive) to hire a 4WD otherwise your choice of stopover will be limited to the lodges accessible in ordinary cars.

You may wish to hire a car in either Harare (Zimbabwe) or Johannesburg (South Africa) instead, and it is often cheaper to do so. The toll road between Johannesburg and Maputo is in excellent condition and the journey takes seven hours if the border is not busy. Known as the Maputo Corridor, it has recently been upgraded with fuel stations and lodges. It goes from Johannesburg via Witbank and Helspruit to Komatipoort. The other route is via Mbabane and Manzini in Swaziland, entering Mozambique at Lomahasha/Namaacha.

The route from Harare to the eclipse path is generally very good though with some bad pot-holes as you approach the Save River Bridge. Many South African-based car-hire companies allow their vehicles to be taken into Mozambique and if you shop around you may find some of them to be cheaper than their Mozambican counterparts. Among the firms offering 4WD the following have good track records and offer vehicles fully equipped for camping safaris:

Avis (Truck Rental) Tel: (27) 39 978 1368; web: www.sco.eastcoast.co.za/avistruck
Buffalo 4x4 and Camper Hire Tel: (27) 11 704 1300; fax: (27) 11 462 5266; web: www.buffalo.co.za
P.F.A 4x4 Hire Tel: (27) 11 472 3453; fax: 11 674 2606; web: www.pfa4x4hire-safaris.co.za

ECLIPSE CENTRES: THE COAST
Overview
The endless golden beaches of Mozambique's southern coast are renowned among South African holidaymakers and are bound to be full on eclipse morning, guaranteeing a jubilant atmosphere and a beautiful setting. The key beach – Xai Xai – is renowned for its good snorkelling and game-fishing, and is rich in birdlife. The only drawback of the coast is that the chance of cloud is higher than it is further inland.

Gateway towns
Inhambane
Situated to the north of the eclipse path, this town is not a practical option for people wanting to get to the eclipse path on the morning by public transport. But by car it is feasible. Alternatively, if you stay at the backpackers' lodge Pachica (email: Inhambane@africamail.com) you may find reliable transport – the proprietor says he will be happy to take interested guests to the eclipse path in his Land Rover.

Xai-Xai
This town lies on the north bank of the Limpopo River and is just 10km from Xai-Xai beach – likely to be a popular eclipse-viewing site. It is a nondescript but busy town, with banks, markets, fuel, supermarkets, telephones and restaurants. It lies on Mozambique's main artery road, the EN1, just 250km north of the capital city Maputo. Most people will probably feel it is worth pushing on to Xai-Xai beach rather than remaining in the town.

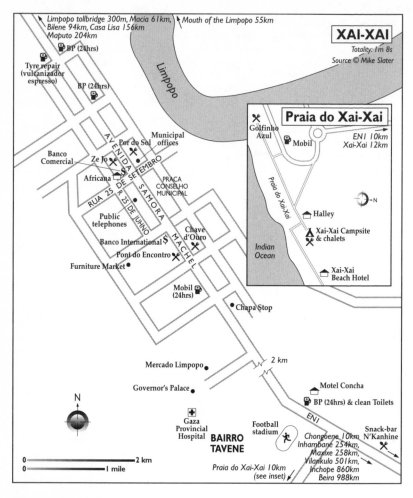

Limpopo tollbridge 300m, Macia 61km, Bilene 94km, Casa Lisa 156km Maputo 204km — Mouth of the Limpopo 55km

XAI-XAI

Totality: 1m 8s
Source © Mike Slater

BP (24hrs)
Tyre repair (vulcanizador espresso)
BP (24hrs)

Praia do Xai-Xai

Golfinho Azul
Mobil

EN1 10km
Xai-Xai 12km

Municipal offices
Por do Sol
Banco Comercial
Ze Jo
Africana
PRACA CONSELHO MUNICIPAL

Halley
Xai-Xai Campsite & chalets

Public telephones
Chave d'Ouro
Banco International
Pont do Encontro
Furniture Market

Indian Ocean

Praia do Xai-Xai

Xai-Xai Beach Hotel

Mobil (24hrs)

Chapa Stop

Mercado Limpopo

Governor's Palace

2 km

Motel Concha
BP (24hrs) & clean Toilets

N

Gaza Provincial Hospital
BAIRRO TAVENE

Football stadium

EN1

Chongoene 10km
Inhambane 254km, Maxixe 258km, Vilankulo 501km, Inchope 860km Beira 988km

Snack-bar N'Kanhine

0 ———— 2 km
0 ———— 1 mile

Praia do Xai-Xai 10km (see inset)

The eclipse zone
Xai-Xai Beach
Getting there and away

From Xai-Xai town take a *chapa* for the 15-minute ride to the beach – or you could walk the 10km if pushed.

Where to stay

Book early because the eclipse is at the beginning of the South African school holidays when accommodation can be hard to find. Xai-Xai beach has a **caravan/camping park** (tel: 22 22 942) with a good restaurant but the atmosphere is a little unfriendly and petty thieving may be a problem. There is also the upmarket **Xai-Xai Beach Hotel** (tel: (27) 31 304 5977, fax: (27) 31 304 8817; email: xai-xai@threecities.co.za; US$100 per person) which is 2km up the coast and very nice. For eating, try Restaurante Golfinho Azul (The Blue Dolphin) on the beach – turn left at the traffic circle and then follow the road down the hill and it is on your left after about 1km. It serves excellent seafood: I recommend the *lulas* (calamari/squid).

Other beach accommodation nearby includes **Paraiso do Chidenguele** (US$50 for four), secluded, serene self-catering cabins 70km from Chidenguele.

Just to the south of Xai-Xai is the isolated, sublime **Zonguene Lodge** (tel: 82 304 189; fax: 82 334 189; web: www.satis.co.za/zongoene; US$130 per person) on the southern banks of the Limpopo river mouth. It may be pricey but you will be staying at one of Mozambique's most unspoiled spots and boats will be available to take you either out to sea, or upriver to view the eclipse.

There are other accommodation options north and south of the eclipse path – again not for those who are relying on public transport on the morning of the eclipse. You can try the accommodation ranging from camping to fully equipped beach houses at Bilene's **Praia do Sol** (tel: (27) 11 828 3533; US$8–150). This is not right on the coast but on the shores of Lagoa Uembje, an impossibly blue lagoon on a blindingly white beach, and offers various watersports. It lies 95km from Xai-Xai town on the Macia turn-off from the EN1.

To the north towards Inhambane, and popular among South African tourists, are several pleasant places to stay, including **Guinjata Bay** (tel: (27) 13 741 3149; **Barra Lodge** (tel: (27) 11 314 3356; fax: (27) 11 314 3239: web: www.barralodge.co.za); and **Barra Reef** (tel: (27) 11 867 3982; email: execupol@mweb.co.za). They are more remote, and have cleaner beaches and better diving.

Where to watch the eclipse

Xai-Xai beach is within the eclipse path but to reach the centre-line you will have to travel about 30km up the coast. You can cover the first 15km, as far as Chonguene, along a track adjacent to the beach, but to get further you will have to use the main road. Driving on the beach is not allowed.

Chonguene beach has the drama of its derelict hotel, which is quite literally sliding into the sea. The access track from the main road is for 4WD only. Alternatively, you could watch from the sea by chartering a ski boat at the campsite, but as this is only just the start of the South African school holidays the folk with the boats may not have arrived yet (the seas are too wild to be suitable for any other type of boat). If boats are available and the weather is clear and calm, charter one and go out over the horizon for an elemental, uninterrupted view of the sky.

Xai-Xai town would be a great place from which to cruise up the Limpopo in a chartered speed boat, as the river criss-crosses the path's centre-line many times before pouring itself into the Indian Ocean. Find a boat at the campsite on Praia do Xai-Xai or from Zonguene Lodge. The skipper will know whether it is better to tow the boat to Xai-Xai town and launch there or to go via the ocean and enter the river at its mouth. Rates will be about US$50–80 per hour plus fuel.

ECLIPSE CENTRES: INLAND MOZAMBIQUE
Overview

Much less compelling than the coast, this is an option for those who want to maximise the chance of clear skies above all else – or want an experience away from the tourists.

The eclipse zone
The Shingwedzi River

If you have a 4WD one of the best ways to combine your eclipse-watching with an unforgettable wilderness experience would be to join the Shangaan Thirstlands 4x4 Trail which enters Mozambique from the Kruger Park (South Africa) and runs down the border as far south as the Shingwedzi River which is dead on the centre-line. For further information call tel: (27) 11 886 7601; email: fourxfour@traidcon.co.za.

Chokwe and Massingir

There is nothing much to recommend this area besides being within the path of totality. However, if the weather along the coast turns cloudy, it may become your last resort because it normally receives far less precipitation than the coast. Massingir, where first contact will be at 07.14 and totality will last for 1 minute 16 seconds, is over 200km from the coast and is therefore well away from the threat of coastal cloud.

Getting there and away

To get there on the morning of the eclipse you will need to stay the night in Maputo or, better, Casa Lisa (see *Maputo*, above) and head out at 03.00 as it will take three hours to get to Chokwe.

If it is open (it's often impassable due to floods and broken bridges), the road across the Limpopo between Chokwe and Chibuto does cross the centre-line; so if you have a 4WD you may be able to get good views as the vegetation here consists of low thorn-trees which will not obscure your views of the heavens.

By public transport the day before the eclipse, there are regular buses (Oliveiras and Virginias) and *chapas* (pick-ups) to Macia where you can change for Chokwe. But after Chokwe you'll be stuck if you don't have your own vehicle. Apart from camping at local villages (ask the *regulo* or *secretario* first), your only option will be the seedy and airless Hotel Chokwe which is not contactable by phone but has a fairly good restaurant (also a disco at weekends). Venture here fully self-supporting and you will be comfortable for a night or two.

Massingir is a three-hour drive from Maputo along a good road, but has no facilities whatsoever (you will have to base yourself in Maputo).

Chibuto and Manjakaze

The turn-off to Manjakaze and Chibuto is 10km after Xai-Xai. As both towns are too close to the coast to be spared from any prevailing bad visibility, I doubt anyone will bother to select either as a viewpoint of choice. And yet who knows? If you have your own 4WD and want to be the only person in the area who knows what an eclipse is, December 4 may just find you perched on your roof-carrier near Chibuto which is, after all, on the centre-line. Chibuto has a hotel. Eating is at local markets where there are basic *quiosques*. Staying overnight is really only feasible for campers.

FURTHER READING FROM BRADT

Africa by Road, Charlie Shackell and Illya Bracht
East and Southern Africa: The Backpacker's Manual, Philip Briggs
Guide to Mozambique, Philip Briggs
Southern Africa by Rail, Paul Ash

Madagascar
Hilary Bradt

Visiting the eclipse areas
OVERVIEW
Last total solar eclipse: May 1901
Next total solar eclipse: June 2095

By fortunate coincidence, the 2001 eclipse crosses the part of Madagascar that has the lowest annual rainfall, at a time of year when the weather in the western and central area is very likely to be cloudless. Add the fact that at the time of totality the Sun is only 13 degrees above the horizon in the west and that sunset into the Mozambique Channel exactly coincides with the end of the eclipse, and it is easy to see why Madagascar is rated as one of the best overall options for the 2001 eclipse. That's the good news. The bad news is that Madagascar's fragile tourist infrastructure, which barely copes with its usual amount of visitors, will be stretched to breaking point with eclipse-chasers. Also, the period of totality will be at its shortest on this island.

This will be the first total eclipse in Madagascar for almost exactly 100 years. No living Malagasy will remember the last one on May 18 1901, so for the local people it will be a very special event. In the highlands north of the eclipse zone this is the season for the *famadihana* (turning of the bones) ceremony, when ancestors who would have experienced the last eclipse will be honoured.

The best place to be for the eclipse will be Morombe, on the west coast. At 15.12 local time the first small bite will be taken from the side of the Sun. After 16.25 the Sun, low in the midwinter sky over the Indian Ocean, will be blotted out, to the cheers of the crowds gathered on the beaches, and darkness will fall. At 16.28, the sky will lighten and one hour later the Moon's shadow will have passed over the Sun. At exactly the time of 4th contact, 17.52, the Sun will set. Unforgettable!

Adventurous, independent travellers with their own tents may prefer to escape the crowds by heading for the Andringitra mountains in the central highlands or the rough roads leading from the town of Ihosy.

An alternative to Morombe is Isalo National Park. The drama here will be the eerie effect of the red-rimmed darkness falling over a landscape that is already

VILLAGE ETIQUETTE
The Malagasy are very courteous people; if you arrive in a small village and are planning to spend the night, whether in someone's home or in your own tent, you should ask for the community leader or *Président du Fokontany*. He will usually speak some French and will allocate you a house or show you where to put your tent. You can also ask for the *gendarmerie*.

MADAGASCAR

Cap d'Ambre

ANTSIRANANA
(Diego Suarez)

Montagne d'Ambre NP
Nosy Mitsio
Ankarana Reserve
Analamera Reserve

Nosy Be
Lokobe Reserve

Iharana
(Vohemar)

Ambanja

Maromokofro
2876m ▲

Marojejy Reserve

Sambava

**Anjanaharibe-
Sud Reserve**

Antalaha

Masoala NP
Maroantsetra

MOZAMBIQUE CHANNEL

MAHAJANGA
(Majunga)

**Nosy Mangabe
Reserve**

**Ankarafantsika
Ampijoroa Reserve**

Mananara NP

Mananara

Ikopa

Soanierana-Ivongo

Île Ste Marie
(Nosy Boraha)

Fenoarivo

**Lac Alaotra site of
Biological Interest**
Ambatondrazaka

Lac
Alaotra

Maintirano

**Ambohitantely
Reserve**

TOAMASINA
(Tamatave)

**Bemaraha
Reserve**

**ANTANANARIVO
(TANA)**

Moramanga

Ambilo-Lemaitso

Ambatolampy

**Analamazaotra
(Périnet) Reserve**

Vatomandry

Belo Tsiribihina

Miandrivazo

**Kirindy
Reserve**

Antsirabe

INDIAN

Mania

MORONDAVA

Ambositra

OCEAN

**Ranomafana
NP**

FIANARANTSOA

Mananjary

Morombe

Mangoky

N

Manakara

Isalo NP

Ihosy

**Andringitra
Reserve**

Zombitse NP

Farafangana

TOLIARA
(Tuléar)

Onilahy

Vangaindrano

Tropic of Capricorn

Path of eclipse 2001

Beheloka

**Beza Mahafaly
Reserve**

**Andohahela
NP**

Berenty Reserve

TAOLAGNARO (Fort Dauphin)

**Lac Anony site of
Biological Interest**

Cap Ste Marie Reserve
Cap Ste Marie

0   200 km
0   100 miles

otherworldly. Isalo is a massif of eroded sandstone, cut by green canyons where lemurs hide. June is the perfect time of year to visit Isalo; the weather is usually sunny but not too hot.

Finally there is Vangaindrano, a small town near the east coast which is seldom visited by tourists, and which lies at the centre of the band of totality. The more easily accessible, so more popular, town of Farafangana is also in the path of the total eclipse. Being on the wet, eastern side of Madagascar, the weather here is unpredictable, even in June, and the chance of cloud or rain is 50%. The eclipse on the east coast will be slightly shorter than on the west coast. However, the atmosphere will certainly be lively, and this area will be free of organised group tours. This makes it an attractive option for independent travellers who are willing to take a big risk with the weather.

A word about camping and safety issues. Independent travellers will often have no option but to camp during the eclipse week. In Madagascar you can put a tent in most places but not near tombs. There are no organised campsites except in a few of the national parks (in the eclipse zone the only relevant one is in Isalo). It is polite to ask permission. Campers do run the risk of robbery, particularly in areas such as Farafangana where there are local people sleeping rough. Perhaps camping in the grounds of a restaurant would be a good option because you can then offer to pay a little for the security.

For updates on Madagascar's response to the eclipse, check the Bradt website on www.bradt-travelguides.com. Madagascar's international telephone code is 261 20.

INTRODUCTION TO SOUTHERN MADAGASCAR

The climatic variations in Madagascar arise because of the range of mountains which runs like a spine down its centre, dividing the island into three distinct climate zones with three very different biosystems. This is what makes the country such a treasure trove of unique plants and animals which have evolved to live in habitats varying from desert to rainforest. The southwesterly trade winds, cooled by the increasing altitude, drop their moisture on the eastern mountain slopes with their covering of rainforest. On the western side of the mountains there is a long dry season and the vegetation has evolved drought-resistant characteristics.

Natural history
The west
Madagascar's most startlingly different flora are found in the 'spiny forest' of the south and west, with some of the best examples within the band of totality. Under threat from charcoal burners and slash-and-burn agriculturalists, the forests form a band running parallel to the coast, from Morombe to Taolagnaro. The most striking trees are from the didierea family. They resemble cacti but are unique to Madagascar. Like giant fingers reaching for the sky, they dominate the horizon. In June these deciduous trees will be bare of leaves which they shed each dry season to reduce moisture loss. Lethal-looking spines arranged in spirals up the trunks and branches deter all but the nimble lemurs which can leap from spiny branch to spiny branch without damaging their soft hands or feet. Towering above the didierea are the baobabs for which western Madagascar is famous, and the smaller bloated moringas which store water in their bottle-shaped trunks. Then there are the numerous species of euphorbia, along with kalanchoe and aloes, all forming an impenetrable barrier to the walker. The most common lemur of the spiny forest is the white sifaka, which never drinks. Ring-tailed lemurs are also found in the region near rivers.

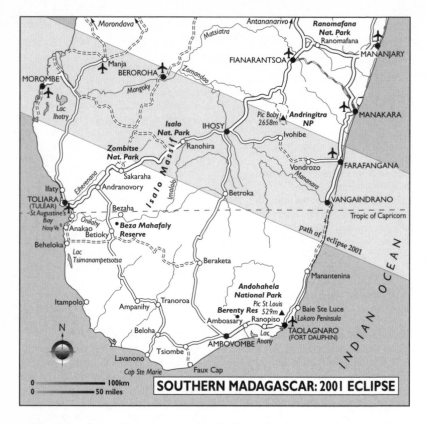

The spiny forest abounds in reptiles. Oplurus lizards mimic the spiny plants with their thorny-looking scales, and chameleons lurk in the branches. Boas and other snakes are common. This is a paradise for birdwatchers, with many endemic species such as the long-tailed ground roller found only in the spiny forest.

The central highlands and Isalo

As you move east along the band of totality, the forests give way to low scrub or coarse grassland dotted with termite mounds. Heavily grazed by cattle, this is mostly an unrewarding area for wildlife enthusiasts but its landscape of mountains and canyons, particularly in Isalo National Park, is magnificent. The new national park of Andringitra combines both superb scenery and the opportunity to see ring-tailed lemurs that have adapted to the cold, high conditions.

The east

None of Madagascar's famous rainforest reserves lies within the band of totality. The forest in this southern region is fragmented and open only to scientists and researchers. It would be better to plan a visit to Ranomafana or Périnet after the excitement is over than to try to combine eclipse-viewing with wildlife encounters.

Ethnic groups

Some interesting ethnic groups live within the path of totality, and enjoying the eclipse with them should be one of the highlights of the trip. The Vezo

> **TIPS FOR INDEPENDENT TRAVELLERS**
> - Take a lightweight tent and sleeping bag
> - Avoid the 'best' places (Morombe and Isalo) which will be crammed with tour groups
> - Choose any western village along the central line of the eclipse
> - Allow plenty of time to get there by *taxi-brousse*
> - Prepare to astound the villagers – you could be the first tourist they've seen
> - Enjoy the eclipse in the company of the locals

(fishermen) and Masikoro (pastoralists) are subclans of the Sakalava who dominated the western region before the Europeans arrived. The Mahafaly, Antanosy, Antandroy and Bara all have their regions in the interior. These southern Malagasy are tough, dark-skinned people, with African features, accustomed to the hardship of living in a region where rain seldom falls and where finding water and grazing for their large herds of zebu is a constant challenge. The Bara are particularly known for their association with cattle: a Bara does not achieve manhood until he has stolen a few of his neighbour's cows.

The Mahafaly and Masikoro people are famous for their decorated tombs. A man who has lived eventfully and died rich will have the highlights of his life perpetuated in the form of wooden carvings (*aloalo*) and colourful paintings adorning his tomb.

The Antaisaka people of the east are an offshoot of the Sakalava, but unlike their cousins they do not build elaborate tombs but keep their mummified dead in a communal burial house.

Regional food and drink

The Vezo people are fishermen so it is not surprising that fish is the main dish served in west-coast hotels along with spiny lobster (crayfish) and shellfish. Rice is more common than potatoes. The central region is cattle country so zebu (beef) dominates most menus. In the east, coconut is a popular ingredient, with *poulet à coco* usually a succulent choice.

There are no special regional drinks, although on the east coast look for *punch coco*, made from coconut milk and rum. Terrific! Three Horses Beer is the most popular beverage with locals and tourists alike.

ORGANISED TOURS

There are several companies offering eclipse tours into the zone of totality. Some will happily arrange for those outside their countries of operation to take part.

UK

Africa Exclusive Tel: 01604 628979; fax: 01604 639879; email: africa@africaexclusive.co.uk. Tailor-made trips.

Discover the World 29 Nork Way, Banstead SM7 1PB; tel: 01737 218800/1; fax: 01737 362341; email: sales@arctic-discover.co.uk; web: www.arctic-discover.co.uk . A 17-night tour of Madagascar, viewing 2001 eclipse from west coast, location to be confirmed.

Okavango Tours & Safaris Tel: 020 8343 3283; fax: 020 8343 3287; email: info@okavango.com. Tailor-made trips.

Rainbow Tours 64 Essex Rd, London N1 8LR; tel: 020 7226 1004; fax: 020 7226 2621; email: info@rainbowtours.co.uk; web: www.rainbowtours.co.uk. 13 nights touring

Madagascar, viewing the eclipse from Isalo National Park. Provisional cost: £2,195. Also, a 14-night tour, viewing the eclipse from Morombe on the west coast.

Reef & Rainforest Tours Tel: 01803 866965; fax: 01803 865916; email: reefrain@btinternet.com. Specialists in Madagascar with a wide variety of tours.

USA

TravelQuest International (see *Planning and Preparation*, page 20), veteran eclipse-chasing company, offering 60 places on an eclipse trip to Morombe.

Cortez Travel Services 124 Lomas Santa Fe Dr, Solano Beach, CA 92075; tel: 619 755 5136 or 800 854 1029; fax: 619 481 7474. Email: cortez-usa@mcimail.com.

Australia

Adventure Associates Pty Ltd 197 Oxford St Mall, Bondi Junction, Sydney, NSW 2022 (PO Box 612, Bondi Junction, NSW 1355); tel: 02 9389 7466; fax: 02 9369 1853; email: mail@adventureassociates.com; web: www.adventureassociates.com.

South Africa

Unusual Destinations PO Box 97508, Petervale 2151, Gauteng, SA; tel: 11 706 1991; fax: 11 463 1469; email: unusdest@global.co.za; website: www.unusualdestination.com.

Madagascar

Boogie Pilgrim Villa Michelet, Lot A11, Faravohitra, Antananarivo; tel: 258 78; fax: 625 56; email: bopi@bow.dts.mg

Cortez Expeditions 25 Rue Ny Zafindraindiky, Antanimena, Antananarivo; tel: 219 74; fax: 247 87; email: cortez@dts.mg

Madagascar Airtours 33 Av de l'Indépendance, Antananarivo BP 3874; tel: 241 92; fax: 641 90

Mad Caméléon Lot II K6, Ankadivato, Antananarivo, BP4336; tel: 630 86; fax: 344 20; email: madcam@dts.mg

Za Tour ID 33 bis, Ambohitsorohitra, Antaninarenina, Antananarivo; tel: 656 48; fax: 656 47; email: za.tour@dts.mg

GATEWAY TOWNS

Given that many hotels in the few towns within the band of totality will be booked solid for months (actually years) before the eclipse, visitors who have managed to secure their own transport (car or boat) can consider staying within driving or sailing distance of the area of totality. Contact details are given for the two or three best hotels for the gateway towns for each region. A full hotel listing can be found in dedicated country guides.

The main gateway is Antananarivo (Tana), the capital. All international flights arrive here and most visitors will need to stay at least one night before continuing to the eclipse zone.

Antananarivo

If you are connecting to a flight south the next day, stay in a hotel near the airport. There are no international chain hotels, but several small, family-run places. **Le Manoir Rouge** (tel: 22 441 04) is probably the best of these, or the lovely **Villa Soamahatony** (email: soamahatony@online.mg; web: http://takelaka.dts.mg/soamahatony) which is the place to stay if you have a few days to spare.

If you want to stay near the centre of town, the **Hilton** (email: sales_madagascar@hilton.com) is as good a bet as any, or the **Hotel Ibis** (email: ibistana@simicro.mg).

GETTING AROUND
By air
Air Madagascar has a monopoly on most domestic flights. The gateway towns of Toliara (Tulear) and Morondava have regular scheduled flights from Tana, and the small towns of Morombe and Manakara have an occasional service. Schedules change twice a year. For the latest information contact Air Madagascar (web: www.air-mad.com).

By public transport
Madagascar has one of the most unreliable and uncomfortable public transport systems in the world, running along some of the worst roads. Even without the heavy traffic expected in the days leading up to the total eclipse, getting around can be problematic. In June 2001, it will be challenging to say the least. A few buses run along the popular routes such as Toliara to Antananarivo (Tana) but every tiny village is served by a fleet of over-crowded, badly maintained bush taxis, or *taxi-brousses*. Thus it is possible to get anywhere in Madagascar provided you are prepared to wait long enough and have a high tolerance for discomfort.

By car
In Madagascar you hire a car with driver. It is risky to drive alone (because of the danger of getting lost and the erratic driving of other road users) and anyway your trip will be far more enriching if you have a driver/interpreter to smooth the way. Car-hire firms in Tana include MTU (tel: 33 11 054 92), and Promotours (tel: 22 408 64/331 84); and in Toliara, Edgar's Car (tel: 94 423 19).

All tour operators can organise cars and drivers.

By bicycle
Independent travellers with bikes and tents will have the best choices of eclipse-viewing sites with the minimum amount of risk and anxiety. A bike can cope with any road and pass any obstacle and can be carried on the roof of a *taxi-brousse* for a small fee. Although there are bicycle-hire places in southern Madagascar, don't risk it – bring your own. Experienced cyclists recommend bringing a spare tyre, tubes, spokes, a tool kit and puncture-mending kit, and a Teflon-based lubricant which does not attract the dust. Allow plenty of time to get to your chosen spot, carry lots of water (remember, this is the dry season) and have a wonderful time!

On foot
A strong hiker with a light backpack should, with careful planning, be able to walk to the most scenic eclipse-viewing spots of all: Isalo National Park, Andringitra National Park, and anywhere in the magnificent mountains of the south-central highlands. The map is inspiration enough.

ECLIPSE CENTRES: THE WEST
Overview
Western Madagascar is characterised by its deciduous forests dominated by vast baobabs and the surviving remnants of spiny forest. The region is flat and relatively prosperous, with two crops of rice harvested each year. The path of the eclipse misses the popular seaside resorts of Morondava and Toliara, bringing unaccustomed attention to the small, formerly sleepy town of Morombe. Roads in the area are either bad or dreadful, with drifting sand making driving and cycling conditions particularly difficult.

Gateway towns
Morondava
Morondava is a good 100km from the total eclipse zone as the crow flies, and much further by dreadful road, so staying in this popular resort town to see totality is not a sensible option. But it is a great place to relax before and after the eclipse. Morondava's best hotels are the **Royal Toera** (tel: 95 520 27), the **Renala** (tel: 95 521 74 or 95 520 89) and **Baobab Café** (tel: 95 520 12; fax: 95 521 86; email: baobab@dts.mg) whose enterprising owners are likely to run tours into the eclipse zone.

Belo sur Mer
Belo sur Mer is an attractive small beach resort some 75km south of Morondava and still about 25km (about three hours' drive) from the area of totality. The hotel **Marina de Belo sur Mer** (tel: 95 524 51 or (in Tana) 22 272 96) is likely to organise boat trips for eclipse watchers along the completely undeveloped coastline to its south. Well worth investigating.

Toliara (Tuléar)
This is the only major town within a day's drive of the western eclipse zone. Route Nationale 7, which runs north to Antananarivo, is one of Madagascar's better roads and it should take only four to five hours to drive the 150 or so kilometres into the totality band. However, this is Madagascar and it only needs one broken-down truck to block the road and ruin the day. Nevertheless, it is a tempting choice because of the large selection of good hotels in the town and for the interest of the drive itself. This is renowned for the Mahafaly tombs to be seen along the way, the delightful small villages, and the strange table mountains that are characteristic of the region.

The three best hotels are the **Capricorne** (tel: 431 12/426 20; fax: 413 20), the **Plazza** (tel: 419 00-2; fax: 419 03) and **Chez Alain** (tel: 415 27, fax: 423 79), but there are numerous small hotels and no doubt private rooms will be available at eclipse time.

Pre- and post-eclipse excursions
In the Toliara area
Toliara is renowned for the excellent snorkelling and diving on the coral reefs north and south of the town. Ifaty, to the north, is the most popular centre but the area south around St Augustine's Bay and the small island of Nosy Ve are equally rewarding.

Toliara is also a centre for birdwatching and for plant enthusiasts, although the spiny forest here is not as impressive as that around Morombe. Do not miss a visit to the **Arboretum d'Antsakay** which has an impressive selection of plant species and offers the chance to see the birds and reptiles that live in this habitat.

Toliara is also the centre for decorated tombs. The **Mahafaly tombs** with their *aloalos* are particularly fine and may be seen along Route Nationale 7 about one and a half hours from Toliara. There are some interesting ones, too, along the road to Betioky.

From Morondava
Most visitors to Morondava take trips to see the **Avenue of the Baobabs**, although if you have come from Morombe you should have had the chance to see some splendid examples of these weird and wonderful trees there. The wildlife reserve of **Kirindy** will be the major attraction. This is famous as the home of the very rare giant jumping rat and its predator the fosa, a cat-like animal more closely

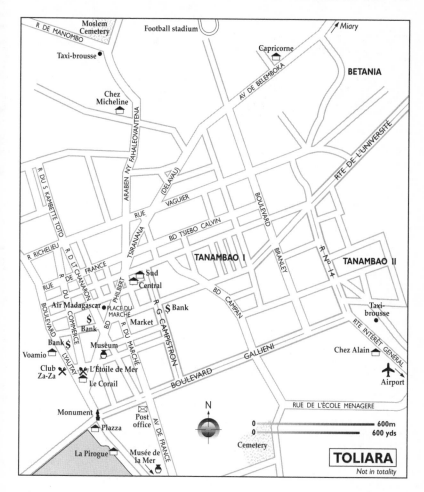

related to the weasel family, and Madagascar's largest carnivore. However, be warned! The giant jumping rat tends to aestevate (hibernate) during the cold winter months. You'll be luckier with the lemurs, however, and may well see a fosa during a night walk.

Adventurous excursions: the Manambolo River

The **Manambolo River** offers a beautiful and exciting trip. A descent of the river, from Ankavandra to Bekopaka, can be arranged through the local tour operator Mad Caméléon (see page 140) or, if you have lots of time, you can do it independently. This is how Herman Snippe and Jolijn Geels did it in 1999. They took a variety of *taxi-brousses* from Tana to Tsiromanomandidy and on to Belobaka. From here they hired a guide to take them on foot to Ankavandra along the Route de Riz used by rice porters. This walk took three days and was 'wonderful' although they warn of a shortage of drinking water in the dry season. Ankavandra is pretty much owned and run by Mr Nouradine, who owns the only hotel and river-worthy pirogues. The trip down the river cost Herman and Jolijn about US$125 (a high price for Madagascar and likely to be even higher at eclipse time).

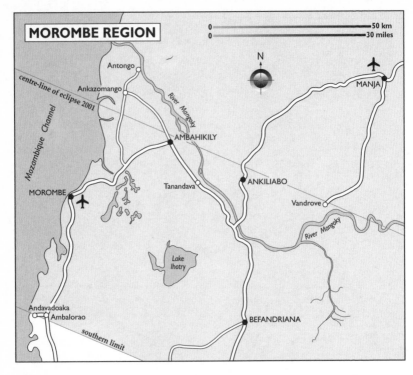

The price included two piroguiers and their food. In April, after rain, the two-and-a-half-day descent of the river was thrilling and spectacularly beautiful, especially through the Gorge de Bemaraha.

Bekopaka is the gateway town for the **Tsingy de Bemaraha National Park**, a wonderful region of limestone karst known as tsingy; the park has only recently been opened to tourists. The hotel in town is Auberge du Tsingy de Bemaraha (often full of tour groups). The tsingy is accessed by boardwalks, ladders and ropes – not a trip for the unfit or nervous.

Getting from Bekopaka to 'civilisation' at Belo sur Tsiribihina is an adventure in itself. Herman and Jolijn walked for a day before finding a *tracteur brousse* – a tractor towing a trailer crowded with passengers – to take them the final stretch.

The eclipse zone
Morombe

Morombe is in for a surprise in June 2001. Accessible only by appalling road and occasional plane, it missed the tourist boom of the 90s enjoyed by other parts of the west coast because it was neither pretty enough nor beachy enough to be worth developing. It has been nominated as the best place to see the eclipse because the entire spectacle will be visible from here, including sunset. Despite its former obscurity it does have a few hotels and a good beach some 45km south: Andavadoaka. The drive to this small fishing village is wonderful, with several species of baobab to be seen near the road. Sadly, however, Andavadoaka teeters just outside the path of totality so it is not a suitable viewing-point.

Morombe's own beach is a pleasant one, fringed with coconut palms. This will be thronged with visitors on the day of the eclipse.

Getting there and away

Morombe is accessible by *taxi-brousse* from Ifaty, north of Toliara. The road is frequently sandy and in very poor condition; the journey takes at least 22 hours by *taxi-brousse* and a full day by 4WD. Local villagers are adept at extricating vehicles stuck in the sand. At the time of writing the *taxi-brousse* runs only twice a week, but it is reasonable to assume that extra transport will be laid on at eclipse time. The scenery en route is lovely, with some of the most beautiful, untouched beaches in Madagascar on one side and intact spiny forest on the other. The road skirts a lagoon offering good swimming. From Morondava it is a nightmare of a journey by boat and on what land transport you can find.

Air Madagascar flies to Morombe twice a week, on Mondays and Fridays. Again, they may put on extra flights.

Where to stay

The best hotels of Morombe are booked by tour groups at the time of writing. These include the **Baobab**, which is on the beach. However, there is always the chance of a cancellation, and almost certainly there will be numerous entrepreneurs in the town only too happy to give a bed to a visitor – for a price.

Camping

There is no organised campsite, but camping places will be established in and around Morombe. Independent travellers should have no problem finding places to pitch their tents.

Where to watch the eclipse

Morombe lies south of the centre of the path of totality, so diehard eclipse-watchers will want to go north, by boat since there is no road that hugs the coast, or to the nondescript village of Ambahikily, where the eclipse starts at 15.12. This village lies at the south side of the Mangoky River and 37km from Morombe; it is on the centre-line and can be reached by road or river. The duration of the eclipse in Ambahikily is 2 minutes 40 seconds, whilst in Morombe it is only 2 minutes 23 seconds. But fourth contact does not occur in Ambahikily until after sunset, so you will not see it. Andavadoaka will fall just outside the total eclipse path so, although it will be a lovely place to stay, eclipse-watchers will need to travel north. Only from Morombe's beach, or one of the beaches over the few miles to the north or to the south, will you have the satisfaction of watching the Sun slip into the ocean at the point of fourth contact.

Nearby excursions

Once the eclipse is over there is nothing to keep you in Morombe or Ambahikily. Andavadoaka is a different matter: the beach and its basic hotel, Coco Beach, are a great base for snorkelling or just lazing.

Apart from the beach and coral, the greatest attraction of the region is the spiny forest, the magnificant baobabs, and the many endemic species of birds that live in this habitat. This seldom-visited area offers some outstanding birdwatching in the virtually untouched forest.

Manja, Befandriana and Vandrove

Manja is a distinct possibility as an alternative to the more crowded seaside towns. It is accessible by Twin Otter which shuttles between Toliara and Morondava via Manja on Mondays, Fridays and Saturdays. There's at least one basic hotel, and a lively market.

The other two small towns also lie in the path of the eclipse and should be able to provide somewhere to stay. If you decide to escape the madding crowds and take pot luck with viewing conditions you could share the experience with the locals, which should be lots of fun. Bear in mind that the vegetation is scrubby and dense and will block your view of the Sun unless you seek high ground or an open area. Make sure you get to your intended destination on June 20 to give yourself time to find the best spot.

The River Mangoky

One of the most romantic and adventurous options would be to hire a pirogue (and paddler) and float down the Mangoky. The whole river lies in the path of the eclipse, and local people in the town of Beroroha, on the upper river, should be willing to provide canoes. Be warned, however, that the price will be opportunistically high, and your boatman is unlikely to understand the importance of being in open country on the afternoon of June 21. You will need to be sufficiently confident of your ability to communicate the importance of this. Or let an expert take over the planning. The agency **Mad Caméléon** (page 140) specialises in river trips and may be running a Mangoky trip for eclipse-viewers.

ECLIPSE CENTRES: THE CENTRAL HIGHLANDS
Overview

For the purposes of this book the Central Highlands cover the area from the Andringitra mountains to Ihosy (Isalo National Park is dealt with separately). It contains the most dramatically beautiful scenery of all and, with the high probability of clear skies, is probably the best bet for self-sufficient independent travellers.

The scenery around Andringitra is marvellous, with huge granite domes of rock dominating the grassy plains. The chance to hike in the newly opened Andringitra National Park should not be missed. For non-walkers there is plenty to see from the road including tombs, some painted with scenes from the lives of the deceased.

Gateway towns
Fianarantsoa

This major town, capital of the Betsileo tribe, is within driving distance of the eclipse zone. The 210km journey to Ihosy usually takes about five hours so with an early start you should reach Zazafotsy, the first small town within the band of totality, and 36km from Ihosy, in ample time to find a good viewing site.

Fianarantsoa, Fianar for short, is divided into the attractive upper town, with its labyrinth of streets and numerous churches, and the dreary lower town where most of the hotels are located. The largest hotel (74 rooms) is the **Sofia** (tel/fax: 75 503 53) but the **Radama** (tel: 75 507 97; fax: 75 513 76; email: radama@hotelsonline.mg) has more charm. In the budget range is the ever-popular **Tsara Guest House** (tel: 75 502 06) run by the hospitable Jim and Natalie.

There are plenty of other hotels so even at eclipse time it should be possible to find a bed.

Ambalavao

Like something out of a fairy story, Ambalavao has wobbly-looking houses with carved wooden balconies leaning over the street. It is the centre for the Antaimoro paper trade. The paper, traditionally made from tree bark and impregnated with dried flowers, is sold as one of Madagascar's unique souvenirs. This is a lovely place to stay and, being 56km south of Fianar, it is within easy reach of the eclipse zone (traffic allowing).

There is one fairly good hotel, **Bougainvillées** (postal address: BP14, Ambalavao 308), and two basic ones. You can also camp at the silk-weaving project (see below).

Pre- and post-eclipse excursions
From Fianarantsoa
Ranomafana National Park
This is the region's most popular rainforest reserve. Don't miss it if you are in the area, although accommodation may be hard to find. If you have a tent, fine, otherwise try to book a tour in Fianar. It is a beautiful place. Twelve species of lemur are found here, along with numerous species of bird, reptile and invertebrate which are easily seen via a network of well-maintained trails.

The train ride to Manakara
Madagascar's most scenic railway runs from Fianar to Manakara on the east coast. The line has recently been improved and locomotives upgraded, so the train no longer labours up the hills only to slide backwards with a screech of brakes. Delays of 24 hours or more are also rare nowadays. The scenery and glimpse of village life at the rural stations make this a treat of a journey if you go first class to avoid the overcrowding. The train runs from Fianar to Manakara on Tuesdays, Thursdays and Saturdays, at 07.15.

Around Ambalavao
Silk-weaving centre at Ankazondandy
This is an inspiring place to visit. An example of grass-roots enterprise, the centre was developed by a group of local women with the help of the charity Feedback Madagascar. Silk production and weaving had all but died out in Madagascar, but since the centre was established in 1996 it has flourished, employing many women from the local communities. There is a good campsite for visitors here as well.

For more information check the website www.feedbackmadagascar.org, or phone (44) 1546 830 240 (Scotland), or the two contact numbers in Madagascar: 22 638 11 (Tana) or 75 501 33 (Fianar).

The eclipse zone
Ihosy
Pronounced 'Ee-oosh', this town is the capital of the Bara tribe, and is best known for being the junction for the two roads to Toliara and Taolagnaro. The road to the former is good; to the latter, bad.

As a junction town, Ihosy has become accustomed to feeding people, and there is a nice little square of *hotelys* (local restaurants) serving tasty and inexpensive food. This would be a good place for viewing with local people as there will be few tour groups here.

Getting there and away
The Central Highlands are easily accessed from Route Nationale 7, the main road running from Tana to Toliara. Buses and *taxi-brousses* run regularly from Tana or Fianarantsoa towards Toliara, and vice versa.

Where to stay
The **Zaha Motel** (tel: 740 83) will be booked solid but there's always the chance of a cancellation. There are several other small, basic hotels – try the **Hotel Relais-Bara**, **Hotel Ravaka** and **Hotel Dasimo**.

If you cannot find accommodation in Ihosy you will need to be self-sufficient with your own tent or travel in from Fianarantsoa, Ambalavao or Andringitra National Park. Cyclists or hikers can take one of the two rough roads leading (eventually) to Taolagnaro (Fort Dauphin) and Farafangana. There will be plenty of places to put your tent, and some sort of transport will eventually pick you up (but check out the safety of the road to Farafangana).

Where to watch the eclipse
The town is quite flat and the eclipse could be viewed from almost anywhere. First contact begins here at 15.16 and totality lasts for a chunky 2 minutes 21 seconds. A road also runs from Ihosy to Farafangana, on the east coast. This is very scenic, lies entirely within the path of the eclipse, and would be perfect for cyclists if it were not for its reputation for bandits. The local *gendarmerie* in Ihosy should be able to tell you the current situation.

Nearby excursions: Andringitra National Park
Andringitra is Madagascar's second peak. Geologically it is one of the oldest rock sites in the country and high enough to have night frosts in June. Its namesake is Madagascar's newest national park and opens up a unique environment to the adventurous visitor willing to rough it a bit for superb scenery. The park entrance is around one hour from Ambalavao.

There are three hiking trails, all in the northern part of the park, just out of the band of totality, but not to be missed before or after the eclipse.

The first is an easy trail which takes you through forest at the base of the main massif, past a dramatic waterfall and then back down to a picturesque campsite. The second goes on to the plateau from 1,700m at the start to around 2,100m. This is altimontane (ie high altitude) vegetation with rare plants such as kalanchoe. There is a spectacular rocky zone that has been eroded into deep streams and gullies. Here you often see ring-tailed lemurs. The trail then descends about 100m to a campsite next to a small river. The entire trail can be done in about 7–8 hours, but it is recommended that you stop at least one night. The third trail goes to the peak, Pic Boby, at something over 2,400m and a fourth trail is being opened in a forest area in the northeast of the park.

Guides are obligatory. Most people stay at the Gîte d'Étape at the village of Namoly, 46km from Ambalavao and at a height of around 1,700m. It is simple, comfortable and clean, with hot water and staff who will cook food for very reasonable prices.

ECLIPSE CENTRES: ISALO NATIONAL PARK
Overview
The combination of sandstone rocks (cut by deep canyons and eroded into weird shapes), rare endemic plants and dry weather makes this park particularly rewarding. There are numerous trails and three- or four-day hiking excursions can be organised.

The eclipse zone
Ranohira
This small town lies 97km south of Ihosy and, although formerly best known as the gateway to Isalo National Park, it is now overrun with sapphire dealers from the nearby mine: accommodation is likely to be next to impossible to find. Campers or the lucky few to secure hotel beds will have dramatic views of the eclipse (weather permitting) from the high spots in the park.

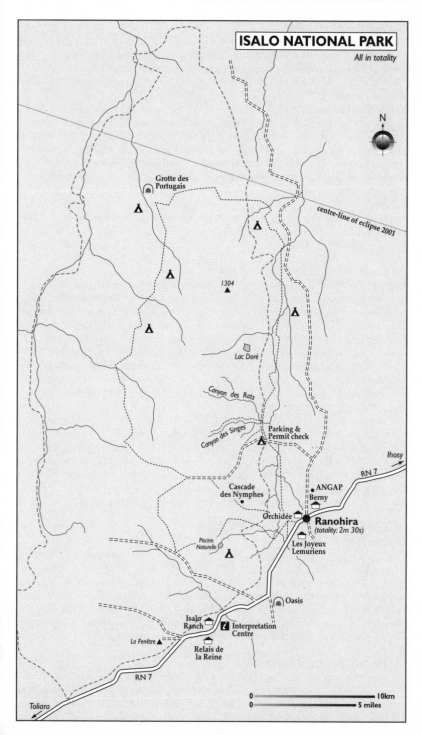

Getting there and away

Getting to Ranohira is usually no problem: about four hours from Ihosy or four hours from Toliara by *taxi-brousse*. Bear in mind, though, that every vehicle in the south will be pressed into service during the days leading up to the eclipse.

Where to stay

Relais de la Reine (tel: 22 785 32; fax: 22 351 67; email: mda@dts.mg) is a lovely, French-run hotel at Soarano, 9km further south, on the edge of the park. Book early as it is often full of tour groups, though it's always worth trying for a cancellation. Your best bet for a room is one of the basic hotels in Ranohira which are difficult to book in advance: **Hotel les Joyeux Lémuriens** and **Hotel Berny**. There are other hotels and no doubt private rooms will be available for let during eclipse week.

Camping

There are already two campsites: the **Oasis**, administered by Hotel Berny, and an area by the Interpretation Centre. Perhaps more will be established in time for the influx of visitors in 2001.

Where to watch the eclipse

Not all of the Isalo massif lies within the national park, so you do not need to pay the admission fee if you stay near the road to the south of Ranohira. You might even jostle for a position watching the eclipse through the windowed rock known as La Fenêtre. This is always a popular place for watching the sunset, and will be crowded, but there is plenty of space nearby where you will get an excellent view.

For an excursion in the park you will need a permit, costing about US$10, which must be purchased at the ANGAP office in Ranohira, and you must take an accredited guide with you. Normally these cost US$5–10. It is difficult to predict whether charges will go up for the eclipse, but this seems likely. Schematic maps of the park are available from ANGAP.

The most popular places in the park, the Piscine Naturelle, a natural swimming pool, and the two canyons, des Singes and des Rats, are likely to be the focus for most eclipse visitors. You need to be a good hiker to visit these on foot, but with the help of a 4WD vehicle you can do both sites in one day. A circular walking tour lasting three days is more rewarding. Everywhere you go in Isalo, you will find perfect high viewpoints. Seeing the strange shapes and wonderful colours of the rocks in the changing light of the eclipse should be utterly magical.

ECLIPSE CENTRES: THE EAST
Overview

The eastern part of Madagascar is the wettest region, and although the southeast attracts less rain than the north, you will nevertheless be lucky to have cloudless skies. The eclipse path is well south of the popular tourist areas, yet two commercially important towns, Farafangana and Vangaindrano, lie in the zone of totality and each has a few basic hotels. The mountains are some 100km away, so the total eclipse will be visible, weather permitting. Sadly there are no good beaches on this part of the coast, and swimming is risky because of sharks.

Gateway town: Manakara

This resort town will not experience a total eclipse and is only about two hours from Farafangana, in the zone of totality, so there seems little point in staying here rather than Farafangana. That said, there are several nice hotels (costing around US$10) including the Hotel Sidi (the best value), the Manakara, which has an

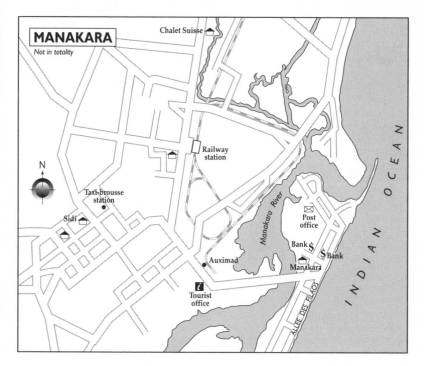

ocean view, and the Parthanay Club, north of the Manakara, which has some recently constructed bungalows.

The Chalet Suisse is recommended for its excellent food.

Pre- and post-eclipse excursions
The train to Fianarantsoa
See page 147 for a description of this train which leaves Manakara on Wednesdays, Fridays and Sundays at 07.00.

Travelling south
If you have a bicycle or a sturdy pair of legs and lots of time you can continue south from Vangaindrano to Taolagnaro (Fort Dauphin). For the first stretch, the road to Midongy Atsimo (no hotel) is not too bad and you will find occasional transport. Simple *hotelys* provide food. Beyond Midongy lies Befotaka (40km) and after that the trip becomes increasingly difficult. Transport in the area is erratic and unpredictable; the roads are very bad. Be prepared to travel over rickety bridges in overladen lorries, walk long distances, and cross rivers in what may appear to be very unstable dugout canoes.

The eclipse zone
Farafangana and Vangaindrano
Farafangana should be a seaside resort, but its position near the mouth of a river means that the beach and ocean are not easily accessible. The locals do not swim because the sea is full of monsters, so they watch football instead – the Farafangana team came top in the Madagascar league in 1998 and 1999. The town is a prosperous commercial centre, with well-stocked shops and a busy market.

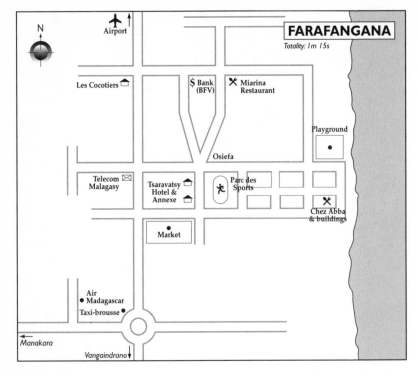

First contact, which begins around 15.17, will only last 1 minute 15 seconds from Farafangana, whereas a trip to Vangaindrano will increase this to 2 minutes 28 seconds, weather permitting. But Vangaindrano is not an inspiring town and lies inland so it lacks the sea view. Its hotels are very basic.

Getting there and away
Air Madagascar flies from Tana to Farafangana and on to Taolagnaro (Fort Dauphin) about twice a week.

A *taxi-brousse* from Tana to Farafangana takes about 24 hours. A more enjoyable option is to take a bus or *taxi-brousse* to Fianarantsoa and then take the train to Manakara (see page 147). Farafangana is only two to three hours away on a reasonably good road. There are also flights to Manakara.

Where to stay
In Farafangana the hotel of choice is **Les Cocotiers** (BP 135, Fenoarivo, Farafangana; tel: 73 911 87/8; fax: 73 911 86). It has en-suite bathrooms with hot water. **Chez Abba** is the best budget hotel (tel: 73 911 85) which costs around US$5 for a seafront bungalow with a simple (bucket) shower. **Tsaravatsy** (tel: 73 910 36) is another option. **Miarina Restaurant** (formerly Tulipe Rouge; still has rooms) is OK but rather damp. You may have to take your chance at finding a bed – the phones in Farafangana rarely work. Vangaindrano has at least four very basic hotels.

Where to camp
There are no designated campsites but plenty of places you can put your tent. However, safety could be a problem because of robbery.

Where to watch the eclipse

There is no obvious high ground in either town, but the area is sufficiently open for you to get a good view of the eclipse wherever you are. A clear western view is essential and you should go to the viewing site at least a day earlier at the same time to check there is an unobstructed view of the Sun. However good your viewing site, the Sun will slip over the horizon before fourth contact.

The truly adventurous can take the road west toward Ihosy from either Farafangana or Vangaindrano. The entire road lies in the path of the eclipse. A *taxi-brousse* runs daily from Farafangana to a village called Vohitranambo, about 50km from Vondrozo. Beyond that, you're on your own! The road on to Vondrozo (and 25km beyond) is passable for vehicles, but after the Vevembe region it is suitable for cyclists or hikers only, and you will need a guide.

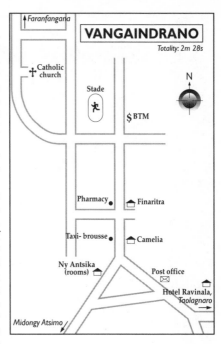

FURTHER READING FROM BRADT

Madagascar: The Bradt Travel Guide, Hilary Bradt
Madagascar Wildlife, Hilary Bradt, Derek Schuurman, Nick Garbutt

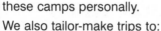

Epilogue

DAUGHTER OF THE SUN
A story in traditional style

They called her Ahmi, which in the old language meant 'small', and indeed at eight years old the sad, silent child stood scarcely higher than her mother's waist. No-one had ever heard Ahmi speak. She was lost in the forest for two days as a baby; and some said her voice had fled to the treetops in terror, or been stolen by the Snake Spirits who live among the tightly twisting creepers. Or perhaps it had been taken by the Forest Giant, whose breath is the rasp of the wind on winter nights, as a gift for his newborn child. Whatever the reason, words were as strange to Ahmi as moonbeams to a hungry jackal.

Nor had Ahmi ever been seen to smile. Her eyes stayed dark as the forest pool and her face tight as the new skin on a wooden drum. She spent her days alone, sitting beneath the big tree or in the shadow of her mother's hut, scratching strange and careful patterns in the dust or arranging small pebbles into cryptic lines and curves. The other village children learnt to avoid Ahmi, for her rage if they teased her or touched her patterns had the ferocity of a cornered beast.

On some days a great sadness swept over the little girl and she broke into heavy sobs, crouching beneath the tree and covering her head as she rocked in grief. At other times the villagers, from kindness, might try to speak to her; but quickly the tears welled up and she turned her head away, or closed her eyes tight in dismissal. Her mother spent more and more time with her other children, ill at ease with this withdrawn and solitary daughter who shrugged off love.

The oldest man in the village – no-one remembered his childhood – was also the wisest, and he watched Ahmi with gentle eyes. 'She knows things that we do not, and feels things that we do not,' he explained to her mother. 'So life for her is a fearsome thing. Spirits torment her in ways we cannot understand.' Of all the villagers, he was the one Ahmi trusted most. Sometimes they sat together beneath the big tree, while Ahmi made her strange patterns and the old man watched sunlight dapple through the leaves. Sometimes he spoke to her, softly and slowly so as not to frighten her, about the moon and the stars and the creatures of the forest; she listened, her eyes locked on to his, but made no sound. Deep in his mind an ancient memory stirred and he began to hatch his plan, waiting until the time was right.

The Sun was high in the sky, throwing fire on to the dusty ground, when he took Ahmi by the hand and led her into the forest. Slowly they walked, the child and the bent old man, until they reached the deep pool whose waters lie dark and smooth as polished stone. In one corner, where the foliage overhead grows less thickly, the sky reflects as if in a mirror, and the Sun, Moon and stars visit the pool's surface day by day. Here, his limbs weary, the old man sank to the ground and pulled Ahmi down beside him, pointing to the Sun as it lay golden in the water.

'Ahmi, little sister,' he told her softly, 'Today you will work a great magic, for I know the power that dwells in your heart. You, Ahmi – you, my little sister – must save your mother Sun, for today a hungry Sky Monster waits to gobble her up. Then darkness will come, and a wind from the edge of space; our bones will grow cold as the flowing river, the old will sicken and the young will not be born. Birds will fall silent and the Sun will have died forever.'

The child's eyes grew wide and full of questions. She clutched his hand. The old man pointed to the pool, where the Sun was changing shape. 'You see, already the Sky Monster has taken a bite,' he whispered urgently. 'We have so little time. Quickly, my sister – you must cry out "Sun!" as loudly as you can. Then the monster will hear and be afraid.'

In great distress, Ahmi gazed up into the treetops, and searched with her eyes among the tightly twisting creepers. She opened her mouth, but no voice came – and all the while the Sky Monster was gnawing away at the Sun. The air grew cold, and far in the distance a harsh wind blew.

Then the old man reached deep into his bones for an even greater magic. He held Ahmi's wrists, and she felt a warmth spreading up her arms and into her heart. The wind became closer and louder, until suddenly standing behind them (although of course they dared not turn their heads to see him) was the Forest Giant, his head bowed in shame and Ahmi's voice cupped gently in his hand. Quickly it flew into her throat.

'S-sun!' she whispered; and then, more loudly, 'Sun!' Throwing back her head, she called into the darkening sky: 'Sun! You are safe! Come back! I am Ahmi, and I have chased away the Monster!'

Slowly, so slowly, light spread once again over the water. The Sun's wounds healed, and shadows reappeared beneath the trees. High overhead, a bird sang joyfully. All was as before.

'Well done, little Ahmi,' sighed the old man, in a voice as fragile as a fallen leaf. 'You see, you have saved your mother Sun. Now she will watch over you every day and turn the hours to gold. You need never be sad again.'

The old man did not return from the forest, for his time had come and his gift to the child ended his life well. When Ahmi reached the village, the hunter sharpening his arrows by the gateway stared in amazement. 'Ahmi is smiling!' he cried, and laughed with such pleasure that Ahmi's smile widened. 'Ahmi is smiling!' cried the fat woman grinding her grain, and chuckled so happily that Ahmi smiled even more. 'Ahmi is smiling!' cried her mother, and wrapped her daughter in a hug so big and warm that the little girl could scarcely breathe.

The months passed, and then the years. If you go to the village today (which probably you will not, because the forest grows thick around it and the walk takes many days), you may see Ahmi sitting under the big tree, making patterns of such intricacy and beauty that the villagers gaze admiringly, and wonder at her skill. She still speaks little, knowing that words are really only useful for chasing monsters, but she smiles a great deal, and so radiantly that those who see her find themselves smiling in return. And if, some day in the far-off future, a Sky Monster again tries to gobble up her mother Sun, Ahmi will have no fear, because she knows she can scare it instantly away.

Appendix 1

ECLIPSE-RELATED LANGUAGE
Angola and Mozambique

It is essential, when in either of these countries, to have some way of communicating in **Portuguese**.

Sun	*sol*	glasses	*óculos*
Moon	*lua*	dangerous	*perigoso*
eclipse	*eclipse*	dark	*escuro*
shadow	*sombra*	Look!	*olha*

It is dangerous to look at the Sun.	*É perigoso alhar para o sol.*
Wear these glasses.	*Usa estes oculos.*
The Moon will hide the Sun tomorrow.	*A lua vai tapar o sol amanha.*
It is safe to look now.	*É seguro olhar agora.*
The Sun will damage your eyes.	*O sol vai danificar os teus olhos.*
Be careful.	*Tenha cuidado.*
Do not look at the Sun until it is completely covered by the Moon	*Não olhe para o sol, até que ele esteje completamente tapado pela lua.*
An eclipse is a happy event to be celebrated.	*O Eclipso é um evento alegre para ser celebrado.*
We have come to see the Moon move in front of the Sun.	*Nós viemos ver a lua mover-se a frente do sol.*

Zambia

Here are a few words in eight of the main Zambian language groups, the most important being Nyanja:

	Nyanja	Bemba	Tonga	Lozi
Sun	*dzuwa*	*akasuba*	*izuba*	*lizazi*
Moon	*mwezi*	*umweshi*	*mwezi*	*kweli*
shadow	*mtunzi*	*ichinshinjwe*	*chinzemwemwe*	*muluti*
glasses	*mandala*	*amaglasses*	*magilazi*	*siponi*
dangerous	*cho-opya*	*ichitinya*	*nchibi★*	*kozi burara*
dark	*mdima*	*ubushiku*	*ku-siya*	*lififi*
Look!	*ku-ona*	*ku-mona*	*ku-langa*	*talima*

	Lunda	Luvale	Kaonde	Namwanga
Sun	*mutena*	*likumbi*	*juuba*	*umusanya*
Moon	*kakweji*	*kakweji*	*ngondo*	*umwesi*
shadow	*mwevulu*	*muvimbimbi*	*kimvule*	*ichinsungwani*
glasses	*yi mbanjilu*	*vibanjilo*	*bimbonyi*	*izilola*
dangerous	*mpodi*	*ponde*	*kizhila*	*ichiwipe*
dark	*mwidima*	*milima*	*mfishi*	*usiku*
Look!	*ku-tala*	*ku-tala*	*ku-tala*	*ku-lola*

★In Tonga there is no word for 'dangerous'. To say, 'It is dangerous to look into the Sun without glasses' (*nchibi kulanga zuba kotasamide magilazi*) one needs to say, 'It is bad...'

Namibia and Botswana

English and Afrikaans should be sufficient in Botswana, and Afrikaans may occasionally work as well.

Zimbabwe

Even in the most remote rural areas one should be able to find someone whose English will allow essential communication to take place. The area within the 2001 path of totality is linguistically pretty uniform, and standard **Shona** is listed below, which will suffice throughout. However, the path of the 2002 eclipse falls over one of the most linguistically varied regions of Zimbabwe. **Ndebele** is the language taught in schools in Matabeleland and almost anyone there will be able to converse in it, though for many it will not be their first language.

Pronunciation

In both languages, vowels are pronounced as follows:

a – ah (as in cheetah)
e – ay (long a sound as in play)
i – ee (long e sound as in see)
o – oh (long o sound as in go)
u – oo (as in rude)

Consonants: 'Sv' and 'zv' are quite like 'sh' and 'zh' respectively, but with more of a whistle. Ndebele is one of the southern African 'click' languages. The difficult 'q' click can simply be approximated with a hard 'g' sound. The simpler 'c' click sounds like a 'tsk tsk' noise and is made by pushing the tip of the tongue against the hard palate behind the upper teeth and pulling downward. The 'hl' and 'dl' sounds in Ndebele can be approximated with 'sh' and 'zh' respectively.

	Shona	**Ndebele**
Sun	*zuva*	*ilanga*
Moon	*mwedzi*	*inyanga*
shadow	*mumvuri*	*intunzi*
glasses	*magogorosi*	*ama'spectacles'*
dangerous	*kuvadza*	*ingozi*
dark	*mumvuri*	*ukungcola*
Look!	*Tarisai!*	*Khangelani!*
The Moon will hide the Sun tomorrow.	*Mwedzi uchaviga zuva mangwana.*	*Inyanga izafihla ilanga kusasa.*
We have come to see the Sun be hidden.	*Tauya kuzo ona zuva richivigwa.*	*Siyabuya ukubona ilanga lifihliwe.*
The Sun will have a shadow.	*Zuva richave nemumvuri.*	*Lizabe lilethunzi ilanga.*
It will be dangerous to look at the Sun without these glasses.	*Zvinokuvadza kutarisa zuva usinamagogorosi aya. lingelamaspectacles la.*	*Kuzabe kulengozi ukukhangela ilanga*

South Africa

The relatively small proportion of people of European descent who live in Northern Province practically all speak **Afrikaans** (a derivative of Dutch) as a first language, though most also speak reasonably fluent English. Oddly, a smattering of Afrikaans will be most useful when talking to Africans in this part of the country. Very few speak any English, but almost everybody can speak a bit of Afrikaans whatever their home tongue. For this reason we have listed a few eclipse-related words in Afrikaans rather than in all of the region's indigenous languages.

Sun	*son*	glasses	*brille*
Moon	*maan*	dangerous	*gevaarlik*
eclipse	*sonsverduistering*	dark	*donker*
shadow	*skaduwee*	Look!	*Kyk!*

The Moon will hide the Sun tomorrow. *Mtre sal die maan die son verduister.*
It will be dangerous to look at the Sun without these glasses. *Dit is gevaarlik om na die son te kyk sonder beskermiing.*
Don't look at the Sun. *Moenie na die son kyk nie!*
Now you can look. *Nou kan jy maar kyk.*
The Sun will damage your eyes. *Die son sal jou ok beskadig.*
You must wear these glasses. *Jy moet hierdie bril dra.*
That is not safe. *Dit is onveilig.*

Madagascar

Phonetic pronunciations are given below for words and short sentences. Long sentences will probably be more than anyone can cope with but a literate bystander will be able to read them and explain to the other locals.

English	Malagasy	Phonetic
Sun	*masoandro*	maswandr
Moon	*volana*	voolan
eclipse of the Sun	*fanakonana ny masoandro*	fanakoonana ni maswandr
shadow	*aloka*	alk
glasses	*solomaso*	soolmass
dangerous	*mety mampidi-doza*	met mampid doos
dark	*maizina*	mice -in
look	*mijery*	midjerr
Look!	*Jereo!*	Dzereo!
Be careful!	*Tandremo masoandro!*	Tandreem maswandr
Look through this thing.	*Mijery amin'ity zavatra ity.*	Midjerr amnity zavitrity
It can damage your eyes.	*Mety manimba maso.*	Mety manimba mass
It is now safe to look at the Sun.	*Azo hatokiana amin'izay ny mijery ny masoandro.*	Azatookeean amzaiy nimdjerr maswandr.
Eclipse of the Sun is a rare event which is much enjoyed/celebrated.	*Tsy fahita matetika ny. fanakonana ka zavatra mandrisika afaliana ary tokony ankalazana.*	
It is dangerous to look at the eclipse directly, as the rays are very strong and can make you blind.	*Mety mampidi-doza ny mijery mivantana ilay alin-kely, satria mahery be ny taratra mipoatra ka mety manimba maso na mahajamba.*	
Do not look at the Sun without glasses until it is completely covered by the Moon.	*Rehefa tampenan'ny volana tanteraka ny masoandro izay vao ampiasana ny masolavitra.*	

Appendix
Aisling Irwin

FURTHER READING
Guides to the heavens
Books

UK Solar Eclipses from Year 1 to 3000 (Clock Tower Press) by Sheridan Williams, Bradt's eclipse expert, is an anthology of 3,000 years of solar eclipses – an intriguing catalogue of the stories attached to Britain's eclipses including those that have started wars, accompanied new kings and symbolised death. What makes the book relevant now is that the author has included a chapter each on the 2001 and 2002 total solar eclipses. He also includes all the eclipse facts you could possibly wish for, a detailed look at eclipse mechanics and astronomical software, a discussion of the practicalities of viewing eclipses and a whole chapter covering observation and photography. There are 21 beautiful eclipse photographs. The book can be obtained through bookshops (ISBN 1 85142 093 2) or direct from the publisher. Send a sterling cheque drawn on a UK bank for £11.95 plus p&p (£1 in UK, £2 Europe/Eire, £3 elsewhere) to: Clock Tower Press, PO Box 5010, Leighton Buzzard LU7 0ZZ. For more details see www.clock-tower.com/eclipse.

Totality: Eclipses of the Sun (Oxford University Press, 1999) by Mark Littman, Ken Willcox and Fred Espenak, is a well-written exposition of the science, culture and history of eclipses, set alight by the authors' enthusiasm.

For a book heavily weighted towards the science side try *Total Eclipses* by Pierre Guillermier et al. This has a less personal tone and is the book for those who really want to get into the history of the scientific study of eclipses.

The most sugared scientific pill I have found is *Eclipse: The Science and History of Nature's Most Spectacular Phenomenon* (Fourth Estate) by J P McEvoy. It is strong on the astronomical and cultural history of eclipses and easy to read.

To understand more of the folklore and mythology surrounding the Sun try *The Book of the Sun* (Courage Books) by Tom Folley and Ian Zaczek.

The definitive scientific guide to any single upcoming eclipse is produced in the form of a bulletin, put together by Fred Espenak and Jay Anderson for the American space agency, NASA. It includes predictions, tables, maps and weather prospects. To obtain one free copy of either *Total Solar Eclipse of 2001 June 21* or *Total Solar Eclipse of 2002 December 04* send a large SAE with sufficient stamps to cover 310 grams of postage, and the eclipse date marked on the bottom left-hand corner, to Fred Espenak, NASA/Goddard Space Flight Center, Code 693, Greenbelt, Maryland 20771, USA. From outside the USA and Canada you must send nine international postage coupons. Alternatively, try to get copies online from the NASA/Goddard Solar Data Analysis centre (address below).

1927: a British Eclipse, by R A Marriott, is an intriguing and amusing account of the response of a nation to a total solar eclipse – from scientific preparations to day-trips – and includes some moving quotes from eye witnesses as well as several disaster stories, many of them due to the fickle weather. It can be ordered from the

British Astronomical Association, Burlington House, Piccadilly, London W1V 9AG, for £3.50 post free in Britain and Europe.

Eclipse-photographers should turn to the authoritative *Cambridge Eclipse Photography Guide* (Cambridge University Press, 1993), or, for a wider range of subject matter, *Astrophotography for the Amateur* by M Covington (Cambridge University Press, 1988).

If humanity's past responses to eclipses have whetted your appetite for the history of astronomy try *The Cambridge Illustrated History of Astronomy* (Cambridge University Press, 1997) or *From Stonehenge to Modern Astronomy* by Fred Hoyle (W H Freeman & Co, 1977). *Historical Eclipses and Earth's Rotation*, by F Richard Stephenson, Cambridge University Press, 1997, is full of interesting quotations about eclipses as well as following – and solving – an intriguing scientific mystery using the eclipse calculations of the Chaldeans.

To find out more about the heavens fleetingly revealed during the eclipse try *A Field Guide to the Stars and Planets* (Houghton Mifflin, 1992) by Jay Passachoff and Donald Menzel.

Videos

Francisco Diego, an exuberant eclipse-chaser, has produced a video that explains the mechanics of eclipses more clearly than can any text and is also packed with moving images of eclipses. *The Magic of Total Solar Eclipses* can be obtained by mail order from UCL Images, 48 Riding House St, London W1P 7PO; tel: (44) 20 7504 9375.

Internet

The internet is packed with eclipse information compiled by dedicated chasers, who are a technologically literate lot.

The internet site http://sunearth.gsfc.nasa.gov/eclipse/toplink.html lies at the heart of all this internet activity. It includes a formidable amount of information produced by scientists who calculate eclipse paths, plot them on maps and deposit them online along with weather forecasts and even analyses of the likelihood of forest fires at your chosen viewpoint. This site will also provide you with links to all the other sites you could possibly want. They include the site for the more astronomically minded, http://umbra.nascom.nasa.gov/eclipse/, which is the official NASA solar eclipse bulletin site. For the uses of eclipses to science, go to www.williams.edu/Astronomy/IAU_eclipses/ and for tutorials try www.earthview.com.

If it is fascinating facts you are after, such as how to say 'total solar eclipse' in over 80 different languages, go to www.mreclipse.com/ , also run by Fred Espenak.

British eclipse links can be found via www.clock-tower.com/eclipse.

Most of the big eclipse tour companies have websites (see *Planning and Preparation*, page 20). A central site with links to many of them is www.eclipsechaser.com, which also includes testimonies and photographs of past eclipses.

There are many stunning eclipse pictures online. For starters, try http://schoenbrun.com/mitch/Eclipse/, which includes a picture of a fabulous diamond ring taken at an African eclipse.

The website of the Astronomical Society of Southern Africa, www.geocities.com/zimastro, promises to be a useful one packed with information on viewing the eclipse in that country. For updates to be used in conjunction with this book, you should of course turn to the Bradt website, www.bradt-travelguides.com.

Don't forget the Bradt website: www.bradt-travelguides.com, which will keep you updated with eclipse-related travel information.

Finally, if you wish to keep up to date on all solar eclipse related matters, the internet provides an ideal forum. You should join the following discussion group, and from then on any emails you send to the group are copied to all members. To subscribe, send an email to listserv@Aula.com. Within the body of the message (not the subject) type: 'subscribe solareclipses name, country'. From then on, any email you send to solareclipses@aula.com will be sent to all subscribers. If you have any problems contact Patrick Poitevin in England by email: patrick_poitevin@hotmail.com.

Guides to Africa

There are Bradt guides to most of the countries in the eclipse path with the exceptions of Angola and Zimbabwe. These guides are listed in the country chapters (for a full catalogue, contact Bradt Travel Guides, 19 High Street, Chalfont St Peter, Bucks SL9 9QE; tel: 01753 893444; fax: 01753 892333; email: info@bradt-travelguides.com; web: www.bradt-travelguides.com. For an Angola country guide see if you can find *Angola: a Fabulous Country* (1995). The publisher's telephone number in Angola is (244) 2 396503.

Zimbabwe features in Bradt's *East & Southern Africa: The Backpacker's Manual* by Philip Briggs. For a full Zimbabwe guide, Rough Guide's *Zimbabwe & Botswana* is informative about the tourist spots but lacks detail about the remoter areas. For more detail on those regions use Lonely Planet's *Zimbabwe, Botswana and Namibia*.

In addition to the Bradt *South Africa* guide by Philip Briggs, the new *South Africa: The Bradt Budget Guide*, written by Paul Ash, travel editor of the popular outdoor magazine *Out There*, will be published in 2001. Although most big travel publishers have dedicated guides to South Africa, it is a measure of the obscurity of the region covered by the eclipse that even the most comprehensive of these books contains little information about anywhere between Messina and the Kruger Park.

Field guides

For a comprehensive catalogue of field guides try the Natural History Book Service, 2 Wills Road, Totnes, Devon TQ9 SXN; tel: 01803 865913. In South Africa, try Russell Friedman books (tel: 011 702 2300/1; fax: 011 702 1403).

For mammals try Chris and Tilde Stuart's *Field Guide to the Larger Mammals of South Africa* (Struik 1997). There are several field guides to birds in the more southerly countries of the eclipse paths: Namibia, Botswana, Zimbabwe, South Africa and Mozambique south of the Zambezi. The most compact is *Field Companion to Robert's Birds of Southern Africa* (John Voelcker Trust, 1997)

Maps

Maps that cover both eclipse paths over Africa and Madagascar are the *Michelin 955 Central and Southern Africa* and GeoCenter World Map entitled *Africa South*.

Index